ROBERT BURNS AND RELIGION

To Jean, my mother,
the great encourager

Robert Burns and Religion

J. WALTER McGINTY

Routledge
Taylor & Francis Group
LONDON AND NEW YORK

First published 2003 by Ashgate Publishing

Reissued 2018 by Routledge
2 Park Square, Milton Park, Abingdon, Oxon OX14 4RN
711 Third Avenue, New York, NY 10017, USA

Routledge is an imprint of the Taylor & Francis Group, an informa business

A Library of Congress record exists under LC control number: 2002038256

ISBN 13: 978-1-138-71478-6 (hbk)
ISBN 13: 978-1-138-71475-5 (pbk)
ISBN 13: 978-1-315-19784-5 (ebk)

Contents

Acknowledgements

My thanks are due to the following publishers for granting me permission to quote from their works: Oxford University Press for *Robert Burns: The Letters, Volume I: 1780–1789* and *Volume II: 1790–1796*, edited by J. De Lancey Ferguson, Second edition edited by G. Ross Roy (1985), and *The Poems and Songs of Robert Burns, Volumes I–III* edited by James Kinsley (OUP, 1968), and *The Letters and Prose Writings of William Cowper, Volume III: Letters 1787–1791*, edited by James King and Charles Ryskamp (OUP, 1982); also to Carcanet Press Limited for *The Religious Poetry of Christopher Smart*, edited by Marcus Walsh (Manchester, 1972); and Taylor & Francis for *The Poetry of Christopher Smart*, by Moira Dearnley (Routledge & Kegan Paul Ltd: London, 1968).

My thanks are also due to Ellen Howden for allowing me to use, on the cover, her photograph of the Robert Burns Memorial Window designed by Susan Bradbury and sited in the Parish Church of Alloway, in the village in which the poet was born.

I am greatly indebted to Dr Kenneth Simpson of the University of Strathclyde for initially encouraging me to further develop my study of Burns's religious thought and for his continued interest in my work. My research was also assisted by the helpfulness of staff at the Carnegie Library, Ayr, and the Mitchell Library, Glasgow.

On a personal note, I want to thank Myra and my family who put up with me, when in the midst of a busy working life my spare time was often spent in research. Thanks too to Nancy for typing the original manuscript of the thesis upon which the early part of this book is based, and to Lois, who, more recently, has helped me towards a calmer use of the computer.

Chapter 1

'The Cultivation of the Finer Feelings of the Heart'

In two of the earliest extant letters of Burns, both to his friend William Niven, a clue is given to an underlying attitude that from time to time surfaces in Burns's writing on the subject of religion. On 3 November 1780, Burns writes to the Maybole merchant:

> I shall be happy to hear from you how you go on in the ways of life; I do not mean so much how trade prospers, or if you have the prospect of riches, or the dread of poverty; as how you go on in the cultivation of the finer feelings of the heart.[1]

Then on 12 June 1781, Burns again writes:

> Our communion was on Sunday se'en night, I mention this to tell you that I saw your cousin there, with some of Mr Hamilton's sons. You cannot imagine how pleased I was to steal a look at him & trace the resemblance of my old friend – I was prepossed [*sic*] in his favor on that account, but still more by that ingenuous modesty (a quality so rare amongst students, especialy in the divinity way) which is so apparent in his air & manner.[2]

I suspect that at that time, Burns was attracted to religion because he saw it as something that could contribute to a development of 'the cultivation of the finer feelings of the heart', but that he was often repelled by some of the attitudes and the behaviour of some of those who professed it. One other thing that emerges from the second letter is that the criticism is made from within a personal relationship with the Church. It is when he is attending the church on a Communion Sunday that he makes the comment on divinity students. This very attendance signals his being a member of the Church as only those who had professed their faith and had been examined on their current understanding of it were admitted to the service to receive the sacrament.

This attraction to religion as a factor capable of helping form 'the finer feelings of the heart', and the opposite revulsion at certain attitudes and behaviour among some of those who claimed to practise it, is a recurrent feature in Burns's writing on the subject of religion and expressive of his own feelings and attitude to it.

In the pages that follow it will become clear that throughout his adult life Burns lived in the tension between having a very full appreciation of the value of religion, and feeling a revulsion at some of those who claimed to practise it, in that their irrational beliefs or inhumane conduct seemed at odds with all that he found good in it.

This underlying attitude which emerges most of all in his letters is perhaps best expressed in his verse epistle 'To the Reverend John McMath'. In the poem, with which Burns had enclosed a copy of 'Holy Willie's Prayer', religion is described as a 'maid divine', that is, as the servant of God in the service of mankind, and the poet asks for religion's understanding lest his remarks about religious people be taken for criticism of her whose reputation is untouched:

> All hail, Religion! maid divine!
> Pardon a muse sae mean as mine,
> Who in her rough imperfect line
> Thus daurs to name thee;
> To stigmatise false friends of thine
> Can ne'er defame thee.[3]

Burns was introduced to religion in the most natural way possible, through the influence of his parents. William Burnes is obviously the model from which the somewhat idealized portrait of a father leading family worship in 'The Cotter's Saturday Night' is drawn. William Burnes was a member of the Church of Scotland and attended the Auld Kirk of Ayr to which the Parish of Alloway had been subjoined in 1690. His minister, Dr William Dalrymple, was called upon to baptise the infant Robert shortly after he was born. From his earliest days the young Burns would have been aware of the importance of religion to his parents.

In another sense, too, Burns came naturally to a religious viewpoint through what seems to have been an early appreciation of the feelings that are evoked as the imagination plays on the beauties, the mysteries, even the terrors of the natural world as it passes through the seasons. His fertile imagination, too, was stimulated by the marvellous range of human feelings as a life makes its way through the years yet is never quite able to fully understand the interior world that equally has its beauties, its mysteries, and its terrors. Burns's religion as it developed related in natural ways to the exterior and the interior worlds that are explored by the imagination.

Religion was a natural part of his early education as we can see from some of the books that William Burnes provided for him to read. Burns gives his own account of some of this early reading on the subject of religion in his letter to Dr Moore. The books listed in that letter include 'Stackhouse's history of the bible, ... Boyle's lectures ... Taylor's scripture doctrine of original sin, ...

and Hervey's meditations'.[4] Gilbert Burns confirms this provision of religious books by their father in his letter to Mrs Dunlop:

> He borrowed *Salmon's Geographical Grammar* for us, and endeavoured to make us acquainted with the situation and history of the different countries in the world; while from a book society in Ayr, he procured for us Derham's *Phisico and Astro-Theology* and Ray's *Wisdom of God in Creation*, to give us some idea of astronomy and natural history. Robert read all these books with an avidity and industry scarcely to be equalled. My father had been a subscriber to Stackhouse's *History of the Bible*, then lately published by John Meuros in Kilmarnock; from this Robert collected a competent knowledge of ancient history: for no book was so voluminous as to slacken his industry or so antiquated as to damp his researches.[5]

These accounts of the early reading of Burns indicate a broadly based diet of religious texts, and although it is possible that Burns did not read Taylor's *Doctrine of Original Sin*, until he did so by procuring it for himself a little later, nevertheless William Burnes provided his son with works that encouraged a detailed examination of the basis of religion. Further to this the father also provided Robert and the rest of his children with a book of religious instruction written by himself, perhaps with some assistance from John Murdoch, *A Manual of Religious Belief in A Dialogue Between Father and Son*. Currie's comment on that book is indicative of the temper of the religion encouraged by William Burnes:

> There is in Gilbert's hands a little manual of religious belief in the form of a dialogue between a father and his son, composed by him for the use of his children in which the benevolence of his heart seems to have led him to soften the rigid Calvinism of the Scottish Church into something approaching to Arminianism.[6]

John Murdoch made a further contribution to Burns's early religious understanding by his choice of Masson's textbooks for schools. His *Collection of Prose and Verse from The Best English Authors* contains much of a religious nature and even his *Spelling Book* has religious overtones.

But the dominant influence in these early years was undoubtedly William Burnes. Burns writes of his father to Dr Moore, 'It was his dearest wish and prayer to have it in his power to keep his children under his own eye till they could discern between good and evil'.[7] Gilbert confirms this in his comment on how much under their father's supervision he and Robert were:

> My father was for some time almost the only companion we had. He conversed familiarly on all subjects with us as if we had been men, and was at great pains while we accompanied him in the labours of the farm, to lead the conversation to such subjects as might tend to increase our knowledge or confirm us in virtuous habits.[8]

It is little wonder then that all this reading of religious texts, which was also accompanied by a reading of the Bible and reinforced by a regular discussion of these matters with an earnest parent, resulted in what Burns describes as his having 'an enthusiastic, idiot piety'. But along with that he also says that he was 'a good deal noted for a retentive memory' and 'a stubborn, sturdy something in my disposition'.[9] These two factors helped Burns develop a view of religion that was always balancing one set of ideas against another, and that refused at times to automatically agree with views no matter by whom they were expressed.

Another important factor in determining Burns's religious views was his early exposure to the folk religion of his neighbourhood through his contact with Betty Davidson, the widow of a cousin of Burns's mother who frequently stayed with the family.[10] Burns comments:

> I owed much to an old Maid of my Mother's, remarkable for her ignorance, credulity and superstition. She had, I suppose, the largest collection in the county of tales and songs concerning devils, ghosts, fairies, brownies, witches, warlocks, spunkies, kelpies, elf-candles, dead-lights, wraiths, apparitions, cantraips, giants, inchanted towers, dragons and other trumpery. This cultivated the latent seeds of Poesy; but had so strong an effect on my imagination, that to this hour, in my nocturnal rambles, I sometimes keep a sharp look-out in suspicious places; and though nobody can be more sceptical in these matters than I, yet it often takes an effort of Philosophy to shake off these idle terrors.[11]

Burns's ability, 20 years after the boyhood experience of Betty Davidson's tales, to remember in detail the huge variety of species of supernatural creatures certainly verifies the retentiveness of his memory. But Burns's admission of how he has to enlist the help of his adult reasoning powers to dispel their continued existence in his imagination is an indication of just how permanent an impression was made upon his mind by the supernatural aspects of folklore, and of how natural it was for him to continue to think in religious terms throughout his life. In his letter to Dr Moore, Burns acknowledges his indebtedness to Betty Davidson as one whose stories 'cultivated the latent seeds of poesy' and in that same letter acknowledges his father as one 'to which I am indebted for most of my little pretensions to wisdom'.[12] As late as July 1790 he acknowledges to John Murdoch that the early years of his life 'owed so much to your kind tutorage'.[13] These three very different people each contributed much to Burns's introduction to religion.

In the extant early letters of Burns, he regularly uses not only religious but Christian terminology. In a rather priggish, stylized and insincere-sounding letter, possibly to Alison Begbie, which is tentatively dated 'Lochlea 1781' Burns writes:

> If you will be so good and so generous as to admit me for your partner, your companion, your bosom friend through life; there is nothing on this side of eternity shall give me greater transport; but I shall never think of purchasing your hand by arts unworthy of a man, and I will add, of a Christian.[14]

In presenting his credentials to the young lady there is an element of boastfulness in his claim to be a Christian, a note that is never sounded in his later writing. This letter also comes from the period when he was consciously developing and experimenting with his letter-writing skills, and its use of such a line as 'nothing on this side of eternity shall give me greater transport' sounds as if it was taken from a model such as he might have found in what Gilbert Burns described as 'a small collection of Letters by eminent writers'. This book had fortuitously been brought to their home by an uncle who had bought it in mistake for a self-help guide *The Complete Letter-writer*.[15]

However, Burns may have tried to use his Christian outlook as an advantage in trying to secure the attention of Alison Begbie, nevertheless he appears to have been genuinely imbued with Christian sentiment when, miserably ill and depressed, he writes to his father from Irvine on 27 December 1781:

> my principal, and indeed my only pleasurable employment is looking backwards & forwards in a moral & religious way. I am quite transported at the thought that ere long, perhaps very soon, I shall bid an eternal adieu to all the pains, & uneasiness & disquietudes of this weary life; for I assure you I am heartily tired of it, and, if I do not very much much [*sic*] deceive myself I could contentedly and gladly resign it –
>
> The Soul uneasy & confin'd from home,
> Rests & expatiates in a life to come.
>
> Pope
>
> It is for this reason I am more pleased with the 15th, 16th & 17th verses of the 7th Chapter of *Revn*: than any ten times as many verses in the whole Bible, & would not exchange the noble enthusiasm with which they inspire me, for all that this world has to offer.[16]

Burns's enthusiasm for these verses is, I think, based on two aspects of religion that he found invaluable. First, religion was a comfort and a source of consolation in the midst of a life that had little hope of material success. Second, it provided a model for conduct in a world in which there were many causes for tears and the need for someone to take it upon themselves to wipe them away. This first aspect of religion is again in evidence when he explains to his friend James Candlish that it was 'experience of the weakness, not the strength, of human powers made me glad to grasp at revealed Religion'.[17] The second aspect of religion comes through in his use of the last verse of the text from Revelation on several other occasions as descriptive of the power that he would like to have, that is, to be able to wipe away all tears from all eyes.

The letter itself has none of the passionate outpouring or sad anger of later letters in which Burns speaks of the usefulness and motivating powers of religion and, by comparison, seems stylized and almost studied, and certainly does not entirely convince of its sincerity by its sudden changes of mood. It leaves the impression of a young man feeling sorry for himself in his debilitated state following a miserable illness, and expressing himself in the religious terms with which he was familiar but which had not entirely gained his wholehearted assent.

Yet despite the hints that may be found in these very early letters of a certain superficiality or lack of deep commitment to the Christian faith, it was from an essentially Christian point of view that Burns viewed his world. It was the Christian religion that provided him with a framework of understanding of his relationship to people, to the world of events, and to the time scale within which he lived, a time scale that for Burns had at its omega point the eternity that might, or might not, hold the prospect of another form of existence. Burns's use of the phraseology of the Christian religion is obvious to anyone who reads his letters. The numerous biblical quotations scattered throughout them indicate his familiarity with the biblical text long before he pays a lighthearted tribute to it in his letter to Margaret Chalmers during the time of his enforced confinement following a fall in December 1787:

> I have taken tooth and nail to the bible, and am got through the five books of Moses, and half way in Joshua. It is really a glorious book. I sent for my book-binder today, and ordered him to get me an octavo bible in sheets, the best paper and print in town; and bind it with all the elegance of his craft.[18]

Burns's interest in the Christian religion was not just expressed in time of illness and its often accompanying depression, nor was his exploration of the Bible only something engaged in in moments of enforced idleness. A letter to his friend Robert Aiken just a few months after the publication of *The Kilmarnock Poems* shows Burns at a time of rising hope expressing himself in terms of faith. He tells Aiken of his feelings of remorse and the overwhelming sense of responsibility toward the children that Jean Armour has just borne to him:

> Even in the hour of social mirth, my gaiety is the madness of an intoxicated criminal under the hands of the executioner. All these reasons urge me to go abroad; and to all these reasons I have only one answer – the feelings of a father. This, in the present mood I am in, overbalances everything that can be said in the scale against it. You may, perhaps, think it an extravagant fancy, but it is a sentiment which strikes home to my very soul: though sceptical, in some points, of our current belief, yet, I think, I have every evidence for the reality of a life beyond the stinted bourne of our present existence: if so, then, how should I, in the presence of that tremendous Being, the Author of existence, how should I meet the reproaches of those who stand to me in the dear relation of children, whom I deserted in the smiling innocency of helpless infancy?[19]

As the letter continues, its next sentence perhaps begins to kindle a suspicion that the writer is taking over from the man, but nevertheless again a faith is being expressed as Burns writes: 'O thou great, unknown Power! thou Almighty God! who hast lighted up reason in my breast, and blessed me with immortality! I have frequently wandered from that order and regularity necessary for the perfection of thy works, yet thou hast never left me nor forsaken me!'

In this letter, too, Burns owns up to having had another view of his life in the past, and this ties in with the attitude expressed in that letter written from Irvine to his father in 1781. Burns writes:

> To tell the truth, I have little reason for complaint, as the world, in general, has been kind to me, fully up to my deserts. I was, for some time past, fast getting into the pining distrustful snarl of the misanthrope. I saw myself alone, unfit for the struggle of life, shrinking at every rising cloud in the chance-directed atmosphere of fortune, while, all defenceless, I looked about in vain for a cover. It never occurred to me, at least never with the force it deserved, that this world is a busy scene, and man a creature destined for a progressive struggle.

In the time between these two letters Burns had moved from a familiarity with religious phraseology and the Biblical text to a more thoughtful and thorough grasp of the issues that religion raised for someone intent as he was to 'study men, their manners, and their ways', which he said to John Murdoch was the joy of his heart.[20]

As early as 3 August 1784, when he wrote to his cousin James Burness who was a lawyer in Montrose, Burns was indicating an independence of judgement that would lead in time to his being regarded as less than orthodox in matters of religion. He gives this account of a religious sect that had caused a considerable upheaval in Irvine:

> Their tenets are a strange jumble of enthusiastic jargon, among others, she [Mrs Buchan] pretends to give them the Holy Ghost by breathing on them, which she does with postures & practices that are scandalously indecent; they have likewise disposed of all their effects & hold a community of goods, & live nearly an idle life, carrying on a great farce of pretended devotion in barns, & woods, where they lodge & lye all together, & hold likewise a community of women, as it is another of their tenets that they can commit no moral sin. – I am personally acquainted with most of them, & I can assure you the above mentioned are facts.
>
> This My Dr Sir, is one of the many instances of the folly in leaving the guidance of sound reason, & common sense in matters of Religion. Whenever we neglect or despise these sacred Monitors, the whimsical notions of a perturbated brain are taken for the emmediate [*sic*] influences of the Deity, & the wildest fanaticism, & the most inconsistent absurdities will meet with abbettors & converts. – Nay I have often thought, that the more out-of-the-way & ridiculous their fancies are, if once they are

> sanctified under the sacred name of RELIGION, the unhappy, mistaken votaries are the more firmly glued to them.[21]

In this account of the Church controversy in Irvine Burns says that he is 'personally acquainted' with most of the parties concerned. He says that the trouble started about two years previously which comes near to the time (summer 1781 to early 1782) when Burns had lived and worked in Irvine in order to learn more about the flax trade.[22] That Burns should be able to display such a detailed knowledge of the events that took place in a town where he had only stayed for a brief period is indicative of the lively interest that he took in religion. Burns accurately describes the parties involved and the principal actors in the drama. In 1761, over a dispute about patronage, Thomas Gillespie, the deposed minister of Carnock, had formed a new Presbtyery of Relief 'for Christians oppressed in their church privileges'.[23] In his letter Burns tells of how a congregation of the Presbytery of Relief had gathered at Irvine and how their minister, a Mr Whyte, was won over by Mrs Buchan and, following this, was deposed.[24] It is significant that Burns's letter to his cousin is almost entirely given over to his description of the Irvine episode, there being only two sentences at its beginning and one at the end that deal with family matters. In the letter, while there is a defence of 'the sacred name of RELIGION', it is a religion that must be in keeping with the equally sacred monitors of 'sound reason & common sense'.

Within a few months of writing this, Burns was to take up the theme of the importance of religion being monitored by common sense in his poem 'The Holy Tulzie'.[25] In his letter to Dr Moore he calls it, 'The first of my poetic offspring that saw the light'.[26] Burns goes on to describe that poem as 'a burlesque lamentation on a quarrel between two reverend Calvinists, both of them dramatis personae in my Holy Fair'. Kinsley points out that as the same letter to Dr Moore says that 'Holy Willie's Prayer' was the next poem to make its appearance, and that that had been occasioned by an event in January 1785, 'The Holy Tulzie' may be dated late 1784 or very early 1785.[27] In this poem Burns displays a knowledge of the local dispute between two Auld Light ministers, Alexander Moodie of Riccarton and John Russel of Kilmarnock, and in the course of the poem refers to no fewer than 11 other ministers in terms that indicate more than a passing acquaintance with them.[28] In what Kinsley deems is the final verse of the original version Burns asserts that the only hope for the success of the Auld Lights' 'orthodoxy' is for 'Common Sense' to be banished:

> Then Orthodoxy yet may prance,
> And Learning in a woody dance;
> And that curst cur ca'd Common Sense
> Wha bites sae sair,

Be banish'd o'er the seas to France,
  Let him bark there. –[29]

In Burns's view, what the Auld Lights claimed as orthodox belief was not compatible with common sense. This same point he made again in 'The Holy Fair' when he castigates one of the representatives of the 'orthodox' party, the Reverend William Peebles who rises to provide a counter view to the previous preacher who has been emphasising the value of 'moral pow'rs an' reason':

In guid time comes an antidote
Against sic poosion'd nostrum;
For*******, frae the water-fit,
Ascends the *holy rostrum*:
See, up he's got the Word o' G—,
An' meek an' mim has view'd it,
While COMMON-SENSE has taen the road,
An' aff, an' up the *Cowgate*
  Fast, fast that day.[30]

The verse quoted and the one immediately preceding it show that Burns is aware of the current theological debate going on within the Church and quite clearly he is also aware of the local exponents of the different views. Some ministers so preached as to seem to have reduced the Christian religion to a moral code, while others sought to emphasise the scriptural message of faith.

By the end of 1784 Burns was becoming articulate about the things that concerned him both in the belief and the practice of Christians. If he was beginning to find his voice in such matters it was a subject that had been introduced to his mind from his early years. One incident from those years is recalled in a letter to Miss Deborah Duff Davies on 6 April 1793, enclosing his song 'Bonie Wee Thing', in which Burns relates an incident in Church:

> I remember, & 'tis almost the earliest thing I do remember, when I was quite a boy, one day at church, being enraged at seeing a young creature, one of the maids of his house, rise from the mouth of the pew to give way to a bloated son of Wealth & Dullness, who waddled surlily past her. Indeed the girl was very pretty; & he was an ugly, stupid, purse-proud, money-loving, old monster, as you can imagine.[31]

That experience obviously remained vividly in his mind. Burns would have seen on many other occasions since that time beauty having to give way to grossness, poverty having to give way to riches, and the worthy commoner having to defer to the worthless of rank, but the fact that this act took place in church, ostensibly in the very face of the God both were there to worship, must have really rankled in his mind, and bitten deep into his soul.

According to his letter to Dr Moore, Burns as a teenager had begun to enter into theological debate with his contemporaries. He writes:

> Polemical divinity about this time was putting the country half-mad; and I, ambitious of shining in conversation parties on sundays between sermons, funerals, &c. used in a few years more to puzzle Calvinism with so much heat and indiscretion that I raised a hue and cry of heresy against me which has not ceased to this hour.[32]

Now in Dr Moore's letter this passage is placed in the account of Burns's life up to his sixteenth year. If we interpret the phrase 'in a few years more' to mean, say, four to five years it means that by the time Burns was an 18 to 20 year-old he was puzzling Calvinism, pondering its asserted certainties against the Lockean denial of certainty, really questioning the tenets of the Christian religion as they were then being preached and taught. This means that by the time he was more publicly making his views known they were opinions that had been a considerable time in the making.

Two letters from what was one of the most creative periods of his life give an indication of the tension to which Burns's hold on religion was subject. In the first he writes to John Arnot of Dalquatswood, 'sometime about the latter end of 1785', of his failure to secure the hand of Jean Armour. But he writes the account so much in the manner of Laurence Sterne's *Tristram Shandy* that it is difficult to know whether to take the things he says seriously or not. However there are some things said in it that I think are indeed indicative of the state of his mind at that time regarding religion. Burns, having related with very deliberate and unmistakable metaphors his action in impregnating Jean Armour, goes on to describe his feelings:

> There is a pretty large portion of bedlam in the composition of a Poet at any time; but on this occasion, I was nine parts & nine tenths, out of ten, stark staring mad. – At first, I was fixed in stuporific insensibility, silent, sullen, staring, like Lot's wife besaltified in the plains of Gomorha [*sic*]. – But my second paroxysm chiefly beggars description. – The rifted northern ocean, when returning suns dissolve the chains of winter, & loosening precipices of long accumulated ice tempest with hideous crash the foamy Deep – images like these may give some faint shadow of what was the situation in my bosom. – My chained faculties broke loose; my maddening passions, roused to tenfold fury, bore over their banks with impetuous, resistless force, carrying every check & principle before them. – Counsel, was an unheeded call to the passing hurricane; Reason, a screaming elk in the vortex of Moskoe strom; & Religion, a feebly struggling beaver down the roarings of Niagara. I reprobated the first moment of my existence; execrated Adam's folly-infatuated wish for that goodly-looking, but poison-breathing, gift, which had ruined him & undone me; & called on the womb of uncreated night to close over me & all my sorrows.[33]

Despite all its literary artifice and all the extravagance of its public posturing this letter reveals much about the state of Burns's mind at that time and casts light upon his attitude to religion. It is a letter revealing of what might be expected to happen if the dictates of 'the man of feeling' were allowed full rein, that is, when feeling and the passions were to be the determinants of behaviour. Burns was later to observe that 'the man of feeling' was not perhaps the best model for a young man to follow if he is 'to make his way into life'.[34] Burns judged that in the experience through which he had passed and about which he was writing toward the end of 1785, he had been a man totally ruled by passion. Counsel and Reason and Religion, although they each made their protest, were nevertheless insufficiently powerful to overcome the man whose passions were paramount.

The three metaphors that he uses are all carefully chosen. Counsel, the wise advice of friends, goes unheeded in the face of the noisy clamour of what he knows and the destructive forces of the hurricane of passion. Reason is described as a screaming elk – a huge animal that is protesting loudly. All its vast bulk and all its cries that would normally be heard and to which we would immediately give our attention are lost in the tumult of the storm of passion. But his metaphor of Religion as 'a feebly struggling beaver down the roaring of Niagara', is masterly, not just in its literary beauty but also in its accuracy in describing the nature of religion. For many people religion is something that helps them swim against the stream. The significant religious leaders have not been those who 'go with the flow' but have tended to be those who have battled against the tide. The beaver is normally able to perform in a very natural way in water which is its natural element but, faced with the roaring of Niagara, it struggles and is inevitably borne downstream. For Burns his religion faced a Niagara of passion and, although it put up a struggle, it had been defeated.

The final sentence in the section of the letter that relates the storm through which Burns's mind has passed, although elaborately working its way through to it, does conclude quite simply, that Burns's knowledge has 'undone' him. All that Burns had hoped would save him – the wise counsel of friends, the understanding acquired by accumulating knowledge, the 'cultivating of the finer feelings of the heart' and the moral strengthening of the will by religion, all of which would lead to virtue – had in the storm not proved sufficient.

The second letter of this period, although much shorter than the one just looked at, tells of the strain on Burns's understanding of himself that had been given him by his religious beliefs. About 1 August 1786 he writes to his friend James Smith at Mauchline. It is quoted in full, for its disjointed nature shows the distracted state of Burns's mind:

> My friend,
> I need not tell you the receipt of yours gave me pleasure. –
> O Jeany, thou hast stolen away my soul!

> In vain I strive against the lov'd idea:
> Thy tender image sallies on my thoughts,
> My firm resolves become an easy prey!
>
> Against two things however, I am fix'd as Fate: staying at home, and owning her conjugally. – The first, by Heaven I will not do! the last, by Hell I will never do!
> The inclosed may divert you. –
> A good God bless you, and make you happy up to the warmest, weeping wish of parting Friendship!
> For me, I am witless wild, and wicked; and have scarely any vestige of the image of God left me, except a pretty large portion of honour and an enthusiastic, incoherent Benevolence.
> If you see Jean tell her, I will meet her, So help me Heaven in my hour of need!
> Farewell till tomorrow morning!
> Robt Burns[35]

Burns's indecision and uncertainty as to what he really wants and what he really feels is obvious as he moves to a vehement denial of any intention to marry Jean Armour immediately after a sentimental expression of his love for her. A benediction is bestowed upon his friend immediately followed by a confession that he has hardly any godliness left within him, and just as quickly he qualifies this by a claim to have certain qualities left within him, all of which are qualities closely associated with religious aspirations. Looking within he sees someone who is quite different from the self-image that the Christian religion has encouraged him to adopt – that he is, as every man, a man made in the image of God. He looks inside and judges himself to be 'witless wild, and wicked' and acknowledges that he has 'scarcely any vestige of God left me'. It is as if at that time Burns discovers that his life is so out of keeping with the life of someone who allegedly has been made in the image of God, and is on the verge of denying that that religious concept is tenable. Yet the very elements of his being that he claims are still left to him are the traces of his having been made by the one who instils honour and a sense of worth and whose own nature is benevolent.

These two letters give us the picture of a man who has enlisted the help of Counsel, Reason and Religion, and yet found them wanting in his struggle with the passions that govern his life. They tell us of a man whose concept of himself as one made in the image of God has been shaken to its foundations by the storms through which his life has passed, yet who refuses to absolutely reject this notion because of the vestigial remains within him that he has to ascribe to the God he still believes in or perhaps just wants to believe in. This paradox is well expressed by Burns in a stanza from 'The Vision', a work whose composition Kinsley places in the time 'after August 1785', that is, the time of these letters, and which was published in *Poems, Chiefly in the Scottish Dialect* (Kilmarnock, 1786). Coila, the poet's muse, is speaking:

I saw thy pulse's maddening play,
Wild-send thee Pleasure's devious way,
Misled by Fancy's *meteor-ray*,
  By Passion driven;
But yet the *light* that led astray,
  Was *light* from Heaven.[36]

Following this period Burns possibly moved away from more specifically Christian beliefs to a more generalised view of religion, one that concentrated its hold on just a few very basic understandings of a person in relation to his God, a God who remained his creator, before whom he was accountable and whose nature was benevolent.

Chapter 2

'A Proven Fornicator'

Burns had come to an understanding of religion through his association with the Church of Scotland in its local manifestation of the church of the parish in which he lived, and so over the years he was attached to the parish churches at Ayr, Tarbolton, Mauchline, Dunscore and Dumfries. Through the various influences of his parents, his schoolteacher and his friends, and as one who conformed to a certain extent to the social pattern of his time, Burns had come into a relationship with the church. At different periods in his life it was to prove a relationship that came under strain but nevertheless it was part of his life right to the end.

The ministers of the first two parishes in which Burns lived were all of the New Light persuasion. Dr William Dalrymple and Dr William McGill of the Auld Kirk of Ayr both came under fire from some of their more orthodox brethren and both were regarded as potential heretics. Dr Patrick Wodrow and his colleague and successor at Tarbolton, the Reverend John McMath, were also recognised by Burns as being of the New Light persuasion. So in the years until he moved to Mossgiel in 1784 he had sat under ministers more liberal than some of their neighbouring contemporaries.[1] The understanding and interpretation of the Christian religion that he formed in his first 25 years made it difficult if not impossible to have a sympathetic understanding of the more rigid beliefs of John Russel of Kilmarnock or William Peebles of Newton upon Ayr.

However it was not theology but morality that brought Burns into contact in his early years with the Church as an institution. His first dealings with the Church were at the receiving end of its censure. That Burns was compeared by the Kirk Session of Mauchline to acknowledge his responsibility for the child conceived by Jean Armour is well documented,[2] but it is very likely that, before that, he had been compeared by the Kirk Session of Tarbolton anent his sexual relationship with Elizabeth Paton, to whom a child was born on 22 May 1785.[3] That this censure occurred is attested only by two poems. In the first 'A Poet's Welcome to his love begotten Daughter; the first instance that entitled him to the venerable appellation of Father', Burns writes:

> Welcome! My bonie, sweet, wee Dochter!
> Tho' ye come here a wee unsought for;
> And tho' your comin I hae fought for,
>   Baith Kirk and Queir;

Yet by my faith, ye're no unwrought for,
That I shall swear!

Wee image o' my bonie Betty,
As fatherly I kiss and daut thee,
As dear and near my heart I set thee,
Wi' as gude will,
As a' the Priests had seen me get thee
That's out o' h—.[4]

The reference to Kirk and Queir probably indicates that Burns had found himself in conflict with the Kirk Session, and had had to stand at the front of the Church in the Queir or chancel area immediately before the pulpit, as one guilty of fornication, and there to receive the rebuke and express his penitence. The next stanza, however, shows his defiant attitude to 'the Priests' who condemned him. The second poem 'The Fornicator. A New Song' is even more explicit in its description of an appearance in church on the charge of fornication. Burns writes:

For I've lately been on quarantine,
A proven Fornicator.

Before the Congregation wide
I pass'd the muster fairly,
My handsome Betsey by my side,
We gat our ditty rarely;[5]

The last line above refers to the harangue of rebuke that would be directed at the couple as they were berated for their sin and urged to an amendment of their lives.

Burns concludes his description of the occasion: 'With rueful face and signs of grace I payed the buttock hire', implying that he went through the motions required of him, but the crudity with which he describes the act that brought him there expresses not only the opinion that he had done no wrong but his contempt for the system that had arraigned him. Unfortunately, the Kirk Session Minutes of Tarbolton Parish for the period when any such censure would have taken place are missing.[6] However as it was the very strictly adhered to practice of the times,[7] it is highly unlikely that Burns would have escaped the censure and if he had he would surely not have written a fictitious account in which he named Betsey and implied that he was 'The Fornicator'.

Shortly after these events, Burns had another learning experience of the Church as an institution in his observation of it at work in the case of Gavin Hamilton's dispute with the Kirk Session of Mauchline. The dispute had started in 1777 over Gavin Hamilton's alleged retention of stent money[8] and was still unresolved at the time when the Kirk Session began pursuing Hamilton on another matter. Undoubtedly there seems to have been an element of intransigence and a certain high-handedness on the lawyer's part, and more than a suspicion of vindictiveness in the manner of the Kirk Session's pursuit of him on charges for non-attendance at church, sabbath breaking and the neglect of family worship. On 4 May 1785 the Presbytery minutes record:

> The Presbytery having heard parties at great length as to some irregularities in Hamilton's conduct alledged by the Kirk Session relating to his attendance on public ordinances, not keeping up the worship of God in his family and unnecessarily riding upon a Sunday, unanimously agreed to accept the Declaration made by Mr Hamilton of his regard for the ordinance of Religion.[9]

The report of the special committee that had been appointed to meet with Dr Auld and the Kirk Session and Mr Hamilton was received and the Presbytery agreed:

> to order the whole minutes relative to this affair to be erazed from the Kirk Session records ... recommend that Mr Hamilton to avoid giving any just cause of offence in the future, and to both parties to live in friendship for the time to come; and declare this affair now wholly at an end.

As far as the Presbytery was concerned that was the end of the matter but it took until 17 July 1785 for the Kirk Session at Mauchline to finally comply and grant a certificate to Gavin Hamilton that 'he was at present free from public scandal or ground of church censure'. But the petty spirit in which this was done is shown by an accompanying note: 'The poor have already suffered in your retaining 5 shillings for 2 private baptisms of your children formerly; due both by act and practice. It is therefore hoped that you will pay 7/6 along with the other dues'.[10]

It was the Presbytery's vindication of Gavin Hamilton and its censuring of the Kirk Session that provided Burns with the raw material for 'Holy Willie's Prayer' which was written after the Presbytery's judgement.[11] The theological content of the poem will be examined later. At present it stands as evidence of Burns's awareness of the workings of the Church as an institution, and of his willingness to offer comment upon it. As it began to circulate in its unpublished form, Burns claims that it got to the ears of the Kirk Session at Mauchline, and in a letter to Dr Moore he writes:

> Holy Willie's Prayer next made its appearance, and alarmed the kirk-Session so much that they held three several meetings to look over their holy artillery, if any of it was pointed against profane Rhymers. Unluckily for me, my idle wanderings led me, on another side, point blank within the reach of their heaviest metal.[12]

Examination of the Mauchline Kirk Session minutes for the period following the Presbytery's decision reveals no hint of concern at anything that Burns had written and it seems likely that anything that might have been talked about in private anent the poem had remained at that, and never reached the level of being recorded in the minutes as a matter raised by any of its members. No doubt Burns would have been apprehensive for a time after he had written it, and the opening verses of 'To the Rev. John McMath, Inclosing a copy of Holy Willie's Prayer which he had requested' seem to indicate this:

My musie, tir'd wi' mony a sonnet
On gown, an' ban', an' douce black bonnet,
Is grown right eerie now she's done it,
  Lest they shou'd blame her,
An' rouse their holy thunder on it
  And anathem her.

I own, 'twas rash, an' rather hardy,
That I, a simple, countra bardie,
Shou'd meddle wi' a pack sae sturdy,
  Wha, if they ken me,
Can easy, wi' a single wordie,
  Louse h–ll upon me.

Prudence was never one of his greatest strengths, and he continues:

But I gae mad at their grimaces,
Their sighan, cantan, grace-prood faces,
Their three-mile prayers, an' hauf-mile graces,
Their raxan conscience,
Whase greed, revenge, an' pride disgraces
Waur nor their nonsense.[13]

Burns is revolting against the outward show of religious people who adopt certain physical poses, who flourish their piety in terms of the lengthiness of their public prayers and who seem to go out of their way to find offence with other people's conduct when their own lives could not bear the same kind of scrutiny.

As his last sentence to Dr Moore indicates, the Kirk Session of Mauchline soon had other cause for his censure in the matter of his own behaviour towards Jean Armour. The details of this episode have recently been documented by James Mackay.[14] I only wish to pick up on the action taken by Burns, and his attitude towards the Church. I want also to consider the attitude of the Church towards Burns as represented by Mr Auld and the Kirk Session.

Burns's proposal of marriage having been rejected, and Jean by this time some six months pregnant, Burns writes to Mr John Richmond on 9 July 1786, informing him of his intention to establish his status as a bachelor: 'the Priest, I am inform'd will give me a Certificate as a single man, if I comply with the rules of the Church, which for that very reason I intend to do.'[15] In between writing that and what follows, Burns has obviously checked out what he has to do, and the letter, prefixed 'Sunday morn', continues, 'I am just going to put on Sackloth [*sic*] & ashes this day. I am indulged so far as to appear in my own seat. Peccavi Pater, misere [*sic*] mei'. Immediately thereafter, and signalling the attitude that Burns is taking to the process of the Church's discipline, he writes on a subject that more greatly concerns him: 'My book will be ready in a fortnight. If you have any Subscribers, return me them by Connell.' The Letter concludes with a flourish:

> The L—stand wi' the Righteous—
> Amen, Amen
>
> ROB[T] BURNS

Burns is obviously playing along with the Church in his obedience to its instructions on the process of penitence, but he is treated with a greater respect than some others who had committed a similar misdemeanour, by being allowed to stand at his own pew rather than at the cutty stool at the front of the church. His appreciation of this is muted as can be detected from his use of the word 'indulged'.

He writes on 17 July 1786 to David Brice, 'I have already appeared publickly in Church, and was indulged in the liberty of standing in my own seat. – I do this to get a certificate as a batchelor, which Mr Auld has promised me. I am now fixed to go to the west Indies in October.'[16] Again this interjection of another subject is an indication of how lightly he looked upon the whole process. But he adds something that seems to indicate again Mr Auld's intention of making this process of discipline as easy as possible both for Burns and for Jean: 'Jean and her friends insisted much that she should stand along with me in the kirk, but the minister would not allow it, which bred a great trouble I assure you and I am blamed for the cause of it, tho I am sure I am innocent.'

Mr Auld's behaviour may have been in order to try to preserve a relationship with the Armour family following Burns's expected departure abroad. Alternatively it may have had something to do with his having perceived that Burns had not been fairly treated by the Armours and so was intended to make it easier for his single status to be firmly established. I think that there may also have been an element of genuine compassion for a young couple caught up in a family feud, combined with a recognition that Burns was genuinely living at a different level of understanding from the people amongst whom he was set. Whatever the real reasons for Auld's behaviour, I suspect that Burns's contempt for the whole system made him oblivious to any compassion or understanding that was being directed at him. Burns appeared again before the Kirk Session on 23 July and 6 August 1786 and on this last occasion Jean Armour and three others who had similarly offended were rebuked by the Minister and thereafter 'absolved from scandal', their formal penitence having been completed.[17]

In June 1788 Burns approached Mr Auld, claiming that he and Jean had some time earlier entered upon an irregular marriage, and sought to have their marital state confirmed by the Kirk Session. There seems to have been some doubt as to whether or not there had ever been an irregular marriage as Burns could not supply any proof of its having taken place. Mr Auld seems to have been extremely diplomatic about it and compeared them before the Kirk Session on 5 August 1788, when it was recorded that, 'The Session taking this affair under their consideration, agree that they both be rebuked for this acknowledged irregularity and that they be taken solemnly engaged to adhere faithfully to one another as husband and wife all the days of their life.'[18] As further evidence of Mr Auld's leniency and discretion no fixed fee was charged, it being decided 'they agree to refer to Mr Burns his own generosity'. Burns gave a guinea to the poor fund. This episode is further evidence of the growing understanding between Auld and Burns, and perhaps should make us question the portrait of Auld so frequently painted in unflattering tones. Perhaps there is greater warmth in the use of the term 'Daddy' than is commonly perceived.

On these two occasions, both involving his sexual behaviour, Burns came under the official censure of the Church, but throughout his life he continued to have a relationship with the Church as an institution. He was a keen observer of its ways and a severe critic of its failings, but his criticism was based upon an inside knowledge of it; it was not a critical condemnatory throwing of stones at it from outside but it was more like the action of someone who had come to worship in a place where he expected to find God and instead found things going on that had no place within it, and things being believed that were of no consequence to those who sought after 'real religion'. His peripheral involvement through his writing in both the Gavin Hamilton and William McGill cases illustrates this. In the one he judged that there was a meanness of spirit and an overwillingness to believe ill being directed against a man he deemed to be honourable, and that such conduct was unworthy of the Church. In the other, he judged that a good Christian man was being pilloried because he had tried to present a more kindly view of God and a more human understanding of the relationship between Jesus and God, in contrast to the more severe image of God and the more transactional relationship between Jesus and God put forward by the ministers who were pursuing on charges of heresy.

Burns's relationship to the Church can best be understood in the light of his central beliefs about the nature of religion itself. On 22 June 1789 Burns writes to Mrs Dunlop, 'Religion, my honoured friend, is surely a simple business, as it equally concerns the ignorant and the learned, the poor and the rich.'[19] From Burns's own observations, he judged that religion was common to all. That in its essentials it was something that was accessible to all and that those who complicated it by over-elaborate theories were departing from its basic simplicity and making it exclusive. Some five years later he writes to Alexander Cunningham: 'Nor would I quarrel with a man for his irreligion, any more than I would for his want of a musical ear. I would regret that he was shut out from what, to me and to others, were such superlative sources of enjoyment.'[20] Religion to Burns was essentially a simple business and a superlative source of enjoyment. When these two things are kept in mind his criticisms of the Church and the Religion it communicated are better understood. Many of Burns's criticisms are directed at the apparent lack of enjoyment experienced by those who lead or participate in church services.

In 'The Brigs of Ayr', Burns puts words into the mouth of the New Brig who, looking at Auld Brig's 'O'er-arching, mouldy, gloom-inspiring coves', says that they are:

> Fit only for a doited Monkish race,
> Or frosty maids forsworn the dear embrace,
> Or Cuifs of latter times, wha held the notion,
> That sullen gloom was sterling, true devotion:[21]

Burns, for whom religion was an aid to the enjoyment of life, mourned the attitude that had confused solemnity with seriousness, and that had to adopt a certain solemn demeanour if it was to convey devotion. This same false gravitas affected the very construction of some of the Presbyterian places of worship. In the summer of 1787 after visiting the church at Linlithgow he commented, 'What a poor pimping business is a Presbyterian place of worship; dirty, narrow, and squalid; stuck in a corner of old popish grandeur such as Linlithgow.'[22]

Some of the ministers of the time contributed to the setting of these false norms. Burns deplored, 'the frigid air of a declaiming Preacher',[23] and declared to Miss Rachel Dunlop:

> I am in perpetual warfare with that doctrine of our Reverend Priesthood, that "we are born into this world bond slaves of iniquity & heirs of perdition, wholly inclined" to that which is evil and wholly disinclined to that which is good untill by a kind of Spiritual Filtration or rectifying process Called effectual Calling &c. The whole business is reversed, and our connections above & below completely change place.[24]

But more than likely he was as much at war with the demeanour and attitude of the ministers who held to and preached such doctrines. It is easy to imagine how believing such doctrines could turn the preacher into a very unattractive and frightening messenger, one who instilled fear and gloom as people contemplated the lost condition that they were told was theirs. No matter whether the preacher went on to deliver the good news of the possibility of escape by means of 'Effectual Calling', the whole theological package made for a very solemn atmosphere in a place of worship.[25]

The extreme manifestations of such theology resulted in bigotry, an attitude that brought out the most virulent criticism from Burns. Writing to Clarinda upon hearing of a comment on their relationship that had been made by one of her friends, Burns contrasts what he hopes is the view of an understanding God with that of their critic. He writes, 'but the half-inch soul of an unfeeling, cold-blooded, pitiful presbyterian bigot, cannot forgive any thing above his dungeon bosom and foggy head'.[26]

Allowing for all the impetus given to his emotion by hearing of an outsider's judgement of matters that they knew little of, nevertheless Burns's indignation gives a clue to his perception of the judgemental attitude that was the stock in trade of the most rigid adherents to such a theology of the fallen nature of man. Burns was not making a generalisation: he had specific people in mind, as is witnessed by his comment to John Logan as he sends him a copy of 'The Kirk's Alarm': 'If I could be of any service to Dr Mcgill, I would do it though it should be at a much greater expence than irritating a few bigotted Priests.'[27]

Burns could be scathingly critical of individual ministers as even the one poem mentioned above will show. Sometimes it was not because of their inappropriate conduct but for a more prosaic reason – their sheer dullness. In a letter written from Ellisland to Alexander Cunningham on 16 March 1791 he apologises for his verbosity:

> But lesst [*sic*] I sink into stupid Prose, so sacriligiously intrude on the office of my Parish-priest, who is himself one vast constellation of dullness, & from his weekly zenith rays out his contradictory stupidity to the no small edification & enlightening of the heavy & opaque pericraniums of his gaping Admirers.[28]

Burns's abuse of the preacher for his dullness of delivery is extended to a condemnation of the content of his message and is further extended to cast doubt on the mental capacity of his hearers. Poor Mr Kirkpatrick, the parish minister of Dunscore, was the butt of that criticism; nevertheless Burns regularly worshipped there and made a point of going along with Jean to visit the minister before they left for Dumfries.[29] Burns's comments on Mr Kirkpatrick are consonant with this heavily ironic remark in a letter of that same period to Mr Peter Hill: 'The Clergy, I pass by – their profundity of erudition, & their liberality of sentiment; their total want of Pride, & their detestation of Hypocrisy, are so proverbially notorious, as to place them far, far above either my Praise or Censure.'[30] Again in a letter to Alexander

Cunningham he castigates religious people for a trait that seems peculiar to them:

> by the bye, will you, or can you tell me, my dear Cunningham, why a religioso turn of mind has always a tendency to narrow & illiberalize the heart? They are orderly; they may be just; nay, I have known them merciful: but still your children of Sanctity move among their fellow-creatures with a nostril snuffing putrescence, & a foot spurning filth, in short, with that conceited dignity which your titled Douglases, Hamiltons, Gordons or any other of your Scots Lordlings of seven centuries standing, display when they accidentally mix among the many-aproned Sons of Mechanical life. – I remember, in my Plough-boy days, I could not conceive it possible that a noble Lord could be a Fool, or that a godly Man could be a Knave. – How ignorant are Plough-boys! – Nay, I have since discovered that a *godly woman* may be a — ! —But hold – Here's t'ye again – this Rum is damn'd generous Antigua, so a very unfit menstruum for scandal.[31]

Yes, maybe Burns was 'fou' when he wrote that, but he was 'nae that fou'. In this passage he gives vent, as it were, to some of his inner thoughts; *in vino veritas*. But notice he uses the phrase 'religioso turn of mind', signalling that his main criticism is directed at religiosity rather than religion, at those who make a display of their religiousness, at those whose religion is so well defined that it is made to cover every contingency in their life, at those whose religion is so daintily packaged that they carry it around with them as something that belongs to them and that cannot be readily shared, and at those whose religion has separated them from their fellow men so much that they begin to think of themselves as those who live on another planet. Here Burns had in mind the 'Unco Guid or the Rigidly Righteous' whom he had once before addressed:

> O ye wha are sae guid yoursel,
> Sae pious and sae holy,
> Ye've nought to do but mark and tell
> Your Neebours' fauts and folly![32]

In his words to Cunningham, Burns allows that such people's lives are orderly, just, even at times merciful, but they so bear themselves in a superior way to their fellow mortals that it is obvious that their religion lacks an inner core of compassion and humility. It is but a veneer, a shallow worthless thing that in the end does more harm than good, so that ultimately a godly man can be a Knave, and, says Burns, it is best left unsaid what a godly woman can turn out to be. Religiosity was his target not religion – ultimately religiosity could only have a bad effect on people, whereas religion continued to have a place of esteem in his thinking. He writes to Mrs McLehose on 4 January 1788, 'Your religious sentiments, Madam, I revere. If you have, on some suspicious evidence, from some lying oracle, learnt that I despise or ridicule so sacredly important a matter as real Religion, you have, my Clarinda, much misconstrued your friend.'[33]

In that same letter he provides a contrast to what he has called 'real Religion' by admitting that there is a possibility that he might still have within him 'a Presbyterian sourness, a hypocritical severity' when he looks upon others whose behaviour is worse than his. Burns's venomous attacks on religious superficiality, be it evidenced by the clergy or by the ordinary Christian, have always to be seen in the context of his respect for religion itself. This attitude comes through at different stages in his life.

A few weeks after Mrs McLehose had challenged Burns on his religious belief, Mrs Dunlop had written chiding him thus on his appearing to have given up religion:

> I fear you have drove away the only friend could supply that cordial [the remedy for his depression] that childish *idiot* the companion of your *early* days, nor will you ever be as happy again unless you are able to recall that discarded friend, unknown in the polite circle and cherish her like a beloved wife, never to be divorced from your bosom ... besides her other qualities the poor idiot is the best sick nurse on earth.[34]

Mrs Dunlop is, of course, referring to the 'idiot piety' Burns had mentioned in his letter to Dr Moore,[35] which, she implies, he has thrown away, and Burns is stung into replying on 12 February 1788:

> Some things, my revered Patroness, in your late letters hurt me: not that *you say them*, but that *you mistake me*. – Religion, my honored Madam, has not only been all my life my chief dependance, but my dearest enjoyment. – I have indeed been the luckless victim of wayward Follies; but, alas! I have ever been "more fool than knave". – A Mathematician without Religion is a probable character; an irreligious Poet, is a Monster.[36]

Burns is 'standing on his dignity' in this letter – witness the terms 'my reverend Patroness' and 'my honored Madam' – but his protestation of what religion means to him is spelled out in no uncertain terms as something that all his life has been important to him as a support and a source of enjoyment. His introduction of that word 'enjoyment' underlines the constancy of his attitude to religion. Six years later, that is just two years before his death, he was to write to his friend Alexander Cunningham, whom unlike Mrs Dunlop he had no need to impress, that religion was one of the 'superlative sources of enjoyment'.[37]

Mrs Dunlop clearly believed Burns's protestation regarding his valuing of religion, for in a letter of 5 November 1788 she informs him thus of an incident in which she defended his religion and his attitude to the clergy:

A gentleman told me with a grave face the other day that you certainly were a sad wretch, that your works were immoral and infamous; you lampooned the clergy and laugh at the ridiculous parts of religion and he was told, were a scandalous free liver in every sense of the word. I said I was certain he must be misinformed and asked if he knew you. He told me he had been in your company and knew it was the case.

"What did I think of your religion?" That it was too exalted and sublime to have any ridiculous parts capable of being laughed at. "What of that illiberal mind that could fall foul of so respectable a body of men as the clergy of Scotland?" That the Scotia Bard was far above it, that no man more regards the pastors of his people when worthy of their calling, but that those he exposed were wolves in sheeps clothing, the bane of the community and too black for his ink, low beneath his pen. But I begged to appeal to the lines left in Dr Laurie's manse as proof positive the clergy were not attacked in a collective body.

Mrs Dunlop continued in a way that implies that she thought that Burns's criticism of individual ministers was justified:

The writers [lawyers] had in my time pensioned three men to quit practice in their callings as their characters were too atrocious for the reputation of the profession. It would be much for the interest of some he [Burns] celebrates that the same delicacy should take place among the divines.
'Twas observed I was too warm ... .[38]

Such a spirited defence of Burns was not made on the basis of friendship but could only have come from Mrs Dunlop's conviction of his sincerity in his stated respect for religion and its honest practitioners. Her friendship was not strong enough in the end to survive Burns's criticism of her friend Dr Moore or Burns's opinion expressed upon the death of the French King and Queen. If ultimately her friendship could break up over such things as these, then she would not have defended Burns on this occasion as she did, if she had thought there was any substance in the allegations being made against him.

Burns again affirms the importance of religion to him when on 6 October 1790 he comments to Mrs Dunlop on the book she has told him she is reading:

I give you joy of the works of Mr Bourne, which you tell me you are reading. I once had the first Volume, & was so delighted with it that I could have almost repeated it verbatim. – We can no more live without Religion, than we can live without air;

But Burns feels that he must qualify this statement and continues:

but give me the Religion of Sentiment & Reason. – You know John Hildebroad's famous epitaph –

"Here lies poor old John Hildebroad;
"Have mercy on his soul, Lord God,
"As he would do, were he Lord God,

"And thou wert poor John Hildebroad".
This speaks more to my heart, & has more of the genuine spirit of Religion in it, than is to be found in whole waggon-loads of Divinity.[39]

Here again is Burns's respect for religion, but it is not the orthodox religion of the time. The religion that emerges is one that reflects the feelings of the heart and the common-sense reasoning of the mind. His quoting of the epitaph signals that Burns's God is one that must at least measure up to the benevolence and the mercy that he would expect to be shown and that he himself would hope to show if the roles were reversed.

To say as he does in this letter that religion is as necessary to us as air, is to signal it as a means by which life is sustained. To talk of religion in this way is to diminish the credal element of it; it is to reduce the importance of detailed beliefs and emphasize the motivating and empowering aspect of it. To pursue the logic of this understanding of religion would be to be able to still acknowledge its utility even if its beliefs were to prove false. This logic is seen expressed in a letter to Mrs Dunlop on 16 August 1788, from Ellisland, in order to ward off a pessimistic mood brought on by contemplating all his responsibilities: 'To counterwork these baneful feelings, I have sat down to write to you; as I declare upon my soul, I always find *that* the most sovereign balm under Heaven for my wounded Spirit.' In this melancholy mood he continues:

> Man is by no means a happy creature. I do not speak of the Selected Few, favored by partial Heaven; whose souls are tuned to Gladness amid Riches, & Honors, & Prudence, & Wisdom. I speak of the neglected Many, whose nerves, whose sinews, whose days, whose thoughts, whose independance, whose peace, nay, whose very gratifications & enjoyments, the instinctive gift of Nature, are sacrificed & sold to these few bloated Minions of Heaven!... It is this way of thinking, it is these melancholly truths, that make Religion so precious to the poor, miserable Children of men. If it is meer [*sic*] phantasm, existing only in the heated imagination of Enthusiasm – "What Truth on earth so precious as the Lie!".

But having opened up the way for expatiating on the falsity of the basis of religious belief, he immediately reverts to the defence of a religious viewpoint by continuing, 'My idle reasonings sometimes make me a little sceptical, but the Necessities of my heart always give the cold philosophisings the lie.'[40]

Religion for Burns springs from feelings that are more powerful than philosophy. Burns's feelings are always challenging philosophy. He writes on a parallel theme to Dr Moore on 2 August 1787 telling of how as a child his imagination had been well supplied with tales of the supernatural and although he regarded them as 'trumpery' nevertheless he confesses:

> [they] had so strong an effect on my imagination, that to this hour, in my nocturnal rambles, I sometimes keep a sharp look-out in suspicious places; and though nobody

> can be more sceptical in these matters than I, yet it often takes an effort of Philosophy to shake off these idle terrors.[41]

For Burns religion was more primal than philosophy and therefore more likely to rise up and challenge the more sophisticated ideas that had been constructed by philosophers.

In the concluding part of his letter to Mrs Dunlop, Burns again seems to be talking about 'real religion' when he indicates that it is to be found not in the expected places, or in overt practice, or among people in the public eye, but in more hidden places and among those who experience the darker side of life. Burns writes:

> Who looks for the heart weaned from earth; the Soul affianced in her God; the Correspondence fixed with Heaven; the pious supplication & devout thanksgiving, constant as the vicissitudes of even & morn; who thinks to meet with them in the Court, the palace, in the glare of public life? No: to find them in their precious importance & divine efficacy, we must search among the obscure recesses of Disappointment, Affliction, Poverty & Distress.[42]

Far from developing an attack on the false premises of religion Burns reiterates its 'precious importance and divine efficacy'. He again seems to stress religion's role as a source of empowerment, a positive consoling agent in the midst of life's distressing circumstances.

One passage from a poem he found in Hervey's *Meditations* is quoted by Burns three times, once in a letter to Mrs McLehose and twice in letters to Mrs Dunlop. From that passage we can gain a sense of the respect that he has for religion and an understanding of his reasons for defending its importance. When writing to Mrs McLehose on 19 January 1788 Burns prefaces the quotation with these words: 'In this light I have often admired Religion. In proportion as we are wrung with grief, or distracted with anxiety, the ideas of a compassionate Deity, an Almighty Protector, are doubly dear.'[43] Burns then goes on to quote from the poem in Hervey (which I have discovered was written by Dr Nathaniel Cotton, the physician who attended to William Cowper during a time of mental illness at St Albans):

> "'Tis this, my friend, that streaks our morning bright;
> "'Tis this that guilds the horrors of our night."[44]

On this occasion Burns does not quote the rest of the stanza, but in his use of the poem with Mrs Dunlop in his letter of 6 September 1789 he does, with the lines that follow,

When wealth forsakes us, and when friends are few;
When friends are faithless, or when foes pursue;
'Tis this that wards the blow, or stills the smart,
Disarms affliction, or repels his dart;
Within the breast bids purest raptures rise,
Bids smiling conscience spread her cloudless skies."

When Burns first quotes these lines to Mrs Dunlop he prefaces them with this remark:

> I know not whether I have ever sent you the following lines, or if you have ever seen them; but it is one of my favourite quotations, which I keep constantly by me in my progress through life, in the language of the Book of Job, "Against the day of battle and of war" – spoken of religion.[45]

Three years later, on 6 December 1792, he uses the lines again in a letter to Mrs Dunlop, and on this occasion he prefaces the quote with these words:

> when I write from the heart, I am apt to be guilty of these repetitions. The compass of the heart, in the musical style of expression, is much more bounded, than the reach of invention; so the notes of the former are extremely apt to run into similar passages; but in return for the paucity of its compass, its few notes are much more sweet. – I must still give you another quotation, which I am almost sure I have given you before, but I cannot resist the temptation. – The subject is Religion. – Speaking of its importance to mankind, the Author says,[46]

The passage from Hervey then follows.

In writing as he does, Burns is avowing the value of religion and clearly commending its usefulness to others. It is the utility of religion, that he has in mind when, in a letter to Alexander Cunningham on 25 February 1794, he writes: 'It is in this point of view, and for this reason, that I will deeply imbue the mind of every child of mine with religion. If my son should happen to be a man of feeling, sentiment, and taste, I shall thus add largely to his enjoyments.'[47]

The passage that follows this statement elaborates on the nature of these enjoyments and gives an insight into what Burns was thinking of when he used the term 'religion':

> Let me flatter myself that this sweet little fellow, who is just now running about my desk, will be a man of melting, ardent, glowing heart; and an imagination, delighted with the painter, and rapt with the poet. Let me figure him wandering out in a sweet evening to inhale the balmy gales, and enjoy the growing luxuriance of the spring; himself the while in the blooming youth of life. He looks abroad on all nature, and through nature up to nature's God. His soul, by swift delighting degrees, is rapt

> above this sublunary sphere, until he can be silent no longer, and bursts into the glorious enthusiasm of Thomson,
>
> "These, as they change, Almighty Father, these
> Are but the varied God – The rolling year
> Is full of thee."
>
> And so on in all the spirit and ardour of that charming hymn.

Burns reins himself in for a moment, and then comes to a cooler assessment of what he is claiming for religion:

> These are no ideal pleasures; they are real delights; and I ask what of the delights among the sons of men are superior, not to say equal, to them? And they have this precious, vast addition, that conscious Virtue stamps them for her own; and lays hold on them to bring herself into the presence of a witnessing, judging and approving God.

Writing to Mrs Dunlop on Christmas morning 1793, Burns similarly defines religion and its utility: 'Now that I talk of Authors, how do you like Cowper? Is not the Task a glorious Poem? The Religion of The Task, bating a few scraps of Calvinistic Divinity, is the Religion of God & Nature; the Religion that exalts, that ennobles man.'[48]

By the time of writing this, Burns has obviously moved on from the natural acceptance of the religion of his childhood and early youth, and has come to hold a less orthodox set of beliefs, whilst not appearing to have relinquished his hold on religion itself. Burns's understanding of religion undoubtedly undergoes change as his reading and his experience of life becomes more extensive, but certain basic religious beliefs remain as constants, as their recurrence in his writings shows. Foremost among these recurring religious themes are a belief in a benevolent God, a speculation on an existence beyond the grave, and an acknowledgement of his own accountability.

Chapter 3

'Still I am a Very Sincere Believer in the Bible'

Burns's independent religious view developed as a result of a number of factors interacting upon him: a questioning of the nature of the Bible, a questioning of Calvinist doctrine, his experience of the Church, and his reliance upon the inner light of the heart and mind. All of these factors, except the last, are mediated to him through people as well as books, and sometimes their message is strengthened or weakened in credibility according to the messenger. As for the last, 'the inner light', this is the understanding that is arrived at by a man of independent mind, a man who claims 'almost all my Religious tenets originate from my heart'.[1] For Burns, his own powers of inner judgement determine what he believes. An examination of the recurring themes of Burns's religion will be left until after we have looked at the factors that made them important to him and helped bring about his particular religious point of view.

Burns's lavish use of biblical texts in his letters is just one indication of his familiarity with a book with which he had a lifelong association. In his introduction to *The Complete Letters of Robert Burns*, James A. Mackay claims that 'There are something like 130 biblical quotations and allusions taken from 34 books of the Old and New Testaments' to be found in Burns's letters.[2] His early understanding of some of these texts would have been coloured by their use as proof texts in *The Westminster Confession of Faith*. But that early understanding might well have come under strain as his experience of literature grew, and he would begin to appreciate the questionable nature of the *Confession*'s method of using texts from widely differing contexts to support the same proposition.

In the *Confession*, Chapter VI: 'Of the Fall of Man, of Sin, and of the Punishment thereof', section IV, man's condition after 'The Fall' is described thus: 'From this original corruption whereby we are utterly indisposed, disabled, and made opposite to all good (1) and wholly inclined to all evil, (2) do proceed all actual transgressions (3).'[3] This proposition is supported by texts, taken out of entirely different contexts and used to justify the statement. A close examination of these texts will soon indicate the contrived nature of the argument, or at least the weakness of their support for the proposition. Anyone with a respect for a literary text's relatedness and coherence to its own contextual relationship will recognize the invalidity of its usage as literary support of an argument in which it has no particular concern. Burns's growing appreciation of the nature of argument – derived from a familiarity with the works of some of the masters of literature and philosophy such as John Locke, Adam Smith, Thomas Reid and Laurence Sterne – must have made him more critical of the way in which the words of the Bible were used by others, even those as respected as the 'Westminster Divines'.

Burns himself uses the Bible in the same way that he uses other works of literature. Biblical quotations are used to illustrate his own arguments, rather than as things that justified them. On occasion he will playfully use the Biblical text or adopt its literary rhythms for lighthearted topics, but he never treats it with disrespect. Yet always there is the sense of his treating it as he would any other book. He never makes a serious reference to the Bible as 'the Word of God'. His only use of the phrase is when he is mocking the Reverend William Peebles in 'The Holy Fair':

See, up he's got the word o' G—,
An' meek an' mim has view'd it.[4]

But as several verses in 'The Cotter's Saturday Night'[5] show, Burns has a thorough knowledge of the Bible and, as his remarks to Margaret Chalmers indicate, he thought of it as 'really a glorious book'.[6] Burns's words on that occasion should be understood in the light of his letter to Mrs Dunlop just one year later on New Year's Day 1789 when he writes, 'Still I am a very sincere believer in the Bible; but I am drawn by the conviction of a Man, not the halter of an Ass.'[7]

Burns had probably been first guided towards this attitude to the Bible by his reading of John Taylor's *The Scripture Doctrine of Original Sin*, which is one of the books that, in his letter of 2 August 1787 to Dr John Moore, he says was part of his early reading.[8] John Taylor writes in defence of the importance of the God-given human understanding, 'For the scriptures can be no rule to us if the understanding God hath given us is not a Rule in judging their sense and meaning. Nothing ought to pass for divine Revelation which is inconsistent with any of the known Perfections of the divine nature ... '[9] In the same passage Taylor goes on to criticize the proof text method of assembling statements of Christian doctrine, as had been done by those who had written *The Westminster Confession of Faith*: 'We should not content ourselves with scraps and single sentences which in Sound may seem to mean one thing but really have, taken with what goes before and what follows after, a quite different signification.'

John Goldie was another writer whose view of the Scriptures seemed to influence Burns both in the matter of what they said about God and in the method by which they should be interpreted. These are brought together by Goldie when he gives the following guidance on the understanding of the

Scriptures, in the first volume of his *Essays on Various Important Subjects Moral and Divine* (1779):

> An infallible rule whereby we may understand the true and proper meaning of the revealed scripture.
>
> (1) We must be extremely careful concerning every particular text to see whether it consists of a literal or figurative meaning.
>
> (2) Bring the text to measure against the "nature and perfections of the true God", and if the literal meaning of the text will not agree therewith it is morally certain that it consists of a figurative sense.[10]

Goldie wants people to use their reason as they interpret the Bible, and to be prepared to make the judgement of a text as to whether or not it should be taken literally or figuratively. He also wants people to judge whether or not the text is in keeping with what they already know of God's nature, that is, the text must be subject to God, not God to the text. Goldie cites Athenasius as his authority: 'Should we understand and take up a great part of sacred scripture literally or in a literal sense, we should inevitably soon fall into blasphemy.'[11]

Later in that same volume Goldie attacks those who 'Sacrifice their reason at that infamous altar of credulity. Everything is infamous that is contrary or inconsistent with the nature and perfections of the Deity, and a putting out of that candle which God himself hath lighted and set up in the human heart.'[12]

It is significant that Burns links the names of John Taylor and John Goldie in his 'Epistle to John Goldie in Kilmarnock, Author of the Gospel recovered' (August 1785). His words make it clear that he approves of them both:

> O GOWDIE, terror o' the whigs,
> Dread o' black coats and reverend wigs!
> Sour Bigotry on his last legs
>   Girns and looks back,
> Wishing the ten Egyptian plagues
>   May seize you quick.

Because of the attacks of 'Gowdie', Superstition is in a 'sad condition', Enthusiasm is 'in a gallopin consumption', and Orthodoxy is 'near unto death'. Burns continues ironically:

> It's you and Taylor are the chief
> To blame for a' this black mischief;
> But could the L—d's ain folk get leave,
> A toom tar-barrel
> And twa red peats wad bring relief
> And end the quarrel.

Burns then gives Gowdie his blessing:

For me, my skill's but very sma',
And skill in prose I've nane ava;
But quietlenswise, between us twa,
Weel may ye speed;
And tho' they sud you sair misca',
Ne'er fash your head.[13]

Taylor's and Goldie's works helped Burns towards an understanding of the Bible as a valuable but not infallible book. He appreciated their open-minded approach to the text and their assertion of the value of the judgement of the individual's own natural understanding, something that they looked upon as God-given.

As Burns questioned the Bible so he questioned the doctrines of the Church as they were in his time expounded by ministers who, as he writes in 'The Holy Tulzie', drank from 'Calvin's fountainhead'.[14] In the last quarter of the eighteenth century that would have included all the ministers in the Church of Scotland, but although all subscribed to the Calvinistic doctrines of *The Westminster Confession of Faith*, there were some among those known as the New Lights who soft-pedalled or chose to ignore some of the more extreme aspects of Calvinistic theology found within the *Confession*. This, for example, was one of the reasons why Dr McGill was suspected of heresy.[15] Burns writes to Dr Moore in 1787 that, some years before, he began 'to puzzle Calvinism with so much heat and indiscretion that I raised a cry of heresy against me which has not ceased to this hour.'[16] Calvinism was synonymous with orthodoxy and so to dispute Calvinistic belief was to be in danger of being guilty of heresy. Burns found himself in opposition to two doctrines that were vigorously expounded by the Calvinists of his day: the Doctrine of Original Sin and the Doctrine of Predestination. His opposition did not spring from an understanding of religion that was totally opposed to Calvinism for, as I shall later show, there were elements of Burns's belief that were entirely compatible with a Calvinistic view.[17]

The ordinary member of the Church of Scotland was confronted by the Doctrine of Predestination in *The Westminster Confession of Faith*, where Chapter III section III states, 'By the decree of God, for the manifestation of his glory, some men and angels are predestinated unto everlasting life, and others foreordained to everlasting death.'[18] This was supported by the following 'proof-texts':

1 Timothy 5:21 I charge thee before God, and the Lord Jesus Christ and the elect angels,

Matthew 25:41 Depart from me ye cursed into everlasting fire prepared for the devil and his angels:

Romans 9:22–23 What if God, willing to show his wrath and to make his power known, endured with much long suffering the vessels of wrath fitted to destruction: And that he might make known the riches of his glory on the vessels of mercy which he had afore prepared unto glory.

Ephesians I:5–6 Having predestinated us unto the adoption of children by Jesus Christ to himself, according to the good pleasure of his will, To the praise of the glory of his grace, wherein he hath made us accepted in the beloved;

Proverbs 16:4 The Lord hath made all things for himself; yea even the wicked for the day of evil.[19]

It is easy to surmise what anyone who had read Taylor and Goldie would make of this hotch-potch of 'proof-texts'. Anyone with any experience of reading the Bible, keeping the criteria of Taylor and Goldie in mind, would soon find themselves questioning the value of such supporting evidence.

But to question the reasoning of the *Confession* was to question the reasoning of the reformer John Calvin, whose teachings to a large extent were adopted by those who brought about the Scottish Reformation and principally by John Knox, and were built in to the very theological and ecclesiastical foundations of the Church of Scotland when it was reformed in 1560. Calvin's *Institutes of the Christian Religion* was published in Latin at Basle in 1536 and at Strasbourg in 1539, then in French at Geneva in 1541 and again in 1559. This immensely controversial, popular and radical work was first translated into English by Thomas Norton in 1561. It became one of the major influences on those who compiled the *Confession*, which had been approved by the General Assembly of the Church of Scotland in 1647.[20] Comparison of the sections of the *Confession* quoted above with this passage from John Calvin's *Institutes* reveals the implications of the acceptance of the Confession of Faith:

> By predestination we mean the eternal decree of God, by which he determined with himself whatever he wished to happen with regard to every man. All are not created on equal terms, but some are preordained to eternal life, others to eternal damnation; and, accordingly, as each has been created for one or other of these ends, we say that he has been predestinated to life or death.[21]

Calvin's arguments are much more broadly based than those of the *Confession*, and reading the *Institutes* brings recognition that to question the authority of the *Confession* was to question one of the most highly respected teachers and founder theologians of the reformed church. In the immediately preceding passage Calvin warns the critics of this doctrine:

> Whoever, therefore throws obloquy on the doctrine of predestination, openly brings a charge against God, as having inconsiderately allowed something to escape from him which is injurious to the Church.
>
> The predestination by which God adopts some to the hope of life, and adjudges others to eternal death, no man who would be thought pious ventures simply to deny . . . .[22]

According to Calvin, to question the Doctrine of Predestination was to malign God, and to deny it was not the act of a pious man. This was the line adopted by those who saw themselves as the defenders of the orthodox position in the Church of Scotland of Burns's time, and it was this doctrine that Burns chose to question in 'Holy Willie's Prayer'.

Burns creates the persona of one of the elect whom we overhear at prayer, so it is that in the opening stanza Burns mocks the Doctrine of Predestination and the concept of God that it encourages:

> O THOU that in the heavens does dwell!
> Wha, as it pleases best thysel,
> Sends ane to heaven and ten to h–ll,
> A' for thy glory!
> And no for ony gude or ill
> They've done before thee.[23]

Burns was probably familiar with John Goldie's *Essay upon What is commonly called Original Sin* (1779). Referring particularly to the Doctrine of Predestination, Goldie writes:

> Men may just as well pretend that there is no God as to believe to his dishonour that he is such a one who not only formed them for damnation but also without reason decreed them over before they had an existence, to everlasting perdition; in which light he is thereby represented as one that delighteth in their misery.[24]

Combined with such ideas, Burns's familiarity with John Locke's view that revelation cannot be admitted against the clear evidence of reason[25] must have caused him to question the Doctrine of Predestination as it was found in the *Confession*. Burns even makes Holy Willie question the reasoning that has caused God to predestine him to be one who is elected to salvation, despite the fact that he is a self-confessed fornicator and even possibly one who has an incestuous relationship with his niece.[26]

> What was I, or my generation,
> That I should get such exultation?
> I, wha deserv'd most just damnation,
> For broken laws

Sax thousand years ere my creation,
  Thro' Adam's cause![27]

Holy Willie expresses his surprise that he should be so predestined to salvation when he knows that he is guilty by association with Adam's sin. Burns ironically makes Holy Willie mention that as the reason for his surprise at finding himself among the elect rather than the more natural reason of his sexual misconduct. But the double irony is in this: Holy Willie uses another doctrine, the Doctrine of Original Sin, as the reason for his surprise at God's choice of him for life instead of death. Two doctrines of the *Confession* are being called into question in this poem, and both are being examined in the light of reason as was advocated by John Locke and later by John Goldie.

Burns's reading was beginning to separate him from some of his contemporaries, both in the Church and in the community, and certainly from the less literate among them. John Goldie expounds the theory that the acceptance of such doctrines has a great deal to do with the illiteracy of the people and their willingness to receive them in an unquestioning way:

> ... the propagating of such doctrines depends much upon the disposition and ignorance of the people who receive them, for if such really knew that there was a God and that he was a just one, it is simply impossible that ever they could either believe or accept thereof; for if people did not from ignorance receive them upon trust, such doctrines as redound to the dishonour of God, they would remain still in the hands of them by whom they were manufactured, but the populace or greatest part of people receive their religion with the different articles contained therein much the same manner that children receive their knowledge, for whatever they hear uttered by their parents or others it is commonly received as the foundation and unquestionable source of their belief. In like manner whatever doctrines the general part of Christians receive from their parents especially if ancient, yea, though it were to unGod the Deity, it will be taken into the calendar of their belief as divine.[28]

Burns uses Holy Willie to further illustrate the irrational nature of the belief in predestination by having him say that if he had not been predestined for life he might have been cast into the eternal torments of Hell at birth:

When from my mother's womb I fell,
Thou might hae plunged me deep in hell,
To gnash my gooms, and weep, and wail,
  In burning lakes,
Where damned devils roar and yell
  Chain'd to their stakes.[29]

The picture that Burns conjures up of a toothless infant being consigned to hell is consonant with the kind of doctrines that Goldie believes 'redound to the dishonour of God'. Burns is painting the extreme picture that nevertheless follows the logic of the Doctrine. He again shows his understanding of the Biblical text by adapting the sentence found in Matthew 8:12 when Jesus is alleged to have said, 'But the children of the kingdom shall be cast out into outer darkness: there shall be weeping and gnashing of teeth.' Burns increases the impact by making his victim so young as not to have teeth, thereby adding to the ludicrous aspect of the Doctrine. What has started out as a serious statement in the *Confession* ends in pantomime as the Doctrine of Predestination is pressed ruthlessly to its conclusion by Burns through the words of Holy Willie.

The other doctrine attacked in the poem is the Doctrine of Original Sin. The *Confession* Chapter VI 'Of The Fall of Man, of Sin, and of the Punishment thereof' declares:

> I Our first parents being reduced by the subtilty and temptation of Satan, sinned in eating the forbidden fruit. This their sin God was pleased, according to his wise and holy counsel, to permit, having purposed to order it to his own glory.
>
> II By this sin they fell from their original righteousness and communion with God, and so became dead in sin, and wholly defiled in all the faculties and parts of soul and body.
>
> III They being the root of all mankind, the guilt of this sin was was imputed, and the same death in sin and corrupted nature conveyed to all their posterity, descending from them by ordinary generation.
>
> IV From this original corruption, whereby we are utterly indisposed, disabled, and made opposite to all good and wholly inclined to all evil, do proceed all actual transgressions.[30]

These statements again claim the authority of a scriptural source according to the proof-text method of the Westminster Divines.

Critics such as John Goldie found fault with this method that relied so heavily on a literal, and disallowed a figurative, interpretation of the texts; moreover it seemed to ignore the context from which they were taken. Goldie calls those who subscribe to the Doctrine of Original Sin 'Originalists'. He accuses: 'they always take sanctuary under the literal meaning of the text for the support of their own hypothesis', and comments that 'the building of doctrines upon the express literal meaning of these figurative texts has been the chief cause why Christianity hath been so much divided, misunderstood and abused among Christians.'[31]

Goldie attacks the interpretation of Romans 5:12ff, which is one of the texts quoted to substantiate the claim of Article III, which asserts that all mankind is affected by Adam's sin. Goldie writes of Romans 5:12ff:

> These ten verses having been taken for the great bulwark upon which the foundation they have built what they call the great Christian Doctrine of Original Sin and which is the very soul of priestcraft (Popery not excepted) and great helm wherewith they

> reduce mankind rational, as fellow creatures to beasts of burden, in order that they may the more passively submit to whatever doctrines they are pleased to impose or load them with.[32]

He goes on to mock the Originalists 'for their illogicality in taking some things literally and others figuratively without any good reason for discerning which is which.'[33] He asks, 'How do the Originalists justify taking Paul literally in this case and not taking Jesus literally when he says 'This is my body, this is my blood?' They should, says Goldie, believe in transubstantiation. Goldie writes rumbustiously and attractively in a style to which Burns would have given a natural and positive response. He displays a sturdy independence of opinion, defying the clerical convention by writing a work of theology, and expressing his views in ways that appeal to reason and yet allow for them to be held with passion, while allied to this is a healthy contempt for the authority of the priesthood. All of this is embraced in his concern for what he calls 'real religion'.

Goldie's appeal to reason, his passion and his contempt of ecclesiastical authority are illustrated in a passage where he discusses the case of a child dying on its day of birth and going to eternal damnation because of Adam's sin. Goldie quotes Augustine as the author of this doctrine and calls it 'A doctrine sufficiently coarse to be expressed by the devil himself because it redounds in the dishonour of the great God ... '[34] He continues:

> Now what a most horrid and shocking theology is this that millions of millions of rational beings, for no fault of their own but only for an offence committed by another (viz an adult person) thousands of years before ever they so much as had an existence should be given up and delivered over to eternal damnation without mercy for ever upon the account thereof.[35]

Burns's understanding of Goldie's theological position and also of these actual words is clear when he writes the first four stanzas of 'Holy Willie's Prayer'. Within their irony is a heart-felt contempt for the theology that has apparently left all reason and compassion behind in its logical pursuit of its own doubtful premises.

Burns had the doctrines of Original Sin and Predestination in mind when he wrote to Alexander Cunningham some years later (10 September 1792) of the 'wizard Power of Theologic Vision' that 'raves abroad on all the winds'. In mocking tone Burns writes of this vision of current theology:

> "On Earth, Discord! A gloomy Heaven above, opening her jealous gates to the nineteen thousandth part of the tithe of mankind! And below, an inescapable & inexorable Hell, expanding its leviathan jaws for the vast residue of Mortals!!!" O, doctrine! comfortable & healing to the weary, wounded soul of man! Ye sons & daughters of affliction, ye pauvres Miserables, to whom day brings no pleasure &

> night yields no rest, be comforted! "'Tis but *one* to nineteen hundred thousand, that your situation will mend in this world;" so, alas, the Experience of the Poor & the Needy too truly affirms; & 'tis nineteen hundred thousand to *one*, by the dogmas of Theology, that you will be damned eternally in the World to come![36]

Burns went on in the letter to describe that as 'nonsense', although in his mocking simulation of the preaching of such a theology he had already made his opinion of it very clear. On 14 February 1790 Burns had written to Alexander Cunningham:

> If there be any truth in the Orthodox faith of these Churches, I am damned past redemption, and what is worse, damned to all eternity. I am deeply read in Boston's fourfold State, Marshall on Sanctification, Guthrie's trial of a Saving Interest, &c. &c. but "There is no balm in Gilead, there is no physician there", for me; so I shall e'en turn Ariminian, [*sic*] & trust to, "Sincere though imperfect obedience".[37]

Burns's quotation from Jeremiah 8:22 indicates that he can find nothing of comfort or healing for his soul in such works. Thomas Boston's *Human Nature in its Four-fold State* (1720) was certainly on the extreme right wing of Calvinism and it is hardly surprising that Burns could not find anything in it for him. It says something about Burns's theological acumen when he puts himself in the opposite theological position of Arminianism.

Dr J.H.S. Burleigh in *A Church History of Scotland* provides an insight both into Arminianism and Thomas Boston in relation to it. In 1715 the Reverend John Simson, Professor of Divinity at Glasgow since 1708, was charged with teaching Arminianism. The case was concluded in 1717 when Simson was acquitted with a warning 'not to attribute too much to natural reason and the power of corrupt nature to the disparagement of revelation and efficacious free grace'.[38]

In 1726 Simson was again in trouble for teaching Arminianism. The Presbyteries were consulted and were almost unanimously unfavourable towards him. In 1729 he was suspended indefinitely from teaching but without deposing him or depriving him of his chair. It is noteworthy that only Thomas Boston dissented from the judgement.

Burns had detected that Boston's work was the very antithesis of the Arminian position that gave credence to the power and the value of reason, that assessed revelation in its light, that did not regard human nature as utterly corrupted by the taint of original sin, nor minimised the human effort that was part of any regeneration of the person. Just five months after claiming to be 'deeply read' in Boston's work, Burns writes to Dr John Moore apologizing in advance for the hurried nature of his letter and asking his forgiveness, even if it be 'as stupid as Boston's *Four-fold State*',[39] and on 17 January 1791 he again expresses his opinion of it in a letter to Peter Hill ordering books for the Monkland Friendly Society:

> You will be so good then as send by the first Dumfries Carrier, all, or as many as you have by you, of the following books:
> The Adventurer – Joseph Andrews – Don Quixote – The Idler – Arabian nights entertainment – Dr Price's dissertations on Providence, prayer, Death & Miracles – Roderick Random – & – the 5th Volume of the Observer – for these books take your fair price, as our Society are no judges of the matter, & will insist on having the following damned trash, which you must also send us as cheaply as possible – Scots Worthies – Boston's 4 fold State – Marrow of Modern Divinity – Cole on God's Sovereignty – Newton's letters – [Watson's (*written over*)] Dodrigde's [*sic*] thoughts – Gib's Act & Testimony – Confession of faith – & Capt Robt. Boyle – I forgot to mention among the valuable books, Blair's Sermons & the latest edition of Guthrie's Geographical grammar, which two books be sure to send us.[40]

Boston's book is listed among the trash, along with another that has come to be associated with it because Boston defended its theology when it was republished in 1718, *The Marrow of Modern Divinity* (1646) by Edward Fisher of Oxford. After a long-running controversy in 1720 The General Assembly condemned the book as heretical, and those who were known as 'the Marrow Men' were formally rebuked by the General Assembly in 1722. Thomas Boston and his friend Thomas Hog of Carnock were among those rebuked. Hog had written a highly commendatory preface to the book he had been responsible for republishing. *The Marrow of Modern Divinity* had offended because of its antinomian statements, and within it the special commission set up by the General Assembly had identified no fewer than five distinct heresies. Undeterred by all of this Thomas Boston went on to publish a new edition of it in 1726, the same year in which the second set of proceedings had begun against John Simson.

Boston's dissent against the decision of the General Assembly in 1729 to suspend Simson indefinitely from teaching without, however, depriving him of his chair was because he thought that the judgement was 'derogatory to the Divinity of Christ'. In his opinion Simson should have suffered the more severe penalty of deposition and of being deprived of his chair.[41] It is probably an indication of Burns's knowledge of Thomas Boston that he lists consecutively the two books with which he was involved, one as author the other as editor. He had identified Boston's theological position and knew it to be diametrically opposed to those who were accused of Arminianism, which in the understanding of the times meant giving too much weight to the importance of man's natural reasoning powers and thereby seeming to take away from the value of revelation and the efficacious acts of a God who was both able and free to do as he graciously chose to do.

In Burns's list of 'trash' is a reference to an author, Watson, the title of whose book has been written over in the manuscript. This is likely to have been Thomas Watson's *A Body of Practical Divinity*. Burns makes the following derogatory reference to this work in an earlier letter to Peter Hill:

> send ... another copy of Watson's body of Divinity. This last heavy Performance is so much admired by many of our Members, that they will not be content with one Copy, so Captn. Riddel our President & Patron agreed with me to give you private instructions not to send Watson, but to say that you could not procure a copy of the book so cheap as the one you sent formerly & therefore you wait farther Orders ....[42]

Watson's book is much more in the mainstream of Calvinistic theology. A well-written work, it was in its seventh edition by 1782.[43] Watson writes methodically, providing a commentary on *The Shorter Catechism*[44] and laying it out in such a way as could be easily followed by the lay reader. He writes in fairly simple language, using homely illustrations and figures of speech, for example in dealing with *The Catechism's* first question and answer, Watson asks, 'Why must we glorify God?', and answers, 'Creatures below us and above us bring glory to God, and do we sit rent free. Shall everything glorify God but man?'[45] Commenting on the Antinomians who reject the Old Testament he writes, 'The two Testaments are the two wells of salvation, the Antinomian would stop up one of these wells, they would dry up one of the breasts of scripture.'[46]

Watson writes imaginatively and, for the time, is quite daringly unconventional. He advises how to read the Bible: 'Read the scripture not only as a history book, but as a love letter sent to you from God.'[47] He offers this cryptic comment that would have interested all those of his day, and ours too, that they should make a connection between the unease of mind and heart, and the disease of the body: 'There had never been a stone in the kidneys if there had not been first a stone in the heart.'[48] Burns might not have condemned Watson's book for its presentation and style, certainly Watson's endorsement of 'the heart' would have appealed to him, but he must have found himself in opposition to its theology and its method of interpretation of scripture.

Watson's view of mankind's corruption due to Adam's sin is unequivocal. He writes:

> Adam's sin is ours by propagation ... the depravity and corruption of his (Adam's) nature is transmitted to us as a poison is carried from the fountain to the cistern. This is what we call original sin. (Psalm 51:5). Adam's leprosy cleaves to us as Naaman's leprosy to Gehazi. (2 Kings 5, 27) ... a man by nature cannot but sin, though there were no devil to tempt, no bad example to imitate, yet there is an innate principle in him that cannot forbear sinning.[49]

A few pages later Watson really warms to his subject, as he writes:

> Let us lay to heart original sin, and be deeply humbled for it. It cleaves to us as a disease, it is an active principle in us, stirring up to evil . . . . Some think, as long as they are civil, they are well enough, ay but the nature is poisoned. A river may have fair streams but vermin at the bottom. Thou carriest a hell about thee, thou canst do nothing but thou defilest it; thy heart like muddy ground defiles the purest water that runs through it.[50]

Watson concludes this section with what might be thought of as bathos, when he writes, 'under our silver wings of grace are black feet'. But however we judge these words, it should not deflect us from the fact that for the writer they were a description of a grim reality.

The same letter to Peter Hill in which Burns had expressed his lack of enthusiasm for Watson's book also shows Burns to be specifically opposed to such views as those quoted above from Watson. Burns writes, 'Mankind are by nature benevolent creatures; except in a few scoundrelly instances, I do not think that avarice of the good things we chance to have is born with us.'[51] Burns clearly believes that man is born with a bias to benevolence rather than vice, and in this view there is no place for a belief in a corrupted nature that is passed on from one generation to another. In this same letter, Burns's view of sin as 'sins', that is, as actions rather than a state of being, is clearly seen as he writes, 'God knows I am no Saint; I have a whole host of Follies & Sins to answer for'.[52]

The early influence of John Locke would also have made him question Watson's view of sin as 'an innate principle'. In his *An Essay Concerning Human Understanding* John Locke wrote a substantial section denying the existence of innate principles. One conclusion reached by Locke, that was of great moment as far as religion was concerned, was his finding:

> If the idea of God be not innate, no other can be supposed to be innate. Since then though the knowledge of God be the most natural discovery of human reason, yet the idea of him is not innate, as, I think is evident from what has been said; I imagine there will scarce be any other idea found, that can pretend to it: since if God hath sent any impression, any character on the understanding of men, it is most reasonable to expect it should have been some clear and uniform idea of himself, as far as our weak capacities were capable to receive so incomprehensible and infinite an object. But our minds being at first void of that idea, which we are most concerned to have, it is a strong presumption against all other innate characters. I must own as far as I can observe, I can find none, and would be glad to be informed by any other.[53]

Locke also subscribed to the idea of sin being equated with acts. In the section where he is dealing with Lord Herbert's book *De Veritate*, in which it is asserted that certain 'innate principles or common notions ... are imprinted on the minds of men by the hand of God', Locke writes on Herbert's proposition, 'Men must repent of their sins':

> Nor is the fourth proposition (viz. "Men must repent of their sins") much more instructive, till what those actions are, that are meant by sins are set down. For the word *peccata* or sins, being put, as it usually is, to signify, in general, ill actions, that will draw punishment upon the doers.[54]

As Burns would have found Watson's theology offensive, so having the natural desire to use his common sense on the Biblical text as he was used to doing with any other book, he would have found Watson's simplistic use of scripture unacceptable. Watson defends the authority of scripture using 'seven arguments as to why it is the Word of God'. Some of these Burns might well have found suspect. Watson writes that scripture should be respected as the Word of God because of its antiquity: 'the grey hairs of Scripture make it venerable'; and because of its preservation: 'the letter of scripture has been preserved without corruption in the original tongue'. He asserts that it should be respected because of 'the matter contained in it ... The Book of God has no errata in it'; and because of its predictions: 'it prophesises things to come which shows the voice of God speaking in it'. It should be respected because of the impartiality of its writers 'who do not spare to set down their own failings'; because of 'its effect upon the souls and consciousness of men' and lastly because of 'the miracles by which scripture is confirmed'.[55]

Watson uses the same proof-text method as that adopted by *The Westminster Confession of Faith* and would be equally unconvincing to any one applying the criteria of John Taylor or John Goldie in scriptural interpretation, or to anyone who wanted to measure the scriptural text in the light of reason. Watson approaches the story of Adam's Fall in a very literal way. He quotes various authorities on when he fell:

> Tostatus says he fell the next day, Pererius, he fell the eighth day after his creation. The most probable and received opinion is that he fell the very same day in which he was created. So Irenaeus, Cyril, Epiphanus and many others ... Adam ... did not take up one nights lodgings in Paradise.[56]

Watson backs up this statement with the quotation from Psalm 49:12 'nevertheless man being in honour abideth not: he is like the beasts that perish'. Here we have an example of a text being dragooned into service. The cynic might say, with Pooh Bah, that it is an attempt at 'Merely corroborative detail, intended to give artistic verisimilitude to a bald and unconvincing narrative'.[57] From this misuse of scripture, the further projection is made in the paragraph that follows:

> From Adam's sudden fall learn the weakness of human nature. Adam in a state of integrity quickly made a defection from God. He soon lost the robe of innocence and the glory of Paradise. If our nature was thus weak when it was at its best, what is it now when it is at its worst? If Adam did not stand when he was perfectly rightious, how are we to stand when sin has cut the lock of our original rightiousness! If purified nature did not stand how shall corrupt nature? If Adam in a few hours sinned himself out of Paradise, how quickly would we sin ourselves into hell, if we were not kept by a greater power than our own! But God puts underneath his everlasting arms (Deuteronomy 33:27).[58]

The literalism with which the text is approached in the first instance has led to a whole theology being built upon a very doubtful premise. Even in the concluding sentence Watson relies on a proof text. But the mischievous might question where 'the everlasting arms' were at the time of Adam's Fall.

Watson provides a good example of the religious nonsense of which Burns was so critical, and it was his familiarity with this book that brought about his putting it into the category of 'trash'. I suspect that even more than their faulty method of scriptural interpretation and their poorly based theological extrapolations, Burns objected to the offence to common sense given by such writings as Watson's.

In Watson's section on 'Effectual Calling', which had had a whole chapter of the *Confession* given to the subject,[59] he quotes approvingly the text from Romans 8:30, which had underpinned the opening statement of the *Confession* on the subject: 'Whom he did predestinate, them he also called, and whom he called, them he also justified, and whom he justified them he also glorified.' Watson writes of 'God's electing love', and continues: 'It is a powerful call. *Verba Dei sunt opera* [the words of God are works]. Luther. God puts forth infinite power in calling home a sinner to himself; He not only puts forth his voice but his arm.'[60]

Having extolled the irresistible nature of the call, Watson goes on to praise God's actions in ways that leave all human sentiment and common sense behind, as he pictures God electing and effectually calling one member of a family while leaving the other behind, presumably to eternal damnation. Watson writes, 'When two are walking together husband and wife, father and child that God should call one by his grace, but leave the other, carry up one in a triumphant chariot to heaven but let the other perish eternally – oh infinite rich grace!'[61]

When Burns was familiar with such writings that could have such horrendous lapses into passages totally devoid of natural human feeling, and so lacking in common sense, it is little wonder that he was moved to write of those who 'soar the wild-goose heights of Calvinistic Theology' or of 'the sightless soarings of SCHOOL DIVINITY'.[62] Watson, for all that he could be considered to have been fairly representative of Calvinistic Theology, still from time to time in his writing ascended to what anyone using common sense as a measure would judge to be the height of nonsense.

Another Calvinistic writer with whose work Burns was familiar was James Hervey. His various *Meditations* were not systematic in the manner of Watson but, rather as the title suggests, writings that dwelt on a certain theme. From Hervey's *Among the Tombs*, Burns probably picked up the phrase for God as 'The Supreme Disposer of Events'.[63] Hervey has a penchant for dwelling on the sombre. The publishers' note to the 1850 edition concludes that Hervey's valuable contribution 'was to lead the young mind to serious reflection and to render the visible objects of nature subservient to the honour and praise of the Creator'.[64] Certainly words like these would lead to serious reflection, as Hervey contemplates the fate of the unrepentant sinner:

> O how will their hearts endure when the sword of infinite indignation is unsheathed and fiercely waved around their defenceless heads or pointed directly at their naked breasts. How must the wretches scream with wild amazement and rend the very heavens with their cries when the right aiming thunderbolts go abroad – go abroad with a dreadful commission, to drive them from the kingdom of glory and plunge them not into the sorrows of a moment, or the tortures of an hour but into all the restless agonies of unquenchable fire and everlasting despair ... so we must warn – "to seek the Lord while he may be found" ... here let the whole force of our benevolence exert itself in exhorting whomsoever we are likely to influence, to take the wings of faith unfeigned, of repentence undelayed, and flee away from this wrath to come.[65]

It is difficult to escape the menacing and malicious thought behind such words. For all their earnestness, there is an unhealthy odour that causes us to understand what Burns means when he writes of the 'children of sanctity [who] move among their fellow creatures with a nostril snuffing putrescence'.[66] Both in the formal theology and in such writings as the *Meditations*, Calvinist Theology in its more extreme forms could become a source of offence to one like Burns who confesses that, 'almost all my religious tenets originate from my heart'.[67]

Burns's religious beliefs were affected by his experience of the Church as an ecclesiastical organization and by the conduct and beliefs of its constituent members. The commonly held opinion of the Church as the body with whom religious truth resides would not have been enhanced for Burns by the unseemly public quarrel that was to provide him the opportunity of his first extended poetical comment on ecclesiastical matters, 'The Holy Tulzie'. Its subject was provided by a dispute over parish boundaries between two clergygmen, the Reverend Alexander Moodie of Riccarton and the Reverend John Russel of Kilmarnock.[68] In the Presbytery of Irvine their debate had apparently been conducted with some heat. Burns expresses his amusement at this spectacle of two clergymen who, although similar in theological outlook and in their view of one of the divisive issues of the time (Patronage), nevertheless engage in a verbal battle over a matter of the boundaries of their respective parishes. Burns uses the poem to point out the theological and ecclesiastical issues of the time and, in doing so, reveals not only his understanding of these but where his sympathy lies. In describing the 'two reverend Calvinists', Burns places them in the Auld Light, orthodox, anti-Patronage faction. He defines their New Light, Moderate opponents in the terms of the abuse commonly levelled against them by Auld Lights, who called them those who preach 'poison'd Arminian stank', by contrast to themselves, the Auld Lights, who drank from 'Calvin's fountain head!'.[69]

Burns's mockery of the two Calvinist ministers' theology and personal behaviour is obvious, and his admiration for the Moderates is clear, but I suspect that his support of their acceptance of Patronage is tinged with irony and perhaps reveals an ambivalent attitude on that subject. Burns writes in verse 15 lines 85ff of 'The Holy Tulzie':

O a' ye flocks o'er a' the hills,
By mosses, meadows, moors and fells,
Come join your counsels and your skills
  To cowe the Lairds,
And get the Brutes, the Power themselves
  To chuse their Herds.[70]

Is Burns really mocking the ability of ordinary members of a congregation to choose their minister, or has he carried the anti-Patronage argument *ad absurdum* to raise doubts about it? Certainly his apparent support of Patronage in the ecclesiastical sphere is in accordance with his own subsequent seeking of Patronage in the matter of his Excise appointments. His apparent mocking of people being able to choose for themselves resulting in calamitous consequences is consonant with his opinion of the poor judgement of the ordinary people who made up the membership of the Monkland Friendly Society in their choice of literature.[71] (Contrast his oft-cited egalitarianism.) But perhaps there remained a rankle in his mind at their exclusion from the choice of their ministers.

Another factor that assisted in the formation of his religious beliefs was his involvement in the Church's disciplinary procedures. His personal involvement, perhaps in an early case with the Tarbolton Kirk Session and certainly later with Mauchline Kirk Session,[72] must have helped him form an opinion. As with any other institution, kindliness and personal consideration can be met with in the individuals who work within it, but when it meets as a body by itself to determine its policy, and perhaps already bound by its own rules, it can come across as cruel and impersonal in its judgements.

Burns seems to have experienced some personal consideration at the hands of the ministers of Tarbolton and Mauchline. In trying to establish whether or not Burns was indeed called to account by the Tarbolton Kirk Session in the case of Elizabeth Paton an interesting opinion held by some of the older residents currently living in the parish was revealed. A recently retired minister of the parish, the Reverend Ian U. Macdonald, observed that if Burns had been brought before Tarbolton Kirk Session for his offence, it would certainly have been part of local folklore, and some anecdotal evidence might still be extant. But there is none, and this is attributed to the friendship that Burns shared with the old minister, Patrick Wodrow, and his colleague John McMath, who may well have turned a blind eye and not compeared Burns before the Kirk Session. However attractive that theory may be, it leaves unanswered the question why Burns wrote 'The Fornicator', in which 'Betsey' is named and his appearance before the Kirk Session is described, if these events did not take place. However, Burns may merely be engaged in a piece of bravado in the poem whose tone at times is similar to the bluster and boastfulness of 'A Welcome to a bastart wean', which although related to a real event nevertheless bears little resemblance to the historical facts.[73] Because of lack of evidence we do not know precisely how Burns was treated at Tarbolton, but we do know of his respect for Wodrow and McMath. In the case involving his being compeared with Jean Armour, Burns meets up with some kindly consideration on the part of Mr Auld, and seems to tolerate a system of discipline of which he disapproves because that is the way in which the Church of the day is structured. Perhaps his involvement in these cases in which he saw the ecclesiastical machine at work helped prompt him into believing that religion ought to be and was essentially a simple business.[74]

Again, as he viewed the action taken by the Church courts against his friends Gavin Hamilton and the Reverend William McGill, Burns must have noticed the ponderous mechanisms and detailed procedures that were engaged in by those who prosecuted such cases.[75] In the case of the financial defalcations that were alleged against his friend Gavin Hamilton, it may well have seemed a monstrous charge to bring against someone whom Burns so well respected. Further, for Gavin Hamilton to be judged by people that Burns deemed were less worthy than his friend seemed iniquitous. His indignation at such conduct is clear in the opening lines of his 'Address to the Unco Guid, or the Rigidly Righteous'.[76] Even more direct are Burns's lines in 'To the Rev. John McMath':

There's *Gaun*, miska't waur than a beast,
Wha has mair honor in his breast
Than mony scores as guid's the priest
  What sae abus't him:
An' may a bard no crack his jest

What way they've use't him?

See him, the poor man's friend in need,
The gentleman in word an' deed,
An' shall his fame an' honor bleed
  By worthless skellums,
An' not a muse erect her head
  To cowe the blellums?[77]

Burns's natural loyalty to his friend Gavin Hamilton must have made the Mauchline Kirk Session's pursuit seem vindictive, although, as noted earlier,[78] they may well have had, and indeed seem to have had, at least a *prima facie* case. However this case could hardly have endeared the local ecclesiastical establishment to Burns, and may well have contributed to an opinion he once expressed to his friend William Nicol, in the only letter he wrote in Scots. Referring to his horse, Burns writes, 'she's as poor's a Sang-maker and as hard's a kirk'.[79] Burns had come up against the hardness and stubbornness of church courts and had discovered that, although individual Christians could be by contrast 'soft' and willing to yield, the Kirk as an establishment could be 'hard'. In that same letter there is a further reference to the Kirk when in the course of describing to Nicol some of the people he had met Burns refers to two women:

> I met wi' twa dink quines in particular, ane o' them a sonsie, fine, fodgel lass, baith braw and bonie; the tither was a clean-shankit, straught, tight, weel-far'd winch, as blythe's a lintwhite on a flowerie thorn, and as sweet and modest's a new blawn plumrose in a hazle shaw. They were baith bred to mainers by the beuk, and onie ane o' them has as muckle smeddum and rumblegumtion as half o' some Presbytries that you and I baith ken.[80]

This lovely piece of fun nevertheless includes within it the judgement that ecclesiastical courts can lack in common sense and that courage and fortitude that declares an independent mind. Burns had witnessed the work of the Presbytery of Ayr in the case of Dr McGill,[81] and it is during the time of this case that he makes use of the particular legal description *fama clamosa* that was applied to the alleged offence for which Dr McGill was being examined before the Church courts.[82] That he had little respect for some of the things that happened in the courts of the Church is seen from an earlier remark made to his friend Mr Alexander Cunningham. Remarking on his son Robert, then only 22 months old, Burns writes: 'By the bye, I intend breeding him up for the Church; and from an innate dexterity in secret Mischief which he posses [*sic*] & a certain hypocritical gravity as he looks on the consequences, I have no small hopes of him in the sacerdotal line.'[83]

Burns was later to observe at close hand all the machinations of certain members of the Presbytery of Ayr and of the Synod of Glasgow and Ayr,[84] and had ample opportunity in that case alone to become sceptical of church courts in their ability to discern the truth. As Burns would see from the procedures followed by the Presbytery and the Synod, the whole process of examining a potential *fama clamosa* is complex, often protracted, seemingly heavily weighted against the accused, and easily manipulated by those such as Presbytery Clerks well versed in church practice and procedure.

In a letter to David Staig enclosing 'The Prologue for Mrs Sutherland's Benefit night', Burns makes imaginative secular use of the ecclesiastical legal term *fama clamosa*: 'if the said Poem be found to contain any Treason or words of treasonable construction or any *Fama clamosa* or *Scandalum magnatum* against our Sovereign Lord the King, or any of his liege Subjects, the said Prologue may not see the light.'[85] In likening the offence to treason or to a scandal of the greatest magnitude, Burns is indeed reflecting the seriousness with which a *fama clamosa* is dealt with in the Church. It is a process that can have a dramatic and extremely serious outcome for a minister. A guilty verdict can result in the loss of his ministerial status, thereby depriving him of his livelihood and further service in the Church.

Another letter written to William Nicol just a month earlier, in February 1790, again shows Burns's awareness of the Presbytery's role in the ecclesiastical scene. Referring to the new theatre that is to be built in Dumfries by subscription, Burns mentions that some of the ministers used to attend the old theatre surreptitiously. Burns writes:

> Some of our clergy have slipt in by stealth now and then; but they have got up a farce of their own. You must have heard how the Rev Mr. Lawson of Kirkmahoe, seconded by the Rev Mr. Kirkpatrick of Dunscore, and the rest of that faction have accused in formal process, the unfortunate and Rev Mr. Heron of Kirkgunzeon, that in ordaining Mr. Nelson to the cure of souls in Kirkbean, he, the said Heron, feloniously and treasonably bound the said Nelson to the confession of faith *so far as it was agreeable to reason and the word of God*![86]

This little piece of local gossip reveals what a detailed knowledge Burns has of the workings of the machinery of the ecclesiastical organization and of the significance of the litigation that is being entered upon. Although deliberately adopting the style of an ecclesiastical lawyer, he displays an acute knowledge of one of the issues that was very much alive at the time, that is, the authority of *The Westminster Confession of Faith* in relation to the authority of the Bible. This was one of the issues in the McGill case[87] and it is interesting to note the continued interest of Burns in his picking up on this aspect of the Dumfries ordination, and feeling that it was sufficiently important to include it in a letter to a friend. He may dismiss the Presbytery matter as a farce, but he knows its plot and its cast, and in his judgement there is sympathy being expressed by the italicized words for the reasonableness of the attitude of 'the unfortunate and Rev Mr. Heron'.

Burns's observation of ecclesiastical courts at work contributed to his determination to exercise his own judgement on matters of religion. In a letter of February 1794 to Alexander Findlater, Supervisor of Excise, Burns writes a facetious, but nevertheless revealing, final paragraph, whereby in linking references to the General Assembly and orthodoxy he is giving an indication of the disregard in which he held them:

> That no scheme to betray a FRIEND, or mislead a STRANGER; to seduce a YOUNG GIRL, or rob a HEN-ROOST; to subvert LIBERTY or bribe an EXCISEMAN; to disturb the GENERAL ASSEMBLY, or annoy a GOSSIPPING; to overthrow the credit of ORTHODOXY, or the authority of OLD SONGS; to oppose *your wishes* or frustrate *my hopes* – MAY PROSPER – is the sincere wish and prayer of
> Robt. Burns[88]

Each important statement is followed by one of much less importance, all of them having the effect of reducing the importance of the preceding statement. In this sequence the General Assembly is reduced to a comparison with gossip, and orthodoxy is said to be of no more authority than a set of old songs.

But while Burns has scant respect for some of the workings of the courts of the Church, he does acknowledge that many of those who work within their framework and recognize their authority are themselves people of integrity. Apart from his references to people like Dalrymple, McGill and McMath, in which his respect for their teaching and character is obvious, Burns refers to the Presbytery of Ayr in respectful terms in the poem he writes to the Reverend John McMath enclosing a copy of 'Holy Willie's Prayer':

> O Ayr, my dear, my native ground,
> Within thy presbytereal bound
> A candid li'bral band is found
> Of public teachers,
> As men, as Christians too renown'd
> An' manly preachers.[89]

Burns sees the faults of the ecclesiastical organization of the Church, but there remains a respect for the individuals who in good conscience strive honestly to live by their beliefs. Nevertheless the pressure of that organization upon its members, that sometimes led them to strange conclusions, perhaps encouraged Burns to attempt an independent religious viewpoint.

Burns's letter to Mrs Dunlop on the 17 July 1789, enclosing a copy of 'The Kirk's Alarm', just about sums up his position in relation to the Church courts and those who are members of them. Burns writes, 'You know my sentiments respecting the present two great Parties that divide our Scots Ecclesiastics – I do not care three farthings for Commentators & authorities – An honest candid enquirer after truth, I revere; but illiberality & wrangling I equally detest.'[90] Burns liked to think of himself as an honest candid enquirer in all things, including religion, and as such an enquirer, one who recognized the insights and understanding gained by the reflective process of the mind and heart.

In a letter written to his good friend Robert Muir, who died less than two months later of consumption, Burns stresses the need to be independent in thought. He writes in hope of Muir's recovery, but nevertheless ventures to discourse on death, and to speculate on what might follow:

> But an honest man has nothing to fear. If we lie down in the grave, the whole man a piece of broke machinery, to moulder with the clods of the valley, – be it so; at least there is an end of pain, care, woes and wants: if that part of us called Mind, does survive the apparent destruction of the man – away with old-wife prejudices and tales! Every age and every nation has had a different set of stories; and as the many are always weak, of consequence they have often, perhaps always been deceived: a man conscious of having acted an honest part among his fellow creatures; even granting that he may have been the sport, at times, of passions and instincts; he goes to a great unknown Being who could have no other end in giving him existence but to make him happy; who gave him those passions and instincts, and well knows their force. – These my worthy friend, are my ideas; and I know they are not far different from yours – It becomes a man of sense to think for himself; particularly in a case where all men are equally interested, and where indeed all men are equally in the dark.[91]

Maurice Lindsay, in his very thoughtful and useful contribution to the subject of Burns and religion in his *The Burns Encyclopedia*, describes this letter as 'stoical', but there is more than stoicism in evidence: there is, however speculative and uncertain, a hope being expressed that some part of us might survive, but, as both Lindsay and Thomas Crawford agree, it is a hope expressed neither in Christian nor in Atheistic terms.[92] Burns is trying to express his own opinion on the subject, drawing not upon the old wives' tales but on what his own perception of the subject leads him to believe. This same attitude is again expressed in his letter to Mrs Dunlop on 9 July 1790 when Burns writes:

> Though I have no objection to what the Christian system tells us of Another world; yet I own I am partial to those proofs & ideas of it which we have wrought out of our own heads & hearts. The first has the demonstration of an authenticated story, the last has the conviction of an intuitive truth. – I have one favorite proof, because (though five thousand have done the same before me), I have discovered it in its native rock, at least hewn it into shape, myself.[93]

In his writing to Mrs Dunlop Burns is usually careful not to cause unnecessary offence, and so it could be thought that he is not being entirely honest in his opening remarks about his having no objection to the Christian view of 'another world', but he is very assertive of his need to work things out for himself. In a letter to his brother William on 10 March 1789 he advocates: 'Whatever you read, whatever you hear, concerning the ways and works of that strange creature, MAN, look into the living world about you, look into Yourself, for the evidences of the fact, or the application of the doctrine.'[94]

This desire to sift the evidence in the light of his own understanding is perhaps the mature manifestation of what Burns had described as a feature of his character as a child, when he says he had 'a stubborn, sturdy something' in his disposition. Then it was accompanied by 'an enthusiastic, idiot piety'; in his maturity, it helped bring about an individualistic outlook on matters of religious belief.[95]

Chapter 4

'Though Sceptical on Some Points of our Current Belief'

Burns's empiricist approach to religion that subjects it to observation and experience may have had the effect of reducing the number of things he believed, but three recurring themes – a belief in a benevolent God, a speculation on an existence beyond the grave and an acknowledgement of his own accountability – remain as constants, as their frequent appearance in his writings indicates. In a letter to his friend Robert Aiken on 8 October 1786, all three themes are enclosed in one paragraph:

> You may, perhaps, think it extravagant fancy, but it is a sentiment which strikes home to my very soul: though sceptical, in some points, of our current belief, yet, I think, I have every evidence for the reality of a life beyond the stinted bourne of our present existence: if so, then, how should I, in the presence of that tremendous Being, the Author of existence, how should I meet the reproaches of those who stand to me in the dear relation of children, whom I deserted in the smiling innocency of helpless infancy? O thou great unknown Power! thou Almighty God! who has lighted up reason in my breast, and blessed me with immortality! I have frequently wandered from that order and regularity necessary for the perfection of thy works, yet thou hast never left me nor forsaken me.[1]

Although it may prove difficult to isolate these three themes from each other, as this letter shows just how related they are to each other in the mind of Burns, that is what I want to attempt, that we might be better able to define what they meant to Burns.

In his letter to Aiken, Burns refers to the deity in ways that indicate his inability to define God with certainty. 'That tremendous Being' signals the awesome nature he ascribes to God. 'The Author of existence' highlights God's creative role and Burns's sense of being like a character on a page of life. But God is also remote – the 'great unknown Power' – hidden, yet at work. He is also 'the almighty God' who has made Burns capable of reasoning and given him a sense of immortality. But the last description of God in this letter is the one that declares him to have been an ever-present feature in Burns's life: 'thou hast never left me nor forsaken me'. For Burns, God might not be knowable in the way that a person can be known, but nevertheless he does not cease to be present to him.

In other letters Burns addresses God in a number of ways, indicating perhaps this unwillingness to settle for any one description of something that he found so difficult to define. The following titles given to God have been abstracted from Burns's letters in chronological order:[2]

Letter	Date	Addressee	Title or Description
I, 45	1 August 1786	James Smith	A good God bless
I, 58–9	8 October 1786	Robert Aiken	That tremendous Being, the Author of existence. O thou great unknown Power! thou Almighty God! who has lighted up reason in my breast
I, 82	[January? 1787]	[Margaret Chalmers?]	the Great Protector of Innocence
I, 94	February 1787	James Dalrymple	that benevolent Being whose image he so richly bears. (Referring to the Earl of Glencairn) ... grand Dieu
I, 113	4 May 1787	Earl of Glencairn	that Great Being whose image you so richly bear
I, 180	December 1787	Gavin Hamilton	the Holy Trinity or the holy Somebody that directs this world
I, 195	4 January 1788	Mrs Agnes McLehose	that Being, my Creator and Preserver and who I have every reason to believe, will one day be my Judge
I, 201	8 January 1788	Mrs Agnes McLehose	He who is our Author and Preserver, and will one day be our Judge ... the Supreme Being
I, 208	15 January 1788	Mrs Agnes McLehose	a good God
I, 210	19 January 1788	Mrs Agnes McLehose	A compassionate Deity, an Almighty Protector ... the Father of mercies
I, 212	20 January 1788	Mrs Agnes McLehose	Thou Almighty Preserver of Men
I, 215	21 January 1788	Mrs Agnes McLehose	O Thou, whose I am and whose are all my ways
I, 225	3 February 1788	Mrs Agnes McLehose	My God ... Thou Almighty Author of peace and goodness and love
I, 227	7 February 1788	Mrs Agnes McLehose	The God of Love
I, 231	13 February 1788	Mrs Agnes McLehose	Thou God of Nature, thou Redeemer of mankind ... the Almighty Judge of men
I, 232	13 February 1788	Mrs Agnes McLehose	Almighty Witness of my actions, some time, perhaps very soon my Almighty Judge ... the Searcher of hearts

I, 233–234	14 February 1788	Mrs Agnes McLehose	Father of mercies ... Almighty Goodness
I, 238	17 February 1788	Mrs Elizabeth Rose	Almighty Spirit
I, 252–253	6 March 1788	Mrs Agnes McLehose	God, my Maker ... approving Heaven
I, 258	7 March 1788	Mr Robert Muir	A great unknown Being
I, 262–263	14 March 1788	Mrs Agnes McLehose	the Divine Disposer of events ... the Lord God
I, 265	18 March 1788	Mrs Agnes McLehose	The Father of Mercies
I, 297	18 July 1788	Mr George Lockhart	Lord God Almighty
I, 320–321	23 September 1788	Robert Graham	Author of Goodness. The GREAT BEING whose image you so richly bear
I, 333	8 November 1788	*Edinburgh Evening Courant*	the Author of all Good
I, 347	December 1788 to January 1789	William Cruikshank	the Great Author of life
I, 349	1 January 1789	Mrs Frances A. Dunlop	those aweful and important realities, a God that made all things
I, 414	4 June 1789	John McAuley	the Great Manager of the Drama of Man
I, 418	21 June 1789	Patrick Miller	some Great Creator
I, 419	22 June 1789	Mrs Frances A. Dunlop	My Creator ... an incomprehensibly Great Being, to whom I owe my existence
I, 424	31 July 1789	Robert Graham	the SEARCHER OF HEARTS & AUTHOR OF ALL GOODNESS
I, 447	1 November 1789	Robert Ainslie	the Great Disposer of Events
I, 448	4 November 1789	Capt. Richard Brown	the BENEVOLENT DIRECTOR OF ALL THINGS
I, 457	13 December 1789	Mrs Frances A. Dunlop	the All Good Being
II, 129	14 January 1792	Mrs Frances A. Dunlop	the Great Disposer of Events
II, 144	22 August 1792	Mrs Frances A. Dunlop	'God was in Christ' ... Le bon Dieu vous benit Ame[n!]
II, 283–284	25 February 1794	Alexander Cunningham	those awful obscure realities – an all-powerful and equally beneficent God and a world to come beyond death and the grave ... nature's God ... a witnessing, judging and approving God.
II, 311	September 1794	Mrs Frances A. Dunlop	I gratefully thank my God for his goodness

II, 333	1 January 1795	Mrs Frances A. Dunlop	Infinite Wisdom & Goodness superintending & directing every circumstance
II, 383	26 June 1796	James Clarke	Him, the Great Unknown, whose creature I am

Only once in the texts quoted does Burns name God in specifically Christian terms, and on that occasion he is quoting from St Paul, who in 2 Corinthians 5:19 writes, 'God was in Christ'. When Burns's letter to Mrs Dunlop is examined, it becomes less clear that this is a belief to which Burns is fully committed. Burns has been discoursing to Mrs Dunlop on the inconclusiveness of the debate on whether or not there is a life beyond the grave. He concludes with the wry empiricist opinion, 'you & I, my Friend, must make the experiment by ourselves & for ourselves'. But he then adds, emphasizing his belief in religion as an enabling influence:

> However, I am so convinced that an unshaken faith in the doctrines of Christianity is not only necessary by making us better men, but also by making us happier men, that I shall take every care that your little godson, & every little creature that shall call me, Father, shall be firmly persuaded that "God was in Christ, reconciling the world unto himself, not imputing unto men their trespasses".[3]

Burns is not saying that he personally believes that 'God was in Christ', or that he has 'an unshaken faith in the doctrines of Christianity', but that he will endeavour to inculcate such beliefs in his children because he is convinced that their lives will be made better and happier by them.

Burns's understanding of God and his awareness of how that understanding relates to Christianity will be more clearly comprehended if the specific references to Jesus Christ in Burns's letters are examined. Apart from the one just quoted, Burns mentions Jesus Christ only four times, and on all these occasions he is referred to with respect. In a light hearted reference to how much he had enjoyed the company with whom he had been dining at Dunlop with Mrs Dunlop's daughter Rachel, Burns writes on 13 November 1788 of the compliments he had received: 'I own they did not lord me over as a Poet does his Patron or still more his Patroness, nor did they sugar me up as a Cameronian Preacher does J–S–S C—st.'[4] Even this passing comment indicates Burns's appreciation of Jesus as a substantial figure whose essential message has been obscured by the preachers who want to make it more palatable to their congregations.

Again there is a brief reference to Jesus Christ set in the context of a letter to Mrs Dunlop and within a discussion of the 'many stories of another world beyond death'. On 13 December 1789 Burns writes: 'Jesus Christ, thou amiablest of characters, I trust thou art no Imposter, & that thy revelation of blissful scenes of existence beyond death and the grave, is not one of the many impositions which time after time have been palmed on credulous mankind.'[5] Burns is clearly attracted by the personality of Jesus, but his very introduction here of the possibility that he is not what he claims to be, or even what others claim him to be, indicates that lack of absolute certainty that characterizes Burns's statements about his own religious belief.

The nearest that Burns comes to defining the relationship between Jesus Christ and God, and also declaring his own conviction of the nature of that relationship, is found in another letter to Mrs Dunlop written some six months earlier. Burns writes:

> I will go farther, and affirm, that from the sublimity, excellence, and purity of his doctrine and precepts unparalleled by all the aggregated wisdom and learning of many preceding ages, though, *to appearance*, he himself was the obscurist and most illiterate of our species; therefore Jesus Christ was from God.[6]

In stressing the words 'to appearance', Burns is indicating his agreement with the traditional Christian proclamation that declares that Jesus is more than a mere man. But he does not follow that line all the way thereby relating Jesus more intimately with God, as in the statement 'God was in Christ', but concludes more ambiguously that 'Jesus Christ was *from* God' (my emphasis). Undoubtedly in so describing Jesus, Burns is full of admiration for him, but even although he is on the point of saying that Jesus is so different as to warrant the belief that God is in him, nevertheless Burns shies away from making that statement. This inability to define precisely to his own satisfaction the relationship between Jesus Christ and God is seen most clearly in a letter to Mrs McLehose on 8 January 1788 in which he makes this almost creed-like statement:

> I feel myself deeply interested in your good opinion, and will lay before you the outlines of my belief. He, who is our Author and Preserver, and will one day be our Judge, must be, (not for his sake in the way of duty, but from the native impulse of our hearts,) the object of our reverential awe and grateful adoration: He is almighty and all-bounteous, we are weak and dependent; hence, prayer and every other sort of devotion. – "He is not willing that any should perish, but that all should come to everlasting life;" consequently, it must be in everyone's power to embrace His offer of "everlasting life;" otherwise He could not, in justice, condemn those who did not. A mind pervaded, actuated and governed by purity, truth and charity, though it does not *merit* heaven, yet is an absolutely necessary pre-requisite, without which heaven can neither be obtained nor enjoyed; and, by Divine promise, such a mind shall never fail of attaining "everlasting life:" hence, the impure, the deceiving, and the uncharitable, extrude themselves from eternal bliss, by their unfitness for enjoying it. The Supreme Being has put the immediate administration of all this, for wise and good ends known to himself, into the hands of Jesus Christ, a great Personage, whose relation to Him we cannot comprehend, but whose relation to us is a Guide and a

> Saviour; and who, except for our own obstinacy and misconduct, will bring us all, through various ways and by various means, to bliss at last.[7]

In 'A Dedication to Gavin Hamilton Esq', Burns applies himself to praising his patron but then after a few lines breaks this off to enter upon a long diatribe against the morals and the theology of the time, then realizing what he has done he apologizes:

> Your pardon, Sir, for this digression,
> I maist forgat my Dedication;
> But when Divinity comes cross me,
> My readers still are sure to lose me.[8]

In the letter to Mrs McLehose, Burns's readers have to follow his reasoning closely or they will get lost in one of the many byways of thought that criss-cross the main credal highway of Burns's statement of faith. The first of these theological byways is found in the words in brackets within which Burns is asserting man's natural capacity to reach out towards God, rather than the initiative having to come from God, as Calvinist thought would have it. Second, he sees prayer not as some church-imposed routine, but as a natural response of dependents. Third, he adopts a stance in direct opposition to the Doctrine of Election as it was preached by some Calvinists, that only the elect had a chance of eternal life. Finally, he challenges the Doctrine of Predestination by suggesting that the virtuous person cannot fail to gain access to heaven. All of this on the way to asserting a belief in Jesus Christ as, 'a Great Personage whose relation to Him [God] we cannot comprehend'. Here is a statement made by a man who is aware of all the theological nuances of the words he chooses, and so in a letter in which he is obviously displaying his theological understanding, he must be intending to be very precise when he describes Jesus Christ's relation to God in the way that he does.

Burns's avoidance of the traditional Christian terminology that seeks to describe the relationship between God and Jesus Christ as that of Father and Son, and that stresses the oneness of substance of the Trinity, has been taken by some writers to indicate that Burns was a Unitarian, or even a Deist. Richard H. Fowler, while admitting that he cannot find 'a single succinct label for Burns's religious persuasion', goes on to write that 'the discernible alignment however is unitarianism verging on deism'.[9] He does allow however that the unitarian label that is sometimes given to Burns is based on negative evidence such as the description of God in *Letters* I, 201 and I, 180 (see page 56), and on the fact that Burns never mentions the Holy Trinity except facetiously in the latter. Fowler's argument relies heavily on one other bit of negative evidence, the letter of February 1793 from William Nicol that addresses Burns as 'Dear Christless Bobbie'. Fowler surmises that the epithet

'Christless' is a result of the confidences exchanged with Nicol on their earlier Highland tour. No doubt on the long days and nights of their holiday the pair would have done just that, but Fowler's conclusion that 'Nicol would not have used the jibe "Christless" unless he knew it was appropriate' and that, 'a true word had been spoken in jest',[10] is hardly justified. As both Nicol's letter and Burns's reply indicate, they were used to carrying their arguments to the outrageous extremes, and when talk between friends is conducted at that level, the jest often goes far beyond what we really believe. Burns seems to indicate this, and is almost apologetic in his explanation prefixed to his reply to Nicol's letter. It is almost as if Burns has been embarrassed by Nicol's form of address because he knows that it is not entirely true. Burns writes, 'As my Friend Nicol, though one of the worthiest, & positively the cleverest fellows I ever knew, yet no man in his humours, having gone greater lengths in imprudence, unholiness, &c. than he; I wrote him as follows'. (*Burns's headnote in Glenriddell MS.*)[11]

Judging by the great respect shown towards the person of Jesus in the admittedly earlier letters and the lack of any retraction or contradictory matter written later, Burns was far from 'Christless'. I suspect that he looked upon Jesus as one of those who provided evidence for, and who gave a good character to, God (a quality for which he had defended Dr McGill).[12] I suspect, too, that the characteristics displayed in the life of Jesus were those that Burns ascribed to the beneficent God in whom he continued to believe long after the 'Christless' letter.

Burns's admission that he did not know exactly what relationship Jesus had to God does not prevent him from recognizing the value of Jesus as one who has truth to offer about what Burns calls 'those awful realities'[13] by which he finds himself confronted. This ability of Jesus to do this for Burns, hardly leaves him 'Christless'. Burns's slightly defensive tone in the prefix to his reply to Nicol's letter may well have been because he appreciated one of the tenets of John Locke, who in his *Essay on the Reasonableness of Christianity* (1695) points out that the mere inability to explain mystery does not in itself stand as a disproof of faith.[14]

John Locke's influence upon Burns's religious thought is again in evidence when the great variety of Burns's titles for God are considered. The freedom with which Burns devises these descriptions of God could have received encouragement from Locke, who in *An Essay Concerning Human Understanding* writes: 'the truest and best notions men had of God were not imprinted, but acquired by thought and meditation, and a right use of their faculties'.[15]

Burns's descriptions of God often seem to reflect his mood or circumstances or even the individual to whom they are addressed. Burns describes God in a great number of ways in his correspondence with Mrs Agnes McLehose. In 15 of the 37 letters of those over-heated months, January to March 1788, he uses a revealing variety of descriptions of God.[16] He uses the word 'Judge' four times and does not use the term to any of his other correspondents. I cannot help but think that he might be protesting too much because of a not entirely clear conscience. In these 'love letters', significantly, Burns refers to 'the God of Love' twice. The only appearances of the phrase 'Father of mercies' are in three letters to Mrs McLehose. In one letter it seems to be used in a way that does cause one to doubt his sincerity. He purports to turn aside to God and pray for 'Clarinda' in the midst of his letter to her:

> Father of mercies! against thee often have I sinned; through thy grace I will endeavour to do so no more! She who, Thou knowest, is dearer to me than myself; Pour Thou the balm of peace into her past wounds, and hedge her about with Thy peculiar care, all her future days and nights![17]

It is all too fullsome and too coated with the religiosity that we know Burns abhors, to be true. It is difficult not to doubt Burns's sincerity, and to escape the feeling that he is just out to impress the lady.

It is not just on this occasion that when Burns describes God he is influenced in his choice of words by the person to whom he is writing. In the titles that Burns gives to God his literary skills are sometimes as much in evidence as his theology, but their aptness need not detract from their sincerity. His letter to a member of the aristocracy, the Earl of Glencairn, combines a compliment to the Earl with the title he gives to God, referring to God as 'that Great Being whose image you so richly bear'.[18] A year and a half later, on 23 September 1788, Burns similarly addresses both God and another important patron, Robert Graham of Fintry, who had helped him obtain his place in the Excise. To Graham, Burns also writes of God as 'the Author of Goodness' (twice) and the 'Searcher of Hearts'.[19] These are significant phrases to write in letters to the person before whom you were purporting to be honest, and who indeed had the power to do good to you. Burns had also used the phrase 'Searcher of Hearts' in a letter to Mrs McLehose before whom he was also pleading his case, this time as an honest lover.[20] 'The Author of All Good' again comes into use when Burns writes to the Editor of the *Edinburgh Evening Courant* and the title's aptness in a letter to one used to dealing with authors hardly needs to be pointed out.[21]

The reason for Burns's reference to God as 'the Great Author of Life',[22] in a letter to William Cruikshank becomes clearer when its context is examined. Burns had stayed with the Cruikshanks from September/October 1787 until he left Edinburgh in February 1788. The tone of the three extant letters to Cruikshank reveals a true respect for him and his wife, and a special tenderness towards their daughter. Burns refers to her as 'my dear little Jeany' and 'my sweet little Rose-bud'; the latter a hint at the song he had written for her.[23] But in the last letter the fullness of the friendship with her parents is indicated by the confidences that continue to be exchanged, and by the warmth and familiarity of its tone. Having previously, in writing of their daughter, used the motif of a rosebud, something that is already pretty but that contains all the promise of a fullness of beauty, Burns offers a benediction in which the title he gives to God has been carefully chosen:

> Many and happy returns of the seasons to you, with your dearest and worthiest friend, and the lovely little pledge of your happy union. May the Great Author of life, and of every enjoyment that can render life delightful, make her that comfort and blessing to you both which you so ardently wish for, and which, allow me to say you so well deserve.[24]

Never casual in his use of words, in the title he gives to God Burns is reflecting his thanks for his having shared in Jeany's young life.

Burns's humour and realism are to the fore when it is remembered that one of his longest and most elaborate titles for God, 'The Great Manager of the Drama of Man', occurs in a letter to John McAuley, the Town Clerk of Dumbarton.[25] Burns well knew the political scene of small towns and all the behind-the-scenes management of men that went on there. Burns is again careful in his choice of title for God when he writes of him as the 'Great Creator' in a letter to Patrick Miller.[26] Miller was known for his creativity and inventiveness in his care of his estate at Dalswinton. Again the appropriateness of the title is seen when God is called 'the Benevolent Director of all things' in a letter to Captain Richard Brown. Brown had opened Burns's eyes to many things when he had encountered him at Irvine. He had impressed the young Burns with his worldy wisdom and directed Burns's attention in a new way toward the fair sex, hence the term 'Benevolent Director' perhaps came to mind.[27] Both Robert Ainslie and Mrs Frances A. Dunlop would have appreciated the appropriateness of God being called 'the Great Disposer of Events', as Ainslie was a lawyer used to having to prepare legal dispositions, and Mrs Dunlop seemed to enjoy her self-appointed role as Burns's patroness disposing her occasional favours on him.[28]

It could be thought that Burns's descriptions of God in some of the letters discussed above owe as much to his literary inventiveness as to his theology, but when the descriptions in the letters to Mrs Dunlop, Alexander Cunningham, Robert Muir and James Clarke are examined, some of Burns's most deeply felt and constant beliefs about the nature of God are revealed. In his letters to Mrs Dunlop and to Alexander Cunningham, Burns seems to engage in the therapeutic release of his inmost feelings.

Writing to Mrs Dunlop in pessimistic mood he breaks off to say: 'To counterwork these baneful feelings, I have sat down to write to you; as I declare upon my soul, I always find *that* the most sovereign balm under Heaven for my wounded Spirit.'[29] As this and other letters show, Burns often writes to her in a serious vein. Similarly his correspondence with Alexander Cunningham displays an intensity that reveals much about Burns's religious thought. Burns begins one such letter, 'Canst thou minister to a mind diseased'.[30] The titles given to God in the letters to Robert Muir and James Clarke should also be treated with the greatest seriousness when it is remembered that they are, respectively, addressed to a dying man and written by a dying man.[31]

Writing to Mrs Dunlop on 'Newyearday morning 1789', Burns expresses his thoughts of God in very careful terms. Having owned up to being moved by the things of nature to what he calls an 'elevation of soul like the enthusiasm of Devotion or Poesy', Burns continues, 'Tell me, my dear Friend, to what can this be owing? Are we a piece of machinery that, like the Eolian harp, passive, takes the impression of the passing accident? Or do these workings argue something within us above the trodden clod?' Burns is then careful to distance himself from both Christian orthodoxy and the views that have been held by many men, when he attempts to answer his own questions:

> I own myself partial to these proofs of those aweful & important realities, a God that made all things, man's immaterial & immortal nature, & a World of weal or woe beyond death & the grave, these proofs that we deduct by dint of our own powers & observation. – However respectable, Individuals in all ages have been, I have ever looked on Mankind in the lump to be nothing better than a foolish, headstrong, credulous, unthinking Mob; and their universal belief has ever had extremely little weight with me.[32]

Burns is fascinated by the discussion of what he calls 'those aweful & important realities' and among these is 'a God that made all things'. But he will not yield his assent to this belief by anything other than his own powers of observation. Burns's empiricist philosophy leads him to set aside commonly-held religious views because they do not match up to experience and observation. It also leads him at times to declare a view of humanity that is at odds with the widely-held perception of him as an almost uncritical egalitarian, a man of the people and an upholder of such ideas as 'the brotherhood of man'.

Six months later he again writes to Mrs Dunlop outlining what he calls his 'creed'. Among the beliefs he declares is 'that there is an incomprehensibly Great Being to whom I owe my existence'.[33] Burns again fails to define God with any precision and certainly does not attempt to make use of the ready-to-hand Christian terminology. Just as when in the earlier letter he is attempting to write of the reality of the confrontation with God, Burns uses the word 'aweful', conveying the idea of the mysterious and the numinous, so in using the word 'incomprehensibly' Burns is emphasizing his inability, even unwillingness, to fully define God. But what does come across again is the sense of the reality of God that Burns has. In the first letter he writes of himself as partial to the idea of 'a God who made all things', therefore including himself as part of a creation, while in the second letter he claims to believe in a

God 'to whom I owe my existence'. Yet however much he senses himself and thinks of himself as God's creature, he is unable to define this God. In two later letters to Mrs Dunlop Burns gives indications of the nature of this God. In September 1794 he writes of the birth of his fourth son, James Glencairn Burns, 'I shall make all my children's names, altars of gratitude. Poor dear little souls, they are all, the finest creatures in the world. I gratefully thank my God for his goodness in that respect.'[34]

Another letter, written on 1 January 1795, adds to our understanding of how he viewed this God. Burns writes:

> I congratulate myself on having had in early days religion strongly impressed on my mind. – I have nothing to say to any body, as, to which Sect they belong, or what Creed they believe; but I look on the Man who is firmly persuaded of Infinite Wisdom & Goodness superintending & directing every circumstance that can happen in his lot – I felicitate such a man as having a solid foundation for his mental enjoyment; a firm prop & sure stay, in the hour of difficulty, trouble & distress; & a never-failing anchor of hope, when he looks beyond the grave.[35]

Burns is again being careful not to claim this belief as his own. He characterizes God as being infinite in Wisdom and Goodness, but although prefacing his statement with his own good fortune in having been introduced early to religion, he is careful to distance himself from the belief that he admires. Yet in this admiration there is a suggestion that he is almost persuaded to believe all that he says he admires and all that he admits is useful, enjoyable and the provider of hope.

There are times in reading the letters where you sense that the barriers are down and that you are enabled to see more deeply into the darkness of a mind that is struggling to make sense of the realities without and within. There are times when the art is secondary to the argument, when although the skill of communication remains, it is stretching to the point where it is in danger of becoming engulfed by the silence of the incommunicable but real. Such a moment is, I think, experienced in the letter written by Burns to his friend Alexander Cunningham on 25 February 1794. The letter begins with the quotation from *Macbeth*, 'Canst thou minister to a mind diseased',[36] and then goes on to reveal a Burns who seems to be just emerging from a period of severe physical and mental debility. He tells of the failure of all the usual comforts that should have lifted his spirit from depression but did not. Burns writes:

> Are you deep in the language of consolation? I have exhausted in reflection every topic of comfort. *A heart at ease* would have been charmed with my sentiments and reasonings; but as to myself, I was like Judas Iscariot preaching the gospel; he might

> melt and mould the hearts of those around him, but his own kept its native incorrigibility.[37]

But then Burns goes on to declare what he has found a help:

> Still there are two great pillars that bear us up, amid the wreck of misfortune and misery. The ONE is composed of the different modifications of a certain noble, stubborn, something in man, known by the names of courage, fortitude, magnanimity. The OTHER is made up of those feelings and sentiments, which, however the sceptic may deny them, or the enthusiastic disfigure them, are yet, I am convinced, original and component parts of the human soul; those *senses of the mind*, if I may be allowed the expression, which connect us with and link us to, those awful obscure realities – an all powerful and equally beneficent God; and a world to come, beyond death and the grave. The first gives the nerve of combat, while a ray of hope beams on the field: – the last pours the balm of comfort into the wounds which time can never cure.

In the opening passage of this letter Burns describes the utterly total nature of his illness: 'My constitution and frame were *ab origine* blasted with a deep incurable taint of hypochondria which poisons my existence.' He goes on to say that all his reasoning did not provide him with cure or comfort but that it was within that experience that he came to rely on the non-rational part of his constitution, 'the senses of the mind'. These are the senses that cannot resist the impressions of the realities that confront them and in this experience there is healing and comfort.

Burns seems to have been influenced by Francis Hutcheson and Thomas Reid in his analysis of how he has come by these beliefs. Setting out perhaps with Reid's dictum in mind – 'Reflection, the only instrument by which we can discern the powers of the mind'[38] – Burns seems to have proceeded on his way of observation and experiment in his own life and to have come to a similar conclusion to Reid who in that same section continues:

> It must therefore require great caution and great application of mind, for a man that is grown up in all the prejudices of education, fashion, and philosophy to unravel his notions and opinions, till he finds out the simple and original principles of his constitution, of which no account can be given but the will of our Maker.

Burns seems to rely on Hutcheson's claim that we have more than just what he calls the external senses of sight, hearing, smell, taste and touch. Burns's 'senses of the mind' are akin to what Hutcheson calls the internal sense and its partners the public and the moral senses and the sense of honour.[39] The quality shared by all these senses is their ability to receive impressions regardless of our will. Burns seems to follow Hutcheson's reasoning to conclude that by our very nature *ab origine*, we are constitutionally able to perceive what he calls 'those awful obscure realities' to which he refers. This influence of Hutcheson's thinking, whether directly from his writings or, as is more likely, indirectly imbibed by Burns from the society that had been so influenced by the philosopher, is confirmed in the concluding part of the letter. In the letter Burns imaginatively projects his son coming to appreciate 'the presence of a witnessing, judging, and approving God' through the beauty of the world around him.[40]

This letter to Cunningham is perhaps the most reliable statement of Burns's religious beliefs when they are at their nadir of certainty. He obviously does not remain constantly in that state of believing, and as earlier and later letters show, he can step back from such beliefs content to understate or to reduce them to a sparer form. Nevertheless the letter reveals more precisely what he claims as the basis of his religion, when he expresses it in different ways to correspondents: 'Mine is the Religion of the bosom' or, 'almost all my Religious tenets originate from the heart'.[41] In using words like these, Burns may be appearing to use the language of sentiment, but behind these words lies a defensible philosophy to which he had given his assent.

In the fullness of his faith Burns perceived God as all-powerful and equally beneficent. That was a conception of God that had been with him from his earliest days; even then, God was all-powerful yet predisposed to do good to mankind, as an excerpt from one of his earliest poems, 'A Prayer in Prospect of Death', shows. The first stanza addresses the all-powerful God while the last one and a half stanzas declare his goodness:

i. O Thou unknown, Almighty Cause
   Of all my hope and fear!
In whose dread Presence, ere an hour,
   Perhaps I must appear!

...

iv. Do Thou, ALL-GOOD, for such Thou art,
   In shades of darkness hide.

v. Where with *intention* I have err'd
   No other plea I have
But *Thou art good*; and Goodness still
   Delighteth to forgive.[42]

This poem also illustrates the recurring themes of the beneficent God, existence beyond the grave and accountability. It also demonstrates Burns's inability to define God, who remains the 'unknown'. Another poem from that same period, 'A Prayer under the Pressure of violent Anguish', again addresses the unknown God:

O Thou great Being! What Thou art,
  Surpasses me to know:
Yet sure I am, that known to Thee
  Are all Thy works below.[43]

But although God remains unknown to the poet, Burns conveys the impression that God knows him, and again, although this time it is expressed negatively, the goodness of the all-powerful God is being asserted when in the third verse the poet writes:

Sure Thou, Almighty, canst not act
  From cruelty or wrath!

Burns could not bring himself to the acceptance of any doctrine that imputed to God any activity that could in human terms be judged as cruel, nor could he conceive of a God who, having made his creatures, would be wrathful toward them. God remained to the end of Burns's life the 'great unknown Being' whom he had described to his dying friend Robert Muir as one 'who could have no other end in giving him existence but to make him happy'.[44] However convinced of the all-powerful and good nature of this God Burns is, God still remains unknown. Burns seems to be striving to be honest in this letter, for if he had just set out to reassure his friend he would have not introduced the possibility of a person being of no greater significance than 'a piece of broke machinery', but would have concentrated on the positive aspects of a better fate than that, at the hands of a good God. This desire to be honest with his friend is further evidenced by Burns's closing remarks where he admits that on this subject 'all men are equally in the dark'.

I started out in this attempt at unravelling this first of the recurring themes, Burns's belief in a benevolent God, by referring to a letter from Burns to Robert Aiken in which, after Burns has described God in different ways, including addressing him as 'thou great unknown Power', he declares of him, 'yet thou hast never left me nor forsaken me'.[45] That was written on 8 October 1786, and nearly ten years later, on 26 June 1796, less than four weeks before he died, Burns still exemplifies that belief when he writes to James Clarke, 'Whether I shall ever get about again, is only known to Him, the Great Unknown, whose creature I am'.[46]

In this, one of the last letters written by Burns, he seems to be writing of God in a very personal way. The style does not seem to be that of someone who is not in the least concerned as to whether or not God exists. If it had been, then God would not have been even facetiously addressed as 'Him'. This form of address is more likely to be adopted by someone who cannot escape the sense of being himself addressed by God, if only by means of those things that he has called 'the senses of the mind'. By using this form of address to God, Burns appears to be someone who finds himself still connected to one of those 'aweful obscure realities', in this case 'Him, the Great Unknown'. Again, from this letter it is clear that although he fears the worst, that is, his own death is imminent, he expresses no fear for himself. Burns continues:

> Alas, Clarke, I begin to fear the worst! As to my individual Self, I am tranquil; I would despise myself if I were not: but Burns's poor widow! & half a dozen of his dear little ones, helpless orphans, there I am as weak as a woman's tear – Enough of this! 'tis half my disease.

The first part of this passage could be read as an expression of stoicism, but the compassionate outburst of the second part shows that it is more than stoicism. Burns is not detached from life in the manner of the stoic, he is still firmly concerned for his family and, as a later sentence shows, for his friends. The tranquillity of which he speaks could be the product of what he has all along maintained as one of his core beliefs, viz. that there is a benevolent God. If there is such a God then there is no need for fear. What lends credence to this claim is that Burns adds to his address to God the assertion, 'whose creature I am'. If Burns did indeed believe in his being part of the creation of a benevolent God then he could have come to a peace with himself as he seems to have done. That is surmise, but what is not in any doubt is the fact that in the last month of his life Burns is still addressing a benevolent God as 'Him, the Great Unknown' and still asserting a relationship to him that he chose to describe with the words 'whose creature I am'. The use of this phrase introduces an element of paradox in that if God were a total mystery to Burns, totally unknown to him, then it would be difficult, if not impossible, to talk of being his creature. There is an outside possibility that Burns, through John Locke who mentions the work of Blaise Pascal, might have heard of the words from the *Pensées* 'Thou wouldst not be seeking me, hadst thou not already found me'.[47] Objective reality is not what is at stake in this argument: what we are considering is the subjective reality of Burns. It would seem from an examination of the texts that his reality encompassed him in a relationship with God, a God perceived by 'the senses of the mind' and whom he addressed and found himself addressed by 'Him, the Great Unknown, whose creature I am'.

Chapter 5

'If There be a Life Beyond the Grave'

Although Burns regularly returns to write about the possibility of a life beyond the grave it is not a subject on which he expresses great certainty. His letter to Alexander Cunningham on 13 February 1790 shows his lack of concern for the matter:

> All my fears & cares are of this world: if there is Another, an honest man has nothing to fear from it. I hate a Man that wishes to be a Deist, but I fear every fair, unprejudiced Enquirer must in some degree be a Sceptic. – It is not that there are any very staggering arguments against the Immortality of Man; but like Electricity, Phlogiston, &c. the subject is so involved in darkness that we want Data to go upon. – One thing frightens me much: that we are to live forever, seems too good news to be true. – That we are to enter upon a scene of existence, where exempt from want & pain we shall enjoy ourselves & our friends without satiety or separation – how much would I be indebted to any one who could fully assure me that this were certain fact!
>
> "Tell us, ye Dead! will none of you, in pity
> "To those you left behind, disclose the secret,
> "What 'tis you are, and we must shortly be!"[1]

From this letter it can be clearly seen that Burns feels that he has quite enough to think about and attend to in this world without having to be concerned about another. He admits that there are no arguments against the possibility of man being immortal, but neither is there sufficient information upon which to be sure about it. Even though Burns seems to appreciate some of the aspects of that projected life, the way he phrases his responses – 'One thing frightens me much' – conveys the feeling that even if it were true he is not convinced that it would be the kind of experience that he would want. In any case no one has come back from the dead to tell us anything about this much-vaunted life beyond the grave. The almost dismissive tone of his letter to Cunningham finds a contrast in a letter to Mrs Dunlop only two months previously. Burns is unwell, and writes: 'I am groaning under the miseries of a diseased nervous System; a System of all others the most essential to our happiness – or the most productive of our Misery.' Burns quotes a little more fully the lines from Blair's 'The Grave', used in his letter to Cunningham, and then continues:

> Can it be possible that when I resign this frail feverish being, I shall still find myself in conscious existence! When the last gasp of agony has announced that I am no more

> to those that knew me & the few who loved me; when the cold, stiffened, unconscious ghastly corse is resigned into the earth, to be the prey of unsightly reptiles, & to become in time a trodden clod, shall I yet be warm in life, seeing & seen, enjoying & enjoyed? Ye venerable Sages & holy Flamens, is there any probability in your many conjectures any truth in your many stories, of another world beyond death; or are they all alike, baseless visions & fabricated fables? If there is another life, it must be only for the just, the benevolent, the amiable & the humane; what a flattering idea, then, is a World to come! Would to God I as firmly believed it as I ardently wish it.[2]

The manner in which Burns deals with the subject does not give me much confidence in the verdict to which he in the end comes. The overdramatic description of dying death and decay, followed by the rhetorical questions, is hardly conducive to the reader taking him seriously and, if anything, both invite the answer 'no'. Burns seems to be coming down heavily on the side of those who regard all speculations on the afterlife as without any factual basis, and yet he leaves room for us to doubt that he does dismiss all of these, by allowing that if there is an afterlife, 'it must be only for the just, the benevolent, the amiable & the humane'. Then just as you think that Burns is changing his mind to believe in it, he performs a reduction of the whole concept by mocking it as a 'flattering idea', that is, flattering to any who think of themselves as benefiting from it. Burns then seems to conclude with the apparently dismissive yet possibly ambiguous, 'Would to God I as firmly believed it as I ardently wish it'. It is difficult to judge what weight to give this last statement. If we concentrate on the first part of it, it most definitely implies that Burns does not believe in the afterlife. But if we dwell on the latter part of the statement it begins to lend some credence to Burns perhaps clinging to a belief and certainly seeming to hope and wish that it were true.

Burns's attitude is made even more obscure when the letter goes on to state his faith in Jesus, whom he plainly trusts in other matters, as one whom he trusts is 'no Imposter' who has further contributed to the false hopes of a life to come.[3] Burns is perhaps making a fair assessment of this letter, when he describes it as a 'distracted scrawl'.[4] But although it gives us no firm idea of what Burns really believed, at that time, its very distracted nature is an indication of the way in which the subject of life after death was exercising Burns's mind.

One thing that does emerge from this with clarity is the natural link that Burns sees between the afterlife and the reward of goodness or the recognition of worth and virtue that had gone unrecognized in this life. This theme is taken up more fully by Burns in another letter to Mrs Dunlop a few months later (10 April 1790). Burns writes of the political leaders in their use of certain words:

> They know the use of bawling out these terms to rouse or lead The Rabble; but for their own private use, with almost all the *able Statesmen* that ever existed or now exist, when they talk of Right & Wrong, they only mean Proper & Improper: & their measure of conduct is, not what they OUGHT, but what they DARE ... However,

> this must be allowed, that, if you abstract from Man the idea of an Existence beyond the Grave, *then* the true measure of human conduct is, Proper & Improper: Virtue & Vice, as dispositions of the heart, are, in that case, of scarcely the same import & value to the world at large, as Harmony & Discord in the modifications of Sound.[5]

In a further letter to Mrs Dunlop on 9 July 1790 Burns again makes the connection between morality and the life after death:

> There are not any first principles or component parts of the Human Mind more truly radical than what is meant by, OUGHT, and, OUGHT NOT; which all Mankind (a most respectable Suffrage!) have, for several thousand years, agreed as synonymous terms with Virtue Vice. – But, except our Existence *here*, have as reference to an Existence *hereafter*, Virtue & Vice are words without a meaning. If *this scene* of Being is the whole of the *Drama* then a man's individual Self, his own pleasures & enjoyments, are & should be the whole of his care; & the true standard of his actions is PROPER and IMPROPER.[6]

From these last two letters it would appear that if Burns has any bias towards a belief in a life hereafter it is being inculcated as much by a view of morality as by an adoption of a theology. It is a moral stance that is being arrived at by observation and experience of a world of division and unfairness and injustice, a world in which true worth is seldom recognized. This is borne out in his letter to Peter Stewart in late August or early September 1789 with reference to the erection of a tombstone to Robert Fergusson, the poet whose worth had not been recognized. Burns writes:

> Poor Fergusson, If there be a life beyond the grave, which I trust there is; and if there be a good God presiding over all nature, which I am sure there is; thou art now enjoying existence in a glorious world, where worth of the heart alone is distinction in the man; where riches, deprived of their pleasure-purchasing powers, return to their native sordid matter; where titles and honours are the disregarded reveries of an idle dream; and where that heavy virtue which is the negative consequence of steady dullness, and those thoughtless, though often destructive follies, which are the unavoidable aberrations of frail human nature, will be thrown into equal oblivion as if they had never been.[7]

Burns's moral indignation at Edinburgh society's neglect of the talented poet, who died aged only 24, and to whom he owed so much, finds consolation in the thought of a life beyond the grave. The brief poems 'On Fergusson' both take up the theme of the 'unhappy fate' that befell Fergusson in this life, and such thoughts provide Burns with the basis for projecting a better life to come. Although the poems themselves do not in any way suggest that life hereafter, Burns's thoughts expressed in the letter are the natural follow-up to them: the injustice Fergusson suffered in this life needs to be compensated for; hence the projected afterlife. Burns writes:

ILL-FATED Genius! Heaven-taught Fergusson,
What heart that feels and will not yield a tear,
To think Life's sun did set e'er well begun
To shed its influence on thy bright career.

O why should truest Worth and Genius pine
Beneath the iron grasp of Want and Woe,
While titled knaves and idiot-greatness shine
In all the splendour Fortune can bestow?[8]

In the three poems he wrote about Robert Fergusson Burns is very much the man of sensibility. In the one quoted above he even applied the phrase 'Heaven-taught' to Fergusson. This was the phrase used by Henry Mackenzie to describe Burns in his review of *The Kilmarnock Poems* that appeared in *The Lounger* in December 1786.[9] The influence of Mackenzie's novel *The Man of Feeling* is in evidence in the tears that feature in all three poems.[10]

This humble tribute with a tear he gives
  [Epitaph. Here lies Robert Fergusson, Poet]

With tears I pity thy unhappy fate
  [on Fergusson (1)]

What heart that feels and will not shed a tear
  [on Fergusson (2)][11]

Burns is writing just two months after Mackenzie's review. However sincere his feelings are he is certainly writing in the rather affected mode of the man of sensibility.

I have written elsewhere an account of the considerable influence of the writings of Adam Smith on Burns, here it is worth mentioning the similarity that is clearly visible in their views on the subject of life after death. In Smith's *The Theory of Moral Sentiments*, a book read as early as 1783 and ever after cherished by Burns, Smith writes:

Our happiness in this life is thus, upon many occasions dependent upon the humble hope and expectation of a life to come: a hope and expectation deeply rooted in human nature; which can alone support its lofty ideas of its own dignity; can alone illumine the dreary prospect of its continually approaching mortality, and maintain its cheerfulness under all the heaviest calamities to which, from the disorders of this life, it may sometimes be exposed. That there is a world to come, where exact justice will be done to every man, where every man will be ranked with those who, in the moral and intellectual qualities, are really his equals; where the owner of those humble talents and virtues which, from being depressed by fortune, had, in this life, no opportunity of displaying themselves; which were unknown, not only to the public, but which he himself could scarce be sure that he possessed, and for which even the man within the breast could scarce venture to afford him any distinct and clear testimony; where that modest, silent, and unknown merit, will be placed upon a level, and sometimes above those who, in this world, had enjoyed the highest reputation, and who, from the advantage of their situation, had been enabled to perform the most splendid and dazzling actions; is a doctrine, in every respect so venerable, so comfortable to the weakness, so flattering to the grandeur of human nature, that the virtuous man who has the misfortune to doubt of it, cannot possibly avoid wishing most earnestly and anxiously to believe it. It could never have been exposed to the derision of the scoffer, had not the distributions of rewards and punishments, which some of its most zealous assertors have taught us was to be made in that world to come, been too frequently in direct opposition to all our moral sentiments.[12]

Smith does not categorically reveal whether he himself believes in 'a world to come', and seems to hint that he is in sympathy with 'the virtuous man who has the misfortune to doubt of it'. Smith is predisposed to believe it, in that he finds it difficult to otherwise explain the dignity, the cheerful bearing, the courage in facing mortality that mankind displays. The belief would also satisfy his sense of justice and morality, that would otherwise be affronted if there were to be no compensation in a life to come. But it is the pronouncement of those very rewards and punishments by those who most zealously proclaim a life to come that also does the most damage to holding such beliefs. From what he says in this passage, he believes on balance in a life to come, in that he finds it intellectually and morally satisfying, but he is almost put off believing by those who so vehemently declare the rewards and punishments to be meted out in the life to come. The crudity and harshness of punishment, the arbitrary nature of the way in which it is dealt out to those who either had the good fortune to be of the elect, or the misfortune to be of the damned, were an affront to his moral sensibilities.

The parallels to be found in the writings of Smith and Burns are such as to suggest that Smith influenced Burns's thinking on the subject of life after death. Both write of it as something that relates to justice and the recognition of worth regardless of rank. Both are repelled by the dogmatism of its most zealous advocates. Both seem unwilling to fully commit themselves to believing in it, yet both seem to cling to a hope that there might indeed be a life after death.

But if Burns's impetus towards a belief in a life to come sometimes arises from a moral base, it also on occasion derives from a belief in the goodness of God. Burns's letter of 9 July 1790, from which I have already quoted, had been written in response to the news of the death of Mrs Dunlop's son-in-law James Henri. In his opening passage Burns draws on the images of 'The Vision of Mirza' as he writes of the suddenness of death:

> What hidden trap doors of disaster, what unseen arrows of misfortune waylay & beset our paths of life! And Heaven, as if to shew its Omnipotence, often from the covert where Suspicion slept as having nothing to fear, looses the Shaft that wounds us to the very soul. – Thomson says finely –
>
> Attach thee firmly to the virtuous deeds
> And offices of life: to life itself,
> And all its transient joys, sit loose
>
> and yet, like many other fine sayings, it has, I fear more of Philosophy than Human-nature in it. Poor David's pathetic cry of grief is more the language of Man; "O Absalom! My Son! My Son!!". A WORLD TO COME! is the only genuine balm for an agonising heart, torn to pieces in the wrench of parting forever (to mortal view) with Friends, inmates of the bosom and dear to the soul! The most cordial of believers in a Future State have ever been the Unfortunate. This of itself; if God is Good, which is I think the most intuitive truth in Nature; this very propensity to, and supreme happiness of, depending on a Life beyond Death & the Grave is a very strong proof of the reality of its existence.[13]

It would appear that Burns is saying that if God is good then the natural corollary is that there is a life beyond death. He supports this argument by saying that a belief in a life after death finds its most enthusiastic supporters among those who have been deprived in this life, and claims that just as they intuitively believe in a good God so they also intuitively believe in an afterlife. As to his own belief, it would then appear he is favouring the case for a life beyond death, a case built on the premise of a belief in the goodness of God and supported by the reassuringly intuitive belief of the unfortunate of this world.

A very early input to Burns's thoughts on the subject of life after death was provided by an article entitled 'The Vision of Mirza' in the school reading book, Arthur Masson's *A Collection of Prose and Verse from the Best English Authors,* used by his teacher, John Murdoch. Burns writes to Dr John Moore on 2 August 1787: 'The earliest thing of Composition that I recollect taking pleasure in was, the vision of Mirza and a hymn of Addison's ... I met with these pieces in Mas[s]on's English Collection, one of my school-books.'[14] Then on New Year's Day 1789 he writes to Mrs Dunlop describing 'The Vision of Mirza' as 'that glorious paper' and as 'a piece that struck my young fancy'.[15]

'The Vision of Mirza' purports to be a translation of an oriental manuscript and tells the story of a man (Mirza) granted a vision as he 'fell into a profound contemplation on the vanity of human life'. The one who leads him to the visionary experience and who, from time to time during it, gives him an explanation of its meaning, is dressed 'in the habit of a shepherd with a musical instrument in his hand'. After some preliminary music which brought forth tears from Mirza, the vision begins: 'I see, said I, a huge valley, and a prodigious tide of water rolling through it. The valley thou seest, said he, is the valley of misery, and the tide of water that thou seest is part of the great tide of eternity.'[16] Mirza notices that the tide arises out of thick mist at one end and loses itself in thick mist at the other. He is told that what he sees is the portion of eternity that is called time. A bridge with 70 arches is standing in the midst of the tide. The bridge, it is explained, is human life. The bridge has innumerable concealed trap doors, through which many people fall into the tide. Some drop through:

> in the midst of mirth and jollity ... some looking up towards the heavens in a thoughtful posture, and in the midst of speculation stumbled and fell out of sight. Multitudes were very busy in the pursuit of bubbles that glittered in their eyes and danced before them; but often when they thought themselves within reach of them, their footing failed and down they sank.

Some are thrust off the bridge by people with weapons in their hands. Birds of prey hover around and these are said to represent 'envy, averice, superstition, despair, love with the like cares and passions that infest human life'. When Mirza sees all this he sighs and says, 'Alas, man was made in vain, here he is going away to misery and mortality, tortured in life and swallowed up in death'.

But then the genius explains that all of this 'is man in the first stage of his existence', in his setting out for eternity. Mirza is then invited to look beyond the mist into which the tide vanishes. It clears and he sees a huge ocean divided into two parts by a rock of adamant, one with clouds still shrouding it, the other with 'innumerable islands that were covered with fruit and flowers with a thousand little shining seas that ran among them. I could see persons dressed in glorious habits with garlands upon their heads.' Mirza wants to go to join them but is told that the only way there is through the gates of death. He learns that these islands are 'the mansions of good men after death'.

The vision concludes with the genius saying:

> Are not these, O Mirza, habitations worth contending for? Does life appear miserable that gives thee opportunities of earning such a reward? Is death to be feared that will convey thee to so happy an existence? Think not man was made in vain who has such an eternity reserved for him.

Mirza is delighted at the prospect but makes one last request:

> Show me now I beseech thee the secrets that lie under those dark clouds that cover the ocean on the other side ... of the rock of adamant. The genius making me no answer I turned about to address myself to him a second time but found that he had left me ... .

What a picture to impose upon the mind of so impressionable a child as Robert Burns. It is little wonder that the themes of 'The Vision of Mirza' were to recur in different ways throughout his works.

Burns continued to wrangle over the mystery of a life beyond death as a letter to Mrs Dunlop two years later shows. On 22 August 1792, Burns writes:

> I hope, & believe, that there is a state of existence beyond the grave where the worthy of this life will renew their former intimacies, with this endearing addition, that "we meet to part no more". Still the damned dogmas of reasoning Philosophy throw in their doubts; but upon the whole, I believe, or rather I have a kind of conviction, though not absolute certainty of the world beyond the grave.[17]

This statement best sums up Burns's attitude toward a belief in a life beyond the grave. It is not so much a belief as a gut reaction. As several of the letters show he respects and almost envies those who firmly believe, but he cannot bring himself to express that belief with certainty. He sees the justice of its existence and its providing a more complete moral framework for human activity. He also sees its consolatory powers, indeed he himself has on occasion drawn comfort from it, but nevertheless he cannot fully commit himself to believe it.

A letter to Mrs McLehose on 22 February 1788 gives a trace of Burns's attitude toward an explicit belief in a life beyond the grave. Writing of a visit to his friend Alexander Pattison, a Paisley manufacturer, Burns jocularly comments on 'His only daughter, who, "if the beast be to the fore, and the branks bide hale", will have seven thousand pound, when her old father steps into the dark Factory-Office of Eternity with his well thrumm'd web of life.'[18] This image of a shadowy place of indistinct shape, where work may be going on, says much about Burns's thoughts of what lies beyond death.

Another brief comment in a letter that Burns wrote to Anthony Dunlop enclosing a copy of 'Holy Willie's Prayer' possibly gives further weight to Burns's lack of a full commitment to a belief in life after death, although it has wider application to religion itself. Burns writes, 'Sir, Inclosed you have Holy Willie, and much good may he do you. I have prefixed a small preface, like a lamp stuck before a Presbyterian Pulpit to throw light not on the subject, that is commonly *light proof*, but on the speaker.'[19] Now although Burns in referring to the 'subject' is probably referring to the dissertation of the typical Presbyterian preacher being often obscure and difficult to penetrate, nevertheless the comment could have a particular reference to the subject dealt with in 'Holy Willie's Prayer', a large portion of which concerns the workings of eternity. Burns was certainly indicating that there are some dark areas of belief upon which the light of reasoning cannot be shed.

Burns found life on earth full of uncertainty, and the older he grew the more that was so, as he writes in a letter to Mrs Dunlop on 6 December 1792:

> I have not passed half the ordinary term of an old man's life, & yet I scarcely look over the obituary of a Newspaper that I do not see some names that I have known, & which I, & other acquaintances, little thought to meet with there so soon – Every other instance of the mortality of our kind, makes us cast a horrid anxious look into the dreadful abyss of uncertainty, & shudder with apprehension for our own fate.[20]

The fact that the uncertainty of this life is a 'dreadful abyss' to Burns is one indication as to the reason he cannot express certainty as he looks into the even darker abyss of eternity. It is the natural concern for what will happen to his dependents when he is gone that causes this anxiety for this world (as the letter shows). He expresses no fear for what might happen to him in eternity. His view of the goodness of God cannot allow for that. In a light-hearted letter on 6 April 1793 to Mrs Deborah Duff Davies, for whom he wrote the poem 'The Bonie Wee Thing', which he enclosed, Burns writes:

> Had I a world, there should not be a knave in it: & on the other hand, Hell as our Theologians paint it, particularly an eternal Hell, is a deeper damnation than I could bear to see the veriest scoundrel in earth plunged into. – But the hand that could give, I would liberally fill: & I would pour delight on the heart that could kindly forgive & generously love.[21]

From the various ways Burns wrote about the good God in whom he said he intuitively believed, it would seem that he was expecting from such a God a magnanimity and generosity at least as great, if not greater than, as that which he himself claimed to be capable of. Such an attitude at the very least prevented a Hell from being included in the darkness of any eternity that he might have in store for humanity. If there was a life beyond death it must relate to the goodness of God, therefore it could only be good. But it seems that Burns could never entirely eliminate that 'if'.

Chapter 6

'I am an Accountable Creature'

The last of the recurring themes to which Burns gives attention is his own accountability. In the letter of 22 June 1789 to Mrs Dunlop Burns states the three intertwining aspects of his religion:

> That there is an incomprehensibly Great Being to whom I owe my existence, and that he must be intimately acquainted with the operations and progress of the internal machinery, and consequent outward deportment of this creature which he has made; these are, I think, self-evident propositions. That there is a real and eternal distinction between virtue and vice, and consequently that I am an accountable creature; that from the seeming nature of the human mind, as well as from the evident imperfection, nay, positive injustice, in the administration of affairs, both in the natural and moral worlds, there must be a retributive scene of existence beyond the grave – must, I think be allowed by every one who will give himself a moment's reflection.[1]

That Burns was brought up to have a sense of responsibility is evident from the many instances of his accepting his responsibilities for his actions. The ignorant often criticize him for his moral lapses, but he accepted responsibility for them, as is witnessed by his provision for the children he fathered out of wedlock (one exception being his treatment of Jenny Clow who was Mrs McLehose's maidservant). Jenny had borne a son to Burns in November 1788,[2] and in a letter of 6 January 1789 he indicates to his friend Robert Ainslie that he wants to meet with her and 'settle that matter with her & free her hand of the process'.[3] But thereafter is silence until November 1791, when Mrs McLehose writes to Burns to tell him that she thinks that Jenny is dying.[4] Burns's response to this information and the plea for his help is found in a letter to Mrs McLehose. The cold, formal tone of this letter might be more easy to excuse had its subject matter not been so intensely personal. But it seems to reveal a much more disturbing attitude – that of someone who claims to have done his best to solve a problem and having failed is almost absolving himself of any responsibility in the matter. However the letter does indicate a willingness to help financially and to meet with Jenny 'and try what is to be done for her relief'.[5] Jenny died in January 1792, leaving a three year-old son,[6] but although in his letter Burns had said that he would have taken her child into his care 'long ago', he never made any attempt, as far as is known, to provide in any way for him after Jenny's death.

To a much lesser extent Burns may have lacked in responsibility towards Mary Cameron, an Edinburgh servant girl who was made pregnant by him in the spring of 1787. Financial payment was made to her and Burns's responsibility for her condition acknowledged, but as no child is ever recorded as having been born to her, the matter ended there.[7] It is in Burns's dealing with Jenny Clow that we see the most serious lapse in his acceptance of his responsibility for his actions. But whether or not in this case he made the reparations that others may judge he should have, he often acknowledged his own shortcomings and accountability. In a letter to Peter Hill, Burns writes revealingly of this accountability, giving it a setting within his understanding of his fellow men and women:

> I am out of all patience with this vile world for one thing. Mankind are by nature benevolent creatures; except in a few scoundrelly instances, I do not think that avarice of the good things we chance to have is born with us; but we are placed here amid so much Nakedness, & Hunger, & Poverty & want, that we are under a damning necessity of studying Selfishness in order that we may Exist! Still there are, in every age, a few souls that all the Wants & Woes of Life cannot debase to Selfishness, or even give the necessary alloy of Caution & Prudence. If ever I am in danger of vanity, it is when I contemplate myself on this side of my disposition & character. God knows I am no Saint; I have a whole host of Follies and Sins to answer for; but if I could, & I believe I do it as far as I can, I would "wipe away all tears from all eyes". Even the knaves who have injured me, I would oblidge them; tho' to tell the truth, it would be more out of vengeance to shew them that I was independant of, & above them, than out of the overflowings of my benevolence.[8]

This letter warrants careful examination. The intimate nature of Burns's remarks in the paragraph prior to the one quoted indicates a close understanding between him and Hill. Burns is writing to someone who knows him well, and with whom he would not succeed if he attempted to tell less than the truth. We glean from Burns's words that he believes that the great majority of men and women are by nature well disposed to each other; circumstances often make them what they are. In these words is a plea for greater understanding in judgement. A few people, however, seem almost impervious to their circumstances, and are not reduced to selfishness. They retain their natural benevolence unalloyed; neither are they brought down to a lower level of conduct by prudence or caution. Burns claims to have in his own nature a bias towards that conduct which is practised by the few that he is describing. He believes himself not to be devoid of selfishness, for he owns up to having sinned and done many foolish things and for these he holds himself accountable. But there remains within him a desire to, if he could, make up for the cause of tears, and he says that he does this as far as he can. He claims that he even does this to those who have done him harm, but he is honest enough to admit that these actions have been a way of showing his superiority rather than his great benevolence. Grasping the nuances of this chapter lays bare the basis of Burns's judgement of others and of his assessment of his own accountability: many people's actions are due to circumstances, therefore judge gently, but judge not only that they are to be accounted for, but that you too will be judged accountable.

This sense of accountability was helped to form in Burns by a number of experiences in his early upbringing. His first awareness of life was in a home where a serious-minded father and an industrious mother instilled their early lessons of diligence in the fulfilling of domestic duties. Burns was introduced to the need to work for a living in order to pay the rent. The bitter lessons of accountability were engraved in his mind by all the striving of his father and mother and eventually himself and his brother to pay their due sum to the Factor (the landowner's agent), while listening to his 'snash'.[9] It is significant that William Burnes taught his sons arithmetic. It was important that they should learn to count that they might learn to be accountable.[10] Burns's early education, sometimes literally at the hands of John Murdoch, also taught accountability, as Burns's reference to those days reveals: 'Though I cost the schoolmaster some thrashings, I made an excellent English scholar.'[11]

Another early influence that encouraged accountability was Burns's introduction to Calvinist teaching through a reading of the *Catechism* and *The Westminster Confession of Faith* and even his school *Spelling Book*. In the *Shorter Catechism* question 84 asks 'What doth every sin deserve?' and answers, 'Every sin deserveth God's wrath and curse, both in this life, and that which is to come.'[12] *The Westminster Confession of Faith* Chapter VI section VI declares:

> Every sin, both original and actual, being a transgression of the righteous law of God, and contrary thereunto, doth, in its own nature, bring guilt upon the sinner, whereby he is bound over to the wrath of God, and curse of the law, and so made subject to death, with all miseries spiritual, temporal, and eternal.[13]

Even in his *Spelling Book* Burns met up with the threat of accountability, as the juxtaposition of words in its first lesson on the use of words of one syllable shows: 'All who sin go in a bad way; do you no ill, nor use the ill way; for the end of it is bad.'[14] From several sources the sense of his own accountability was inculcated in the young Burns. It was to remain with him all his life.

In a letter to Mrs McLehose on 7 March 1788 Burns discusses the things given in friendship and love. The letter was defaced, but from what is left of it Burns seems to be mourning that much that is given is not reciprocated, and expresses his pleasure in finding someone like Mrs McLehose whom he likens to 'an honest Merchant who is qualified to deal with us in our own terms'. Burns says that this is a rarity, and that 'with almost everybody we must pocket our pearls, less or more; and learn, in the old Scots phrase – 'To gie sic-like as we get'.[15] It is as if he would like always to be more generous in his giving but as this is seldom reciprocated, he has learned on most occasions just to adopt the normal canny calculation that ensures at least that he gives an honest return for what he has received. Honesty is again a component part of his sense of accountability. Writing to James Hamilton on 26 May 1789, enclosing an account of five copies of his *Poems*, Burns includes the homily, 'Among some distressful emergencies that I have experienced in life, I ever laid this down as my foundation of comfort – "THAT HE WHO HAS LIVED THE LIFE OF AN HONEST MAN, HAS BY NO MEANS LIVED IN VAIN!" '[16]

In another letter written just a few days later, on 4 June 1789, to Mr John McAuley, Town Clerk of Dumfries, Burns again refers to his own accountability:

> Though I am not without my fears respecting my fate, at that grand universal inquest of right and wrong, commonly called *The Last Day*, yet I trust there is one sin, that arch vagabond, Satan, who I understand is to be king's evidence, cannot throw in my teeth, I mean ingratitude. There is a certain pretty large quantum of kindness for which I remain, and, from inability, I fear must remain, your debtor; but, though unable to repay the debt, I assure you, Sir, I shall ever warmly remember the obligation.[17]

However pleasantly the compliment is delivered and however smoothly the words flow, the warmth and sincerity of this letter is its lasting impression. It is written by someone who appreciates what he owes to others and who himself is accountable. This sense of accountability will not be altered in any easy way by a theology that can have a tendency to distort the individual's responsibility by an almost exclusive emphasis on the Sovereignty of God, with its corollary beliefs of Predestination and Election.[18] One of the reasons that Burns seems to baulk at the corollaries is their tendency to diminish human responsibility, as for example in Antinomianism the belief that the elect are not subject to the moral law. This understanding perhaps lies behind his words addressed to the Reverend George Husband Baird on 28 February 1791. Burns has generously offered his help in making available some of his unpublished poems for printing in a volume that will help support the mother of the deceased poet, Michael Bruce. Burns writes:

> You shall have the choice of all the unpublished poems I have ... Nor need you give me credit for any remarkable generosity in my part of the business. – I have such a host of Peccadillos, Failings, Follies, & Backslidings (anybody but myself might perhaps give some of them a worse appellation) that by way of some balance, however trifling in the account, I am fain, so far as my limited power reaches, to do any good I can to my fellow-creatures, merely for the selfish purpose of clearing a little the vista of Retrospection. – You who are a Divine, & accustomed to soar the wild-goose heights of Calvinistic Theology, may no doubt look down with contempt

> on my creeping notions; but I who was forced to pick up my fragments of knowledge as the hog picks up its husks, at the plough-tail, can understand nothing sublimer than this debtor & creditor system.[19]

The genuineness of Burns's generosity is not done justice by what he writes in his letter, but it is conveyed by the activity that it is signalling. A less self-conscious motive is at work here. He is not just reflecting a debtor and creditor mentality, but is perhaps exercising what he in another letter called 'the morality of the heart'. The activity in which he engages springs from a generous understanding of humanity. He once wrote to Patrick Miller upon seeing a wounded hare. The poem itself is one of his poorest but the sentiment expressed in the letter is of a higher order and perhaps relates more to humanity than to the animal that set the thoughts in motion. Burns writes:

> such an action is not only a sin against the letter of the law, but likewise a deep crime against the *morality of the heart*. We are all equally creatures of some Great Creator; and among the many enormous instances of capricious partiality in the Administration of this world which cry to Heaven for retribution & vengeance in some after state of existence. I think it is none of the least flagrant, that power which one creature of us has to amuse himself by and at the expense of another's misery, torture & death.[20]

Something deep within Burns knew himself to be responsible, a creature accountable both to man and to God. In this letter the three recurring themes in the religion of Burns are again in view – a belief in a benevolent God, a speculation on a life beyond the grave and a sense of his own accountability. Trying to isolate these themes from each other has proved extremely difficult if not impossible, for in Burns's thought they are so interrelated, and at times interfused, that any one of them cannot be discussed for long before there is a need to speak of it in relation to one of the others. Together and separately these three themes so dominate his thoughts on religion that he seems to be following his own instructions on another occasion given to a friend and parodying St Paul: 'Think on these things, and think on!'[21]

Chapter 7

William Cowper

The first sign of Robert Burns's awareness of William Cowper and his poetry appears in a letter to Peter Hill, his bookseller, on 18 July 1788. After ordering several novels by Tobias Smollett, regardless of their condition, Burns writes, 'I am nice only in the appearance of my Poets – I forget the price of Cowper's Poems, but I believe I must have them.'[1] However, by September he has been given a present of the book by a friend, William Dunbar, and writes, 'Accept my thanks for your letter; your Cowper's Poems, the best Poet out of sight since Thomson.'[2] Five years later he is still enthusiastic in his praise of Cowper, writing to Mrs Dunlop on Christmas Morning 1793 'Now that I talk of Authors, how do you like Cowper? Is not the Task a glorious Poem? The Religion of The Task, bating a few scraps of Calvinistic Divinity, is the Religion of God & Nature; the Religion that exalts, that ennobles man.'[3] Burns's last mention of Cowper comes just over a year later, in January 1795. He writes to 'The EDITORS of the Morning Chronicle', complaining about the non-delivery of his copy of the newspaper that caused him to miss an important speech by the Marquis of Lansdowne. He playfully quotes from Cowper's 'Retirement' in his reference to the speech, in which, Burns says, that the Marquis had 'made the great though ineffectual attempt, (in the language of the Poet, I fear too true,) "to save a Rotten State"'.[4] The phrase from Cowper is used out of context and does not contribute to our understanding of Burns's appreciation of Cowper, but it does indicate his continued familiarity with the work of the English poet.

As for Cowper's awareness of and attitude to Robert Burns and his work, five letters – 24 July and 27 August 1787, and 31 March, 12 April and 27 May 1788 – make this clear.[5] In the first letter, Cowper finds much to admire in the poems, and perhaps even more, in the poet. He claims to have read the poems through twice, even though he says that they are in a language new to him and on subjects that he deems are much inferior to the author's ability. Cowper's upper middle class attitude peeps through as he writes:

> He is I believe the only Poet these kingdoms have produced in the lower rank of life, since Shakespeare, I should rather say since Prior, who need not be indebted for any part of his praise, to a charitable consideration of his origin, and the disadvantages under which he has laboured.

Cowper sees Burns as a poet in his own right, for whom no allowances need to be made because of his humble origins. But Cowper cannot prevent himself from criticizing the language used by Burns, and concludes, 'It will be a pity if he should not hereafter divest himself of barbarism and content himself with writing pure English, in which he appears perfectly qualified to excel.' Cowper also judges that Burns is lacking in *gravitas*, and adds, 'He who can command admiration, dishonours himself if he aims no higher than to raise a laugh.' Cowper returns to the theme of Burns's language in a further letter to Rose, asserting that Burns will not get 'his deserved praise in this country [England] through our ignorance of his language'. But Cowper, although obviously having trouble with understanding the language, takes time to use the glossary provided, and ends up quoting the word 'ramfeezl'd', which he had found in the second 'Epistle to J. L ***** k'. He clearly likes the word and uses it again in a later letter to Lady Hesketh on 31 March 1788.

In a lengthier passage, in a further letter to Lady Hesketh, Cowper displays his admiration for Burns but with several qualifications:

> It is true that he was a Ploughman when he composed these, [poems] but being a Ploughman in Scotland where the lowest of the people have yet some benefits of Education, makes the wonderment on that account less. His poetical talent has however done that for him, which such a talent has done for few; it has mended his circumstances, and of a ploughman has made him a Farmer. I think him an extraordinary Genius and the facility with which he rhimes [*sic*] and versifies in a kind of measure not in itself easy to execute appears to me remarkable.

But although Cowper acknowledges the genius of Burns and his technical proficiency in working within the framework of an intricate and difficult poetic form, he again baulks at both the language and the structure used by Burns, qualifying his praise by saying, 'But at the same time, both his measure and his language are so terribly barbarous, that though he has some humour and more good sense, he is not a pleasing poet to an English reader.' Cowper again makes the point that the average reader will not either have the time, or take the time to understand Burns's language, 'or he will never account it worth his while to study a Dialect so disgusting'. Cowper had earlier written to another friend:

> Poor Burns loses too much of his deserved praise in this country, through our ignorance of his language. I despair of meeting with any Englishman who will take the pains that I have taken to understand him. His candle is bright but shut up in a dark lantern. I lent him to a very sensible neighbour of mine, but his uncouth dialect spoiled all and before he had half read him through he was quite "ramfeezled".

It is easy to conclude that it is Cowper's 'refinement' or English insularity that cannot allow him to see the legitimacy of the language that Burns uses, but

Cowper is no different from some of the elements of the Scottish literati such as Henry Mackenzie and the Reverend Hugh Blair who would have preferred if Burns had refrained from using Scots and written only in English.

Cowper's last reference to Burns is made in response to a letter from Lady Hesketh in which she had expressed her approbation of several poems by Burns. From the nature of Cowper's reply, it would appear that Cowper was again of the opinion that it would have been better if they had been written in English. He writes:

> Could a Nightingale be so unhappy as to acquire the scream of a Jay, she would furnish an instance somewhat resembling the case of a good poet writing in a destestable language. A man may whistle well, but if his breath be offensive one would [not w]ish to sit within wind of him. Poor Burns [is eve]r in this predicament.

'Poor Burns' indeed, according to Cowper; a genius, but fated to use a language that was 'uncouth', 'barbarous', 'disgusting', like 'the scream of a Jay', 'detestable', like an 'offensive' breath, and, in fact, not a language at all, but a 'dialect'.

When the albeit few remarks that each poet makes of the other are examined, Burns's emerge as the more generous, while Cowper's seem tainted with an air of assumed superiority. Cowper's are words spoken from the insularity of retirement and self-imposed exile, while Burns's are uttered by one immersed in the affairs of the world. Cowper's words appear to be written by one looking down from the heights of a Parnassus already conquered, while Burns's are full of natural admiration, qualified only by a personal opinion about religion, but from one who seems to acknowledge that he is still on the climb, aspiring to the same mountain of the Muses that has been gained by Cowper.

Before attempting a more detailed comparison on the poets' writings, it might be useful to consider their contrasting lifestyles and attitudes that emerge from their two vastly different life experiences.

William Cowper was born in 1731 into a privileged home. His father, John Cowper, was rector of Great Berkhampstead and a Chaplain to George II. His mother, Anne Donne, claimed to be descended from the poet John Donne. Robert Burns was the son of William Burnes, a gardener and a cotter, who in time became a tenant farmer, but who never achieved a living above the subsistence level. Cowper, upon his mother's death, was sent as a six year old to a boarding school where he was unmercifully bullied, barely surviving and marked for life by the experience. His later schooling at Westminster, a prestigious English Public School favoured by the then Whig oligarchy, was much more pleasant. Burns, born in 1759 in the cottage built by his father, had little formal education. Starting around the same age as Cowper, Robert and his brother Gilbert were taught by a young trainee teacher, John Murdoch, hired by William Burnes and a few of his neighbours. This lasted for two and a half years until Murdoch moved on to a teaching appointment in Dumfries in 1768. Apart from a 'summer quarter', shared week about with Gilbert, at Dalrymple School, where they had both been sent to improve their handwriting, and a further three week spell with Murdoch (who had returned to Ayr) to brush up his English (which was so good that the teacher spent the last fortnight introducing Robert to French), and a brief few weeks at Kirkoswald School to learn 'mensuration', this was all the formal education that Burns was to know. It should be said that the input of William Burnes to his children's education in the home was considerable. He taught them arithmetic, encouraged the habit of reading and above all conversed with them in ways that were calculated to give them a sense of the importance of equipping themselves with knowledge and an understanding of the world in which they lived. William Burnes's move from the cottage to the farm at Mount Oliphant in 1766 was partly because he wanted to be able to keep his children at home in order to be able to continue to care for their development, rather than to place them with others as farm servants. Burns's educational experience was enriched by his father, but it was also tempered by the harsh working life of a small farm in which he and his siblings provided the labour force.

Cowper went on to become articled to a solicitor and eventually a barrister, but it seemed a dilettante dabbling in the law with little work coming his way, and when the prospect of it did, he could not face the strain and suffered a nervous breakdown. He was cushioned against financial hardship by an allowance from his family and throughout this period he did not know what it meant to be hungry and poor. Burns, by contrast, lived with these two factors for most of his life, even in his later and more comfortable years at Ellisland, when he combined for a short time the life of a farmer with that of an Exciseman, he was still haunted by the twin spectres of hunger and poverty that ever existed in his mind, even if only more as a threat than as part of his everyday experience. These are some of the material differences in the lives of the two poets.

When we turn to consider the relationships that they each had, an even greater difference begins to emerge in their life experience. Cowper had a lovingly intense relationship with his mother in the short time he knew her, and an almost non-existent, certainly distant, relationship with his father. Burns was brought up in a small cottage and later in a not much bigger farmhouse, where in crowded conditions he had to get used to the regular additions of brothers and sisters as the family grew to the time when in 1771 he was the eldest of seven children. Cowper, on the other hand, had only one brother, John, and had been brought up in the spaciousness of a Rectory. Burns's father conversed with his children and treated them as those for whom he was responsible, instilling in them a sense of their own worth and a desire to learn more about the world in which they were set, and to this end inculcating the habit of reading and encouraging it by providing books on history, geography and the Bible, and discussing the issues that they raised. Although Burns's mother, Agnes Brown, could only barely read and write, she was familiar with the Psalter and with Scottish folk song, and by her singing introduced her children to music. In the home, too, a helper in the work of the farm, Betty Davidson, brought a wealth of stories and folklore to the knowledge of the children. So although raised up in a materially poorer home than that of Cowper, Burns probably had the more enriching experience, and in all likelihood emerged from it the better equipped to face the world.

Cowper's intense, although brief, relationship with his mother, perhaps combined with a distant relationship with his father and then being sent off to Boarding Schools from the age of six, seems to have badly affected his ability to relate to women in any other way than that of son to mother or brother to sister. In his early life he did not venture beyond the family in his male-to-female relationships, seeking the company of his cousins Harriet and Theodora, whom he might possibly have married but for the intervention of her father, who perhaps had become aware of Cowper's mental instability. But underlying his relationship with Theodora there seems to have been an attitude of Cowper's that would have ultimately prevented marriage. It is hinted by his biographer, David Cecil, that Cowper had some physical or sexual defect that he thought made him different and therefore basically unacceptable, even to God, and perhaps, he thought, even to any woman with whom he might fall in love.[6] His relationship with Theodora seemed to be conducted more in the manner of brother and sister than that of two lovers, that is as far as Cowper was concerned. Theodora might have had other ideas if the anecdote related by David Cecil is true. When she was asked by her father what she would do if she married Cowper, she is alleged to have replied, 'Wash all day, and ride the great dog all night.'[7] Apparently she loved him in a different way from the way that he loved her. Cowper's second, or third if we count his mother, important relationship with the other sex was with Mrs Mary Unwin, the wife of a clergyman who with his wife and family befriended him and after a short time took him in as a lodger. When Mr Unwin died some two years later William and Mary continued to live together, defying convention. Shortly after Unwin's death, and under the influence of their newly acquired friend, John Newton, they moved to Olney in Buckinghamshire, where Newton was Curate. Cowper's relationship with Mary is difficult to fathom. David Cecil tells of how Cowper writes to a friend, 'Mrs Unwin looks on me completely as a son' and comments: 'but it is not natural to live in a filial relation to a woman only a few years older than yourself, to whom you are not related and whom you had never seen until you were thirty-three.'[8] Cecil offers this explanation, 'Passion ... was alien to Cowper's nature; his deepest feelings were all affections', and puts it down to what he calls Cowper's 'etherial, hyper-civilized' disposition. I tend to think that Mary was fully in love with Cowper, but that he was physically, mentally and emotionally incapable of making any response other than that of a loving son or brother.

Cowper seemed to need people who could organize him and make decisions for him. The strange episode of his move to Olney with Mrs Unwin, under the dominating and domineering presence of the fiercely evangelical John Newton, tells us a great deal about Cowper. He was almost incapable of making decisions. His dithering over his protracted relationship with Theodora lost him a marriage. His lack of decisiveness regarding the post as Clerk to the House of Lords brought him to the brink of suicide. His unawareness of the flirtatious nature of his relationship with Lady Austen nearly cost him his relationship with Mary. He delayed proposing to Mary until another breakdown was nearly upon him and then came her illness and again he was too late. Throughout his sad life he was overly dependent upon others, and even more sad, he seemed to enjoy it.

Burn's relationships with the opposite sex are well documented. He had passionate relationships with several women, and in all his association with the many other women who were his friends and acquaintances, there are often sexual undertones. Burns had a robust relationship with men, whether as friends or acquaintances or in his business dealings. He was appreciative of their help and generous in his response for anything that they did for him. But he did not shy away from dispute or hide his true feelings from them. One huge difference between the two men was that while Cowper seems to have been content with a few select friends, and to live in seclusion with them, Burns had a much wider circle and loved to renew his acquaintance with them at regular intervals and to share with them in the social scene. Cowper's relationship with his male friends and associates was quite different. Cowper allowed himself to be moved by his brother following his first breakdown, taken into care by the Unwins, dominated by John Newton, gently managed by Mary, manipulated by Lady Austen (until Mary put her foot down and delivered him an ultimatum), accepted without question the spiritual direction of Samuel Tweedon (the schoolmaster at Olney), and allowed a much lesser scholar, William Hayley, to interfere in his work.

Turning now from the relationships that the poets had with people, their relationship with nature is revealing of further differences between them. Cowper saw the natural world as a source of wonder that had come from the hand of a Creator God. He saw it as expressing the attributes of God. He also saw it as mirroring the drama of life and death and resurrection, as a type of Jesus Christ and God's plan of redemption. Burns looked upon the world of nature with an equal wonder, but seemed to see it more with the eye of a farmer. For him the natural world was a source of nurture and a place of beauty, but one in which the farmer toiled, the cotter eked out a living and the ditcher and the ploughman got themselves dirty and weary. Burns also saw it occasionally in romantic ways as the world of nature whose splendour could cause the uplifting of heart, mind and spirit. For Burns the world was a natural mystery rather than a supernatural one. It was a world set in motion by a Creator God, sustained by a providential God, but it was never revealing of God in every aspect. It was capable of making us think about a Creator God, but it was not necessarily a means of knowing God. Most decidedly different from Cowper, the natural world was never seen by Burns as revealing or paralleling the redemptive work of Jesus Christ, which now brings us to a consideration of the religious poetry of Cowper and Burns.

Cowper's poetry often reflects the Christian beliefs that were then in vogue. Two books by William Derham, published in the early eighteenth century, were still selling well in its last quarter: *Physico-Theology: or a Demonstration of the Being and Attributes of God from His Works of Creation*, published in 1713, and its sequel *Astro-Theology: or a Demonstration of the Being and Attributes of God from a Survey of the Heavens.* A measure of Derham's popularity at the time of Cowper is witnessed by the fact that the editions of the two books that I was consulting show that the first volume was in its third Scottish edition in 1758 and the sequel in its seventh edition in 1757. His books have an evangelical purpose and work from the one premise: that the universe has been created by God and that his nature can be discerned from his work. The first book deals with the earth and the second with the heavens, but the very same argument is applied to both. I find that I can hardly justify the word 'argument', in that every claim that is made for anything on earth or in the heavens having been created by God is substantiated by a sentence that runs like this, 'Surely, such design, or utility, or congruity, or inter-relatedness, or variety, or magnitude, or minuteness etc. etc. has come from a Creator's hand.' A naivety prevails throughout both books and no attempt is made to deal with any counter arguments to the premise. In the concluding paragraph to Book One of *Physico-Theology*, Derham writes:

> And now from this transient view of no other than the outworks, the bare appendages of the terraqueous globe, we have to manifest a sample of the wisdom, power and goodness of the infinite Creator, that it is easy to imagine the whole fabric is of a piece, the work of at least a skillful artist. A man that should meet with such a palace beset with pleasant gardens, adorned with stately avenues, furnished with well-contrived aqueducts, cascades, and all other appendages, conducing to convenience or pleasure, could easily imagine that proportionable architecture and magnificence were within, but we should conclude the man out of his wits that should assert and plead that all was the work of chance, or some other skillful hand.[9]

That kind of argument is repeated throughout the books. Although hugely detailed and thoroughly researched, it is nevertheless superficial in its treatment of the subject, in that it only very superficially seeks to answer some of the real difficulties that people, even in the eighteenth century, had with some aspects of the natural world.

Derham writes of volcanoes:

> Although they are some of the most terrible shocks of the globe, and the scourges of the sinful inhabitants thereof, and many may serve them as emblems and presages of hell itself; yet even these have their uses too, being spiricals [*sic*] or tunnels to the countries where they are to vent the fire and vapours that would make dismal havoc, and oftentime actually do so by dreadful succussions and convulsions of the earth.[10]

Although they pre-date the publication of Voltaire's *Candide* in 1759, Derham's two books bring to mind Voltaire's Dr Pangloss and present a somewhat similar view to his, that all is for the best in the best of all possible worlds.[11] In his section on what the eyes can do for us Derham writes:

> They can with admiration and pleasure behold the glorious works of God; they can view the glories of the heavens, and see the beauties of the flowry fields, the gay attire of the feathered tribe, the exquisite garniture of many quadrupeds, insects and other creatures; they can take in the delightsome landscapes of divers countries and places; they can with admiration see the great Creator's wonderful art and contrivance of the parts of animals and vegetables, and in a word, behold the harmony of the lower world, and the globes above, and survey God's exquisite workmanship, in every creature.[12]

These samples from one of the popular books of the time that tried to build a bridge between theology and science were known to both Cowper and Burns. It would appear that Cowper was more influenced by them than Burns, as might be revealed when we come to further examine their respective attitudes to the natural world.

Burns's view of the natural world is simple: he seems to accept that it comes from a Creator God's hand, but his theology as to the nature and purpose of that God is not well defined. Although often expressing a belief in God as Creator, he does not claim to be able to define the connection between this Creator and Jesus Christ. In this respect he clearly deviates from the orthodox Christian beliefs of the time. He is more generally than specifically Christian. Burns settles for Jesus Christ as a good model for humans to follow. He believes in Jesus Christ as having been sent by God, but he cannot be specific about the precise relationship between Jesus and God. There is nothing very remarkable or unusual about this in the Christian Church today, where there are many people who would be hard pushed to be precise about the exact nature of that relationship, but who nevertheless think of themselves as Christian. But in Burns's time, such views as these would not be tolerated and anyone declaring them would have been regarded as not being a Christian. Burns appreciates the ethical message of Jesus, and believes that those who use him as their guide will be made better and happier as a result. It probably would be true to say that Burns saw Jesus as someone who could save men and women from the their sins in this earthly life, but that he was not greatly concerned about the eternal dimension of salvation, rather preferring to entrust that to his belief in a benevolent God. These conjectures are derived mainly from the religious views expounded in Burns's letters, for although the Creator God appears in his poetry, he makes no mention there of Jesus Christ or any plan of redemption. That whole area of what might or might not happen after death remains a mystery to Burns, but it is a mystery that he is content to leave in the hands of God, whom he deems will be benevolently disposed towards the creatures he has made.

In their different attitudes towards this final mystery that faces humanity, the two poets are sharply contrasted. Cowper's religion torments him; Burns's religion is a comfort to him. Considering Cowper's underlying mental condition (which was never far below the surface at any time) and Burn's basically more 'laid back' disposition, this is hardly surprising. When Cowper finished his training as a solicitor, he moved into rooms in the Middle Temple to begin to equip himself as a barrister. But when after two years had elapsed and no briefs had come to him he grew depressed, but on this occasion found himself helped by religion and in particular by a book by George Herbert (1593–1633), an Anglican priest. The book was likely to have been *A Priest to the Temple*, which showed what the life of a country parson might be in terms of humility and in loving care of his parishioners. Stephen Neill, in his history of Anglicanism writes, 'One who wishes to know what Anglicanism is and has not much time for study cannot do better than to pay attention to the life, the poems, and the prose of George Herbert.'[13] Cowper read and prayed, 'the fierce banditti' were dispersed and peace returned to his mind. He was only 21. Just over ten years later, in 1763, he went into a serious mental breakdown; this time there was no gentle George Herbert brand of religion to restore him, but a much stronger medicine.

Cowper was unfortunate to come under the influence of a set of religious beliefs that work well for those whose confidence in them is not undermined by doubt. But for those prone to doubt, or those of a more searching disposition, once doubt sets in they are undone, excluded by the very faith that had initially brought them to a sense of having been saved by God. When that faith has been destroyed by doubt, the result for a mind already depressed can be a sense of being damned beyond all hope. Such was the experience of the unfortunate and probably clinically depressed Cowper. Following his second mental breakdown, and while still in the convalescent period, he was introduced to the evangelical belief in a personal salvation through an acceptance of Jesus Christ as the one who has died for your sin. Upon adopting this belief, Cowper knew an almost immediate joy, and lived for a brief time bathed in the white light of certitude. However, as this certitude yielded to doubt, the joy changed to the blackest and bleakest despair, so that far from his having been elected for salvation, he reasoned himself into thinking that he had been singled out for damnation.

Cowper had come under the influence of the evangelical wing of the Church of England and the enthusiasm of the Wesleys and Whitefield. There had come into the religious thought of the time a concept that had long remained dormant. Following the theological and ecclesiastical conflicts of the sixteenth and seventeenth centuries in Scotland and England, there had risen to prominence a concern for individual salvation, one that was dependent upon right doctrine and a personal decision. These were the things that determined whether or not one's faith was truly 'a saving faith' and were the only correct responses to the call of God. This was a departure from the long held, and more commonly accepted, belief in a salvation that was guaranteed merely by becoming a part of the community of faith that was the Church, and by accepting the general beliefs proclaimed by the Church. By contrast, the evangelical faith elevated the concept of individual salvation to the point where if anyone was not aware of their having been saved, it was almost certain that they had not, and therefore were in danger of damnation.

The evangelical influence upon Cowper caused him to worry about his own salvation. Whereas the more liberal approach of the Moderate theology absorbed by Burns allowed him to sit more lightly to the state of his own individual soul and, for example, to be happy to accept Jesus Christ as that 'Great Personage' who could be an ethical guide to him as he made his way through the world and who would lead him, as far as he could, towards salvation and the expected acceptance of God. Burns had been led towards this attitude by means of his early introduction to the Christian religion through his father, whose Calvinism was tempered by enlightened thinkers like Adam Smith, Thomas Reid and his own parish minister the scholarly William Dalrymple of the Auld Kirk of Ayr, who in turn had been greatly influenced by Francis Hutcheson.[14] The inherited views would have been further nurtured by his own extensive reading. Authors like the local lay theologian John Goldie and the earlier John Taylor of Norwich contributed to a Christian faith that felt free not to have to take the Bible, in every respect, as literally true, but to allow for its figurative interpretation and for an application of common sense to those elements of it that seemed to be derived from superstition, or from beliefs that were no longer tenable in the light of new knowledge.[15] Having reached his religious beliefs in these ways, Burns was able to sit more comfortably and in a less worried way with some aspects of the Gospel story, and to exercise a more common sense attitude to all of scripture and to those who built a theology upon it.

Cowper, by means of the evangelical teaching, was made even more afraid than ever of his own real or imagined sin, and feared exclusion from the mercy of God because of it. Burns was well aware of his own sin, or more accurately of his sins, but it was the sins of commission and omission that concerned him, not some genetic defect or any inherited original sin that traced its genealogy to Adam. Again, while Cowper was made afraid by the prospect of hell and eternal damnation, Burns could not conceive of a God who had set out to make a hell and plan the torture for the very creatures he himself had made. Therefore Burns did not have any fear of an eternal damnation. Cowper had only briefly known religion as a source of happiness following his first mental depression, whereas from his childhood Burns had lived with the understanding that religion was one of the factors that contributed to men and women becoming better and happier human beings.

Cowper's life was overshadowed by his religious beliefs, even after he ceased to fully believe them. He then became troubled by the doubt that the things that he had rejected might indeed be true, and if so he was then in even greater danger of damnation. Burns sat much more lightly to anything that he believed, and was more willing to live with the mystery of life, trusting that any God he believed in would at least be more generous spirited than any human being; and that being so, because he knew others and even himself to be generous spirited, gave him hope that despite all his short-comings, of which he had many, in the providence of God there would be a place for him and an acceptance of him. So far as Burns was concerned, Hell was not part of his understanding of Eternity.

Sometimes Cowper's madness has been understood to have been the result of a religious mania. But this is to forget that Cowper was a very disturbed young person long before the onset of his first depression. David Cecil, in *The Stricken Deer, The Life of Cowper*, makes this judgement: 'Cowper the child was like Cowper the man: a defeatist, hating decisions, frightened of the unknown, not the creator of his own destiny; liking someone or something on which to lean.'[16] He had such a fear of illness and death that it could be said that he had no confidence in life. Cecil remarks, 'For such ills, religion was the only real remedy', but if, as Cecil implies, Cowper thought like that, then Cowper was wrong, for religion would only deal with the surface fears that were but the symptoms of a much more deep-rooted disease from which he had suffered perhaps from as early as the death of his mother when he was a six year old. Living in such a fearful way, Cowper did turn to religion, but having done so he began to fear that he might not be able to live up to its precepts, and this only added to his distress. Following that first illness when he was 21, he was helped by the form of religion prescribed by George Herbert, which seemed to provide a sufficient crutch for about ten years, but in those years there were several crises that eventually proved beyond its power to overcome. In those years, his engagement to Theodora was broken off, his father died and he lost a close male friend, Russell. He was not being successful in obtaining work as a barrister, his income was low, and when the opportunity came, by means of his cousin Major Cowper, to apply for the lucrative post as Clerk to the House of Lords, he became fearful of there being other candidates and of having to be examined for the position, and suffered a violent nervous breakdown that resulted in him attempting suicide.

Cowper was filled with revulsion at his suicidal behaviour and now had an even greater consciousness of his sin and more cause to fear the wrath of God. His brother John, who had moved in with him, brought in their cousin Martin Madan, who was part of the new Evangelical Party, to see if he could help. Madan assured Cowper of his certain salvation if he would repent, but to no avail, and five months later Cowper broke down completely and was admitted to Dr Nathaniel Cotton's Home for Madmen at St Albans.[17]

Cotton, who at the time was considered progressive in his treatment, was an evangelical Christian but also a poet. Oddly enough, Burns quotes from one of his poems in four different letters, two to Mrs Agnes McLehose and two to Mrs Frances Anna Dunlop,[18] although at the time he probably did not know Cotton's name. Burns had come across Cotton's poem in Hervey's *Meditations* where it appears in a preface and is said to come from 'A Physician'. In one letter Burns quotes only lines three and four, but in the others he uses the last eight lines. Cotton's complete verse is as follows:

For let the witling argue all he can,
It is religion still that makes the man.
'Tis this my friend, that streaks our morning bright;
'Tis this that gilds the horrours of the night.
When wealth forsakes us, and when friends are few;
When friends are faithless, or when foes pursue;
'Tis this that wards the blow or stills the spirit,
Disarms affliction, or repels the dart;
Within the brest bids purest rapture rise;
Bids smiling conscience spread her cloudless skies.[19]

Burns's use of this passage indicates how important it is to him. However, it also illustrates how he saw religion as a useful tool to help a person cope with their worst fears, the loneliness, the disappointments, the antagonists, the blows, the hurts, the lowliness of spirit, the unease and the diseases of life; and of how it is capable of renewing hope, dealing with conscience, and eventually restoring a sense of well being and happiness.

Burns writes to Mrs McLehose as a lead in to quoting lines three and four, 'I have often admired Religion. In proportion as we are wrung with grief, or distracted with anxiety, the ideas of a compassionate Deity, an Almighty Protector, are doubly dear.'

Writing to her again the following month, after quoting the last eight lines, Burns reveals how long he has known and used the poem, 'I met with these verses, very early in life and have them by me, copied at school'. Eighteen months later he again quotes the eight lines, this time to Mrs Dunlop, prefacing them with these words, 'it is one of my favourite quotations, which I keep constantly by me in my progress through life, in the language of the Book of Job, "Against the day of battle and of war"'.

Burns's last use of the quotation is over three years later, when he writes to Mrs Dunlop in a letter in which he apologises for perhaps having used the quote before, but saying, that 'when I write from the heart, I am apt to be guilty of these repetitions'. This adds significance to his use of Cotton's words, which Burns says are used by the author when 'speaking of its [Religion's] importance to mankind'.

Burns has clearly been deeply impressed by the verses now known to be by Cotton. It is I think legitimate to surmise that the theology that lay behind such words would have undergirded everything that Dr Cotton would have to say to Cowper, and in the fragile state of Cowper's mind have had an even greater impact.

Alexander Chalmers, who contributed a 'Life of Nathaniel Cotton' to accompany Cotton's poems in Johnson's *The Works of the English Poets from Chaucer to Cowper*, Vol. XVIII, quotes from a letter by Cowper of 4 July 1765, in which Cowper attests both to Cotton's great care and of his willingness to speak of religion:

> I was not only treated by him with the greatest tenderness when I was ill, and with the utmost diligence, but when my reason was restored to me, and I had so much need of a religious friend to converse with, to whom I could open my mind upon the subject without reserve, I could hardly have found a better person for the purpose. My eagerness and my anxiety to settle my opinions upon that long neglected point, made it necessary, that while my mind was yet weak, and my spirits uncertain, I should have some assistance. The doctor was as ready to administer relief to me in this article likewise, and well qualified to do it as in that which was more immediately his province. How many physicians would have thought this an irregular appetite, and a symptom of remaining madness! But if it were so, my friend was as mad as myself, and it is well for me that he was so.[20]

However seemingly pleased with Cotton's treatment Cowper was, it is now easy to see the inherent danger in implanting new suggestions of a religious nature into a mind still recovering from the trauma of a suicidal state, and that was already clearly obsessively concerned with religion.

Although the elements of what seems a religious mania are liberally scattered throughout this and other parts of Cowper's life, there is one tiny incident recorded by Cowper during this recovery period with Cotton that again signals that whatever its cause, the source of his mental disturbance lies in his early childhood. Cowper had been much troubled by terrifying dreams, but in his convalescence, as David Cecil tells, he had dreamed, 'of a child of about four years old who came dancing up to his bedside, radiant and beautiful as an angel from heaven and at the sight of it an indescribable sense of peace and freshness came into his heart.'[21] Was this the child that he had been before his life had been irrevocably marred by the death of his mother when he was a vulnerable six year old? Perhaps if the good Dr Cotton had pursued a line of questioning from this starting point instead of using the ready-made tool of religion, the outcome for Cowper might have been different.

But instead, Cowper's recovery was steered on a different course. A few days after his dream he picked up a Bible and was greatly moved by the story of the raising from the dead of Lazarus (John 12), and then went on to read from Romans 3:25 of the sacrifice of Christ as the price he paid to God for the sins of men. According to Paul, Christ was the one, 'Whom God set forth to be a propitiation through faith in his blood, to declare his righteousness for the remission of sins that are past, through the forbearance of God.' Cecil records Cowper's reaction to Paul's words: 'Immediately I received strength to believe it. I saw the sufficiency of the Atonement he had made, my pardon sealed in his blood and all the fullness and completeness of his justification. In a moment I believed and received the gospel.'[22] In immaculately orthodox evangelical fashion, Cowper declares himself roundly converted. But in reality he had but swung from one extreme to the other. After leaving St Albans in May 1765, he went to stay for a short time with his brother John at Huntingdon. John, upon hearing Cowper praising God for his salvation, 'thought Cowper's apocalyptic rejoicings only less insane than his apocalyptic despair.'[23]

Burns knew no such 'conversion' experience. His faith, such as it was, had been acquired in a more gradual way. He had never attained the heights of 'enthusiasm' as Cowper had, consequently if at times his faith reached a low point, he had less far to fall. But sadly it was this 'all or nothing' faith of Cowper's that let him down, whereas the more general faith of Burns seems to have remained with him all his life.

Cowper's loss of sanity was not brought on by 'religious mania', but neither was it helped by it. Perhaps if he had been led to a less 'either–or' form of religion, one that offered less all-encompassing assurance and certainty, he might have been led towards a more balanced and satisfying life. But these extreme evangelical beliefs that were adopted by him at a time of great instability of mind seemed to have the effect, in the long term, of undermining the new stability that they had initially brought to him.

However, Cowper, with the help of his newly acquired faith, entered upon a period of some stability that began with him meeting up with Mary Unwin, who, says David Cecil, 'was Theodora, Harriet and his mother all in one'.[24] First of all as a lodger, while her husband was alive, and then as her companion, he lived with Mary for over 20 years until her death in 1796. Following the death of Mary's husband Morley Unwin, Cowper and Mary were persuaded by John Newton, who had come to visit them, to move to

Olney where he was Curate.[25] For a time, Cowper assisted Newton, visiting the sick and acting as a reader. They collaborated in the production of a collection of hymns for worship, published in 1779 as *The Olney Hymns* and to which Cowper contributed 68 and Newton 280.[26] However, in the beautiful 'O for a closer walk with God', two verses tell of Cowper's lessening faith:

Where is the blessedness I knew
When first I saw the Lord?
Where is the soul-refreshing view
Of Jesus and his word?

What peaceful hours I once enjoy'd!
How sweet their mem'ry still!
But they have left an aching void,
The world can never fill.[27]

However good and kind a friend John Newton was, and he indeed was generous in his care of Cowper, he was probably not the best person to nurture Cowper's new found faith and fragile disposition. One of John Newton's own hymns paints a portrait of a wrathful God that is demanding retribution for sin. Referring to Christ as the protection against an accusing God, Newton writes:

Be Thou my Shield and Hiding place
That sheltered near Thy side,
I may my fierce accuser face,
And tell him Thou hast died.[28]

No wonder Cowper's old fears returned and he entered his third mental breakdown in 1773. He slowly came out from under Newton's influence and was further helped towards a greater equilibrium when Newton left for a living in London in 1780.[29] There then followed a period of relative calm during which Cowper produced the humorous romp 'John Gilpin' and his major work 'The Task' before again succumbing to mental illness in 1785. His last notable poem, 'The Castaway' (1799), sadly signals the way in which he thought of himself in what was to be the year before his death in 1800.

Religion for Cowper became an obsession, but sadly an obsession that failed him. He continued to believe in its truths as far as other people were concerned, but his own disposition and mental attitude towards himself led to his excluding himself from its benefits. Because of the insecurity of his own basic nature and his lack of a sense of self-worth, he placed himself beyond the reach of any gospel. There was no good news of a God who accepted him and who loved him. Yet strangely, he could still present the image of that God to others. It was as if he had placed himself beyond the pale, a castaway by virtue of his own nature, a stricken deer that had to leave the herd, a drowning man who had been washed overboard by the heavy seas of life – all of these images are from his poetry and are indicative of a man in whom a deep-seated fear of life would not allow him to find any temporary hope, far less a permanent peace from the religion by which he was obsessed.

In total contrast, religion for Burns was an aid to the enjoyment of life. He freely acknowledged that it had not saved him at a time of crisis, but that it had enabled him to think more honestly about himself and the world in which he lived. Religion for him is not a man-made thing, it is as natural to adopt it as to breathe, especially if you are a poet, one sensitive to all that is around you. He writes to Mrs Dunlop, 'Religion, my honored Madam, has not only been all my life my chief dependance, but my dearest enjoyment ... A Mathematician without Religion, is a probable character; an irreligious Poet, is a Monster.'[30]

But this natural thing that religion was to Burns although something that could be fostered within the Church, could equally be found outwith it. In a sense, the poet was expressing a personal belief when he allowed the 'Jolly Beggars' to raucously sing of 'Churches built to please the PRIEST'.[31] Burns knew that many things had come into religious practice that had been contrived by men, as much according to their own predilections as by any divine revelation, whether from the Bible, or from any source of holy tradition. While Burns might want his children to be brought up with a knowledge of religion and specifically with an understanding of Jesus Christ, he steps back from making the same commitment in a statement of personal faith.[32] Whereas Cowper is quite explicit in expressing his faith in specifically Christian terms, Burns never does. Although both Jesus Christ and God are discussed in Burns's letters, Jesus Christ does not feature in any of Burns's poems, and while God is mentioned in them, it is never with any accompanying Christian terminology. In his poetry Burns expresses himself as a Theist rather than as a Christian, a broad believer in religion as against the Christian Faith. It is only in his letters that what can be called his Christian beliefs emerge. Yet the strange thing is that while Cowper dies doubting, Burns seems to die hoping; that while Cowper comes sadly to the end of it all in distress of mind, Burns's last days are faced with a kind of Christian stoicism that signals a man at peace with the less complicated God in whom he still believed.

'The Task'

If at times Burns seems to have reduced his Christian faith to something more resembling Theism, nevertheless he retains a great deal of sympathy for Cowper's religious stance, despite it containing elements of 'Calvinistic Divinity'. Burns calls the religion of 'The Task' 'The Religion of God and

Nature; the Religion that exalts, that enobles man.' It is not my purpose here to assess the whole poem, but rather to offer comment on the religious elements of it that might have evoked Burns's approval or caused him to want to counter them.

In Book I of 'The Task', Cowper's walk takes him to a bower upon which the locals have carved their names, and he muses:

> So strong the zeal t'immortalize himself
> Beats in the breast of man, that even a few
> Few transient years, won from the abyss abhorr'd
> Of blank oblivion, seem a glorious prize.
> And even to a clown.[33]

Burns and Cowper are just a little more sophisticated in their carving of their names in verse rather than on wood. Like Cowper, Burns is driven to 'immortalize' himself in his poetry, and is also aware of the transience of life and of the abyss at the end. But for Burns the vision stops there and does not continue into the horrors of Cowper's view of life after death.

The man-ennobling religion that Burns perceives in 'The Task' is sometimes expressed in secular terms, as in Cowper's distress at 'Man's inhumanity to man':

> My ear is pained.
> My soul is sick, with ev'ry day's report
> Of wrong and outrage with which earth is fill'd
> There is no flesh in man's obdurate heart
> It does not feel for man: the nat'ral bond
> Of brotherhood is sever'd as the flax
> That falls asunder at the touch of fire.[34]

Cowper then goes on in that same book to condemn racial discrimination and slavery; views that raise the status of humanity and that express an ennobling compassion. However, in the very next book Cowper sees a recent earthquake (there was one in Sicily in 1783) as an instrument of God's wrath. He declares that those affected by the Sicilian earthquake are not more guilty than other people but that God has disrupted nature to issue a warning to all. Cowper writes:

> No, none are clear
> And none than we more guilty. But where all
> Stand chargeable with guilt, and to the shafts
> Of wrath obnoxious, God may choose his mark
> May punish if he please, the less to warn
> The more malignant. If he spare not them

Tremble and be amazed at thine escape
Far guiltier England, less he spare not thee.[35]

Burns would list those words as part of the 'Calvinistic Divinity' that he could not accept. They are an indication of Cowper's belief that what others might call the aberrances of nature, such as tempest, earthquake and flood, are indeed the loosing of God's control over nature as an expression of his wrath and an instrument of his punishment. Burns could not believe in that kind of God, who like Holy Willie's:

Sends ane to heaven and ten to h–ll,
A' for thy glory!
And no for ony gude or ill
They've done before thee.[36]

Nor could Burns agree with Cowper's assessment of all men as guilty men and his view of the world as a kind of playground for God as Cowper seems to imply:

What is his creation less
Than a capacious rescevoir of means
Form'd for his use, and ready for his will.[37]

Another aspect of 'The Task' that stems from the Calvinism of the eighteenth century is the elevated view that it has of the clergy, and the authorial role of the preacher in the pulpit. In Book II Cowper scorns the poet's use of satire, saying:

What vice has it subdued? whose heart reclaim'd
By rigour, or whom laugh'd into reform?[38]

He turns to the pulpit as the better instrument of reform:

The Pulpit (when the sat'rist has at last
Strutting and vap'ring in an empty school
Spent all his force and made no proselyte) –
I say the pulpit (in the sober use
Of its legitimate, peculiar powers)
Must stand acknowledged, while the world shall stand
The most important and effectual guard,
Supported ornament of virtue's cause
There stands the messenger of truth;
There stands the legate of the skies.

Cowper goes on to acknowledge the faults of the pulpiteers, but then returns to the theme and paints an ideal picture of one who from the pulpit is 'a messenger of peace to guilty men'. Burns could not have agreed with Cowper's assessment of the pulpit. Burns values satire as an instrument of change, and although he has a good relationship and respect for several Church of Scotland ministers, as his verse epistle to the Reverend John McMath tells, he sees them 'as men, as Christians too renown'd / An' manly preachers', not as 'legate[s] of the skies'.[39] Burns, however, would find himself in accord with Cowper's final comment on the preacher, 'I seek divine simplicity in him / Who handles things divine'. This last word would have found a ready assent from Burns who believed that religion was essentially a simple business.

In Book III Cowper likens himself to 'the stricken deer that left the herd', and uses the same image to describe how he was found by Jesus Christ, himself 'hurt by th' archers'. The poet claims that he was healed by Christ and bade to live. But unlike Burns's concept of religion, Cowper is not made happy by his 'healing'. Indeed as he recollects it, it seems to have affected him in the same way as the writer of Ecclesiastes, who declares of the world, 'Vanity of vanities, saith the Preacher, vanity of vanities, all is vanity'.[40] It is as if Cowper knows the theory of the Gospel that Jesus Christ is a saviour, but cannot apply it in practise to himself. He claims to have been healed by this saviour, but his life gives no evidence of it. It is as melancholy as it was before the encounter with the one whom he claims 'healed me and bade me live'. The only result of his 'healing' seems to have been that he has become more aware of how empty are the dreams of his fellow men and how vain is their search for a 'fancied happiness'. Religion has not succeeded in making him happy. If anything, as it is related in 'The Task', religion seems to make Cowper harsher in his judgement of his fellow men. In Book IV he expresses a very conventional upper middle class view of poverty, declaiming imperiously:

> But poverty with most, who whimper forth
> Their long complaints is self inflicted wo; [*sic*]
> Th' effect of lazyness or sottish waste.[41]

He is equally hard on those who frequent the tavern:

> There sit involved and lost in enticing clouds
> Of Indian fume, a guzzling deep, the boor
> The lackey, and the groom, the craftsman there
> Takes Lethean leave of all his toil
> Smith, cobbler, joiner, he that plies the shears
> And that kneeds the dough, all loud alike
> All learned, and all drunk![42]

Cowper's conversion experience seems to have made him more critical, and as the tone of the above passage reveals, condemnatory of the pleasures sought by working men. How different are the convivial scenes portrayed by Burns, as Tam and his friends, or the Jolly Beggars, enjoy a drink, a 'crack' and a song. It is a little surprising that Burns, as far as is known, does not offer comment on this rather judgemental attitude of Cowper. However it is viewed, Cowper's attitude towards his fellow men seems to lack understanding when they come from what he would deem the lower classes.

Burns would have greater sympathy with Cowper when he considers the origins and function of kingship. Cowper outlines the growth of the power of kings from what he asserts is their origin in the strong killing leader, to their elevation by the people, and puzzles at the attitude of the more mature and developed societies that cannot free themselves from the servitude of kings. In the course of this passage he claims that the British do not seem to be able to learn from the experience of other countries like America and France, and Burns must have been nodding in approval as Cowper muses over why this should be so:

> Such dupes are men to custom, and so prone
> To reverence what is ancient and can plead
> A course of long observance for its use
> That even *servitude*, the worst of ills
> Because deliver'd from sire to son
> Is kept and graded as a sacred thing.[43]

Cowper then goes on to rejoice in the fall of the Bastille and laud individual liberty:

> For he who values liberty confines
> His zeal for her predominance within
> No narrow bounds; her cause engages him
> Wherever pleaded.[44]

Burns's radical blood would have been stirred by such words, for he himself had been moved to express his support for both the American and the French revolutions.[45] In the case of the French, possibly even attempting to assist it by the sending of a carronade acquired when he impounded a ship he had boarded as a custom's officer. Liberty was the theme taken up in several poems, sometimes whimsically as in 'To the Beautiful Miss Eliza J—n', or in celebration of a fox's escape in 'On Glenriddel's Fox Breaking his Chain', but also more seriously, as in 'Ode [For General Washington's Birthday]', when Burns defiantly declares:

But come, ye sons of Liberty,
Columbia's offspring, brave as free
In danger's hour still flaming in the van:
Ye know, and dare maintain, The Royalty of Man.[46]

In 'The Jolly Beggars' he choruses, 'Liberty's a glorious feast' and in 'Here's a Health to them that's awa' he prays, 'May Liberty meet wi' success / May Prudence protect her frae evil.' But most famously in his battle cry for freedom, 'Scots Wha Hae', he concludes with the words, 'LIBERTY's in every blow / Let us do or die.'[47] Burns was not just concerned for national liberty but also for individual liberty, and so Cowper's words that followed on from those on liberty knowing 'no narrow bounds', would have contributed to Burns's opinion of the 'glorious' nature of this poem, as Cowper writes:

Tis liberty alone that gives the flower
Of fleeting life its lustre and perfume
And we are weeds without it.[48]

Man's need for personal freedom and personal liberty are dear to Burns, and without these things life would be as worthless as a weed. But unlike Burns, whose thoughts might have developed these sentiments in more human directions, Cowper uses them as a lead in to a religious, indeed a specifically Christian statement:

But there is yet a liberty unsung
By poets, and by senators unpraised
. . .
Tis liberty of heart derived from Heaven
Bought with his blood, who gave it to mankind
And sealed it with the same token.

Cowper suggests that man can only be fully free when he has been liberated by Jesus Christ – freed from the consequences of his sin by the sacrificial death of Christ – redeemed at the cost of the blood of Christ. He finally poses the question:

Is liberty a flight into his arms
E'er yet mortality's fine thread gives way
A clear escape from tyrranising lust
And full immunity from penal wo?

Here in the explicitness of Cowper's version of an evangelical faith, Burns must have felt uncomfortable. Here the tortured mind of Cowper is harking back to the Olney period, when much under the influence of John Newton, he could write in a hymn:

There is a fountain filled with blood
Drawn from Immanuel's veins
And sinner's plunged beneath that flood
Lose all their guilty stains.[49]

Then having stated the purpose of this fountain, Cowper claims that just as the dying thief who was crucified with Christ took advantage of it, so did he:

The dying thief rejoiced to see
That fountain in his day
And there have I, as vile as he
Washed all my sins away.

Yet in truth, Cowper was no further on, no more free from his haunting sense of being damned for all eternity. No matter what his hymns or his poetry protested or theorised, the reality of a man unable to accept his own acceptability to God remained, and comes across in 'The Task' as he still poses the question to which he cannot find an answer, 'Is liberty a flight into his arms?'[50] Burns is untroubled by such questions, for he believed that if there was a God, then he would have to be a benevolent God, far beyond the limited perceptions of humanity, and therefore far more capable of being more generous spirited than man in the judgement of those who are his creatures.

As Book V comes to its close, Cowper again turns to the theme of God and Nature. He seems to follow two different lines of thought: first, that until man awakens to the existence of God he will not see the world as his creation, and second, that the world itself reveals God and leads men to an appreciation of him. It is difficult to detect which of these two ideas Cowper most favours. In Richard Feingold's *Nature and Society, Later Eighteenth Century Uses of the Pastoral and the Georgic*, he points out:

He [Cowper] seems to move somewhat carelessly between two attitudes. On the one hand there is the advice to "Aquaint thyself with God if thou wouldst taste his works" [Book V, 779–80]. On the other hand is the assertion that Nature itself is the road to God. An observer sensitive to the changing season will understand that,

From dearth to plenty, and from death to life,
Is Nature's progress when she lectures man
In heavenly truth; evincing, as she makes
The grand transition, that there lives and works
A soul in things, and that soul is God. [Book VI, 181–5][51]

I suspect that Burns would share Cowper's dual approach. Nature speaks to him through a bird, a mouse, a flower, a rainbow or a snowflake, and passing these things through the catalyst of his mind it generates thoughts of himself and his place in the world. He measures himself against the known darknesses of the past and the unknown darkness of the future, and from those thoughts of the transient nature of life he is led to consider his own creatureliness as part of nature and the work of a Creator. But he too approaches nature from the standpoint of a creature who sees in his fellow creatures the handiwork of God, and would have empathized wth Cowper's experience that caused him to recognize:

A loud hosanna sent from all thy works
Which he that hears it with a shout repeats
And adds his rapture to the gen'ral praise
In that blest moment, Nature throwing wide
Her veil opaque, discloses with a smile
The author of her beauties.[52]

Burns knows that same exaltation of spirit that is provoked by nature's beauty and although he does not make as immediate a connection with God as its author and creator, the experience does bring him, after some deliberation, to thoughts of God:

I have some favorite flowers in Spring, among which are the mountain-daisy, the hare-bell, the foxglove, the wild brier-rose, the budding birk & the hoary hawthorn, that I view and hang over with particular delight. – I never hear the loud, solitary whistle of the Curlew in a summer noon, or the wild, mixing cadence of a troop of grey-plover in an Autumnal-morning, without feeling an elevation of soul like the enthusiasm of Devotion or Poesy. – Tell me my dear Friend to what can this be owing? Are we a piece of machinery that, like the Eolian harp, passive, takes the impression of the passing accident? Or do these workings argue something within us above the trodden clod? I own myself partial to these proofs of those aweful & important realities, a God that made all things, man's immaterial & immortal nature, & a World of weal or woe beyond death & the grave, these proofs that we deduct by dint of our own powers & observation.[53]

In Book VI Cowper continues the theme of the relation of nature to God, and borders on pantheism as he writes:

The Lord of all himself through all diffused
Sustains and is the life of all that lives
Whose cause is God.[54]

The wavering between the God in all things of pantheism and the Creator, sustaining, providental God of the Christian Faith is again seen. But Cowper has only been toying with this idea, and explicitly denies pantheism, indeed he goes on to be extremely assertive, identifying the Creator God with the pre-existent Christ as the word of God who was with God as the creative force in the very beginning:

> But all are under one. One spirit – His
> Who wore the platted thorns with bleeding brows –
> Rules universal nature.
> But shows some touch, in freckle, streak or stain,
> Of his unrivall'd pencil.[55]

Any dabbling with pantheistic interpretations has been utterly renounced, and in this Christianising of the Creator, Cowper departs entirely from any resemblance to any concept of a Creator that is held by Burns.

Cowper introduces another element of 'Calvinistic Divinity' when he asserts the corruption of nature as well as humanity as a result of Adam's sin, claiming:

> Though winter had been none, had man been true
> And earth be punish'd for its tenant's sake.[56]

The poet, taking much of his imagery from the prophet Isaiah, then projects to an idyllic time, in which the earth will enjoy 'an eternal spring' and all nature will be at peace, when, 'All creatures worship man, and all mankind One Lord, one Father' (Book VI 759–804).[57] Cowper then offers a portrait of a man who is already sharing that 'happier life to come':

> He is the happy man, whose life ev'n now
> Shows somewhat of that happier life to come;
> Who, doom'd to an obscure but tranquil state,
> Is pleas'd with it, and, were he free to choose,
> Would make his fate his choice.[58]

If this is, as I think it is, a self-portrait, then Cowper is either suffering from a delusion or he is being less than honest. I suspect that this is how he would like to see himself, or perhaps how he thinks he should see himself if he believes the things that he once believed. But when these words are measured against what is known of his sad life, they do not ring true. Michael Schmidt, in his *Lives of the Poets*, makes this observation: 'for him [Cowper], poetry was the means of talking himself back from the edge'.[59] Just as Burns used a 'burst of execration' to expel his anger, so Cowper used his statements of faith to assuage his doubts.[60] Schmidt relates how D.J. Enright compares Cowper with George Herbert: 'Cowper asks that we assent to his presentation of faith, while Herbert's representations are faith as experience.' Schmidt continues, with a comment from Coleridge, who admires 'The Task ... for the vein of satire which runs through that excellent poem, together with the sombre hue of its religious opinions'. To which Schimdt comments: 'Opinions is the right word, opinions argued and affirmed, only seldom conveyed to the pulse.'[61] By contrast, Burns's religious statements, although far fewer than Cowper's, have about them something that seems to have been felt on the pulse of experience.

Chapter 8

Christopher Smart

There is a strand in Burns's thought that affects his attitude to religion. It has to do with the view that comes across so often, that somehow or other many of those who proclaim the Christian faith have got it wrong. That in trying to explain man's behaviour, their proclamations have missed the mark. That the God for whom they stand as advocates is not at all like the portrait that they present of him. Burns rebels against the doctrines that have emanated from what he sees as this misunderstanding of both the nature of God and the nature of man, thus he rebels against the Doctrines of Original Sin, Election and Predestination, and the concept of an eternal hell. There is a nagging doubt at the heart of all of Burns's questioning of what is claimed to be orthodoxy, that it has failed to properly consider the whole man. This comes out in different ways, but it is summed up by a conviction that even when elements of man's nature lead him astray, those very elements are part of his nature, that they are in fact elemental, of his very being and in it by design. In 'The Vision', the 'heavenly seeming Fair' muse tells the poet:

> 'I saw thy pulse's maddening play,
> 'Wild – send thee Pleasure's devious way,
> 'Misled by Fancy's *meteor – ray*,
> 'By Passion driven;
> 'But yet the *light* that led astray,
> 'Was *light* from Heaven.[1]

Burns's muse is asserting that what drives him, what comes from the heart, what is felt on the pulse, what is derived from his quick bright imagination, what is passionately experienced is part of the nature that has been given him from heaven. 'Fancy' – imagination (the ranging of the mind over other possibilities) – that which brings light and insight, is from God. 'Passion' – the strong feelings that are felt on the pulse – that comes from the heart, is from God. These things, imagination and passion, can lead astray, yet without them our humanity would be deprived of two of its most distinguishing and enriching characteristics. Man is not just a religious 'soul', but has a body, a mind and a spirit that are all part of his nature and can be thought of as coming from nature, whether that be envisaged as a Creator God or, more neutrally, from whatever is the natural source of being. The muse is imparting to Burns the insight that even though his imagination and passion have led him astray, they are part of what God has given him. The way he is is not because of some defect brought about by his one-time ancestor, Adam, disobeying God. It is not something for which he is to be held responsible and that brings him inevitably to be held to account and punished for. But that it is part of his natural, God-made self. This is what did not seem to be taken account of by those who purveyed the orthodox Christian faith then current, and caused Burns to rebel against some of their proclamations and to label them as religious nonsense.

This tension between what was often proclaimed by the Church and what the poet really believed was felt by more than Burns. Other poets had been troubled by the same tension. John Milton struggled to 'assert Eternal Providence, / And justify the ways of God to men', and possibly failed.[2] William Blake found the traditional understanding of the Christian faith somewhat lacking in meeting his own view of human nature and the God whom he believed confronted him in the midst of life.[3] William Cowper had known the strain of trying to conform to what other religious practitioners had told him that he should believe, and as has been seen it seems to have had the effect of leading him into an even deeper depression.[4] Christopher Smart, a poet less well known than these others, bears his own testimony to the cost of the tensions felt when the poetic mind attempts to grapple with traditional Christian beliefs in the light of an understanding of the complexities of human nature, in the setting of the natural world about which more and more is becoming known. In this chapter I want to explore some of the ways Christopher Smart attempted to come to terms with these tensions and how he relates to the tentative, emerging theology of Robert Burns.

Christopher Smart was born in Shipbourne, Kent, in 1722. His father Peter was steward of the wealthy Vane family's estate at Fairlawn. After his father's death, when Christopher was 11, he spent his youth in Durham with another branch of the Vane family, passing his holidays with them at Raby Castle, Staindrop. The Vanes also very generously helped him to Cambridge, where he was a diligent scholar. While there, his poetic talents led him to translate Pope's 'Ode on St. Cecilia's Day' into Latin. Pope later signalled his approval. Again at Cambridge he had composed Tripos verses. He had shown an early interest in poetry and wrote his first verse as a precocious four year old. He had fallen in love with a girl three times his age who had shown him affection.

Teasing him, a gentleman had said that he would marry the girl, and if she would not have him, he would send his son to marry her. Smart was stung into responding with these lines to thwart his rival and to restate his own case to his 12 year-old lover:

Madam, if you please
To hear such things as these.
Madam, I have a rival sad

And if you don't take my part it will make me mad.
He says he will send his son;
But if he does I will get me a gun.
Madam if you please to pity,
O poor Kitty, O poor Kitty![5]

Perhaps not too much should be read into these words of a four year old, although Michael Schmidt suggests that they show Smart 'already in infancy insecure in love, already subject to the teasing and treachery of the adult world'. At Cambridge, however, Smart's circle of friends was widened through his friendship and association with Charles Burney the organist and composer, through whom he got to know Dr Samuel Johnson and those who gathered round him. Smart graduated as Bachelor of Arts in 1744, became a Fellow of Pembroke College in 1745 and graduated as Master of Arts in 1747.

In five out of the six years from 1750 to 1755 Smart won the Seatonian Prize, which had been established by the Reverend Thomas Seaton for a poem to the 'Honour of the Supreme Being'. In those years he successfully submitted poems on the 'Attributes of the Supreme Being' as follows: eternity, immensity, omniscience, power and goodness. The Seatonian Prize for the year 1754 was won by George Bally for his poem 'On the Justice of the Supreme Being'. It is not known whether Smart entered for the competition that year or just failed to please the judges.[6]

Smart had another aspect to his character. In 1743 he had written a comedy, 'A Trip to Cambridge, or, The Grateful Fair'. In 1750–51, as well as entering religious poems for the Seatonian Prize, he was a frequent contributor to the magazine 'The Student' and also to 'The Midwife or The Old Woman's Magazine'. Smart and John Newbery (1713–67) were almost the only contributers to 'The Midwife', with Smart using the pseudonym 'Mrs Mary Midnight'. Newbery, its publisher, was also one of the first to publish books intended for children. At this period, too, Smart not only wrote for 'The Midwife', but on at least one occasion performed on stage at the Castle Tavern in Paternoster Row as 'Mrs. Mary Midnight, the Male Midwife'. Smart had been introduced to Newbery through Charles Burney, who tells of how Smart, 'ruined himself by returning the tavern treats of strangers who invited him as a wit and an extraordinary personage'.[7] Smart describes himself in these very self-deprecating terms:

> In the first place then, my stature is so very low that it has executed the jealousy of a *Dutchman* lately come over for a show from Holland, and who, like some persons, I don't care to mention, expects to be a great man by no other merit than his distinguished *littleness*. My eyes, which are extremely small and hollow, may truly be styl'd of the *amorous* kind, for they are always looking at one another. In the rest of my person there is nothing very singular, saving that when I take the air, having neither horse nor vehicle, I am obliged to do it upon a pair of bandy legs.[8]

In 1752, Newbery published a collection of Smart's poems. It was well enough received although there also was some criticism. Smart reacted badly to the criticism, and supposing that the critic was Dr John Hill afterwards Sir John Hill, he took his revenge by publishing 'The Hilliard' in 1753, which Chalmers rates as 'one of the most bitter satires ever published.'[9] Smart, however, gathers his dignity about him and, rather disdainfully, writes:

> The critic's censures are beneath our care,
> We strive to please the generous and the fair.
> To their decision we submit our claim,
> We write not, speak not, breathe not, but for them.[10]

But he had revealed how easily he could be hurt.

In 1753, Smart married Ann Maria Carnan, the daughter by a former husband of Mary, the wife of John Newbery, and by 1756 had two daughters. However he was not good with money. While at Cambridge, his biographer Chalmers writes that Smart had:

> a habitual neglect of pecuniary matters, a convivial disposition that led him at the same time to associate rather too frequently with men who were of superior fortune, while pride kept him from avowing his inability to support their expenses ... in all other respects Smart was a man of blameless conduct.[11]

In 1747 Smart had been arrested for non-payment of debts to his tailor. Now the sporadic nature of his income from his writing, combined with his convivial nature and his new responsibilities of a wife and family, were inevitably putting greater pressure upon him, and probably contributed to his increasingly eccentric behaviour.

One manifestation of Smart's eccentric behaviour is attested by Dr Samuel Johnson. James Boswell records this episode which takes place on Boswell's very first visit to Johnson, on 24 May 1763, when in the midst of a discourse on 'madness', Johnson refers to Smart:

> Madness frequently discovers itself merely by unnecessary deviation from the usual modes of the world. My poor friend Smart showed the disturbance of his mind, by falling upon his knees, and saying his prayers in the street, or in any other unusual place. Now although, rationally speaking, it is greater madness not to pray at all, than to pray as Smart did, I am afraid there are so many who do not pray, that their understanding is not called in question.[12]

Boswell, in a paragraph immediately following this quote from Dr Johnson, further records:

> Concerning this unfortunate poet, Christopher Smart, who was confined in a mad-house, he [Johnson] had, at another time, the following conversation with Dr. Burney.
> BURNEY. "How does poor Smart do, Sir; is he likely to recover?"
> JOHNSON. "It seems as if his mind had ceased to struggle with the disease; for he grows fat upon it."
> BURNEY. "Perhaps, Sir, that may be from want of exercise."
> JOHNSON. "No, Sir; he has partly as much exercise as he used to have, for he digs in the garden. Indeed, before his confinement, he used for exercise to walk to the alehouse; but he was carried back again. I did not think he ought to be shut up. His infirmities were not noxious to society. He insisted on people praying with him; and I'd as lief pray with Kit Smart as any one else. Another charge was, that he did not love clean linen; and I have no passion for it."

The first anecdote of Johnson's recorded by Boswell regarding Christopher Smart is unequivocally dated as having been given on 24 May 1763, the very year that Smart emerged again into society after a period of seven years hidden away in a 'mad-house'. It is also the year in which 'A Song to David', perhaps his best-known work, and two other small volumes of his poetry were published. Dr Johnson's kindly and balanced assessment of his 'poor friend' seems to be saying that there had been no need for Smart to have been confined for his 'madness', indeed in the second anecdote Johnson implies that if Smart was mad, then Johnson was as mad as he was, for they both had the same symptoms: they both prayed and neither saw the great importance of clean linen. But perhaps that is to unfairly reduce the real distress of mind and no doubt the other indications and symptoms of mental disturbance that caused Smart's mental breakdown to precipitate him into confinement in a madhouse in 1756.

The public manifestations of Smart's illness only offer slight clues as to its true nature. Certainly the desire to kneel before God in public places displays an exuberance that might make others uncomfortable, but it also perhaps indicates a sense of someone who deems himself not worthy to remain upright in the presence of God. Such abject behaviour is perhaps understandable in relation to God, but less understandable when the same posture is adapted before people. The poetry of Smart shows this over-willingness to prostrate himself before those whom he deems are of a higher rank in society than himself. Moira Dearnley comments, 'One of the main driving forces in Smart's personality as a poet was his need to metaphorically kneel before the people he admired, to thank them for being such dazzling mortals, so sublime, so transcendent and so condescending as to notice his poetry, "this rough unbidden verse"'.[13]

Although the reference to his poetry can be paralleled by Burns's apologetic words in his verse epistle 'To the Rev. John McMath', when addressing 'Religion':

Pardon a muse sea mean as mine,
Who in her rough imperfect line
Thus daurs to name thee,[14]

the poets are still at opposite ends of the scale in terms of their self confidence.

There might have been a hint of paranoia in Smart's reaction to his critics following the publication of his poems in 1752, but the first sign of serious illness occurs in 1756, when Smart writes to his physician, Dr Robert James, 'this is the third time that your judgement and medicines rescued me from the grave; permit me to say in a manner most miraculous'. In gratitude, when Smart publishes his poem 'A Hymn to the Supreme Being' he prefaces it with these words acknowledging Dr James's part in his recovery but claiming that he was the instrument of a Divine Providence:

> Having made a humble offering to Him, without whose blessing your skill, admirable as it is, would have been to no purpose, I think myself bound by all the ties of gratitude to render next acknowledgements to you, who under God, restored me to health from as violent and dangerous a disorder, as perhaps man ever survived.[15]

In 'A Hymn to the Supreme Being' Smart uses the analogy of the healing of King Hezekiah's illness related in the book of the prophet Isaiah.[16] But Hezekiah could claim a blameless life, Smart says, therefore God healed him, whereas he – Smart – could make no such claim. By this reasoning he makes himself out to be more of a sinner, thereby asserting that his healing is even more miraculous than that of Hezekiah. Smart describes his mental state at the onset of his illness:

But, O immortals! what had I to plead
When Death stood o'er me with threat'ning lance
When reason left me in the time of need
And sense was lost in terrour or in trance.
My sinking soul was with my blood inflam'd
And the celestial image sunk, defac'd and maim'd.[17]

In the next verse, God is described as eternal, immense, omniscient, good, illimitably powerful and intensely loving, but, and it is a hugely significant but, that in Smart's understanding qualifies all that has already been said of God:

But yet whose justice ne'er could be withstood
Except thro' him – thro' him, who stands alone
Of worth, of weight allow'd for all mankind to atone.

The poet sees Jesus Christ as the one who by standing on one side of the scales can counterbalance the weight of the sins of the world and thus make atonement. The poet is restating the substitutionary theory of the atonement, the idea that by the death of the sinless Jesus Christ, the Son of God, the justice of God – which required the death of men for their sins – was satisfied, having been fulfilled by Christ standing in their place. This theory, which had been adopted as a doctrine, was much used in the preaching and writings of the evangelical elements of the Churches both in England and Scotland. Burns's friend, the Reverend Dr William McGill, was attacked by the Reverend John Russel for appearing not to give due weight to the theory in his book *A Practical Essay on the Death of Christ* (1786).[18]

The next verse describes Smart's conversion experience, which apparently happens when he is clearly suffering physical and mental distress and is in a debilitated condition:

My feeble feet refus'd my body's weight.
Nor would my eyes admit the glorious light
My nerves convuls'd shook fearful of their fate
My mind lay open to the powers of night
He pitying did a second birth bestow
A birth of joy – not like the first of tears and woe.

And so the poet, by the intervention of God in Jesus Christ, has been rescued not just from a present death threat but from an eternal death, and pledges himself to live by God's laws and endlessly to uphold God's glory:

Ye strengthen'd feet forth to his altars move
Glow, glow my soul, with pure seraphic fire
Ye heav'n directed eyes, o'erflow with love
Deeds, thoughts and words no more his mandate break
But to his endless, glory work, conceive and speak.

In response to what he sees as a quite miraculous second birth and a strengthening of his physical and mental state, the poet seems to tell himself that he must from this time on worship this God who has brought him to life again, that he must live his life with glowing zeal and turn his eyes always towards him, giving him utter obedience and forever offering his work and thoughts and words to his glory. Smart even hopes for greater things to come through his penitence, as he concludes:

O! penitence, to virtue near allied
Thou can'st new joys e'en to the blest impart
The list'ning angels lay their harps aside
To hear the music of the contrite heart
And Heav'n itself rears a more radiant face
When charity presents thee to the throne of grace.

Although it is intended to express the contrition of the poet, this last verse has a strange element of pride showing through it. It is as if the poet is so pleased with his own new-found state of grace that he has begun to see some merit in his penitence, rating it as almost a virtue in itself. There is also a pride in the picture of the angels ceasing their praise of God in order to listen to the music of the poet's contrite heart. The last two lines of the poem even seem to indicate that God is pleased with the poet for turning to him, implying that the poet has by his penitence done something to alter God's attitude to him. This attempt to express his gratitude to the God who has saved him becomes in the end a means of self-congratulation.

But the newly found security in the arms of his Saviour and accepting God did not last. Within the same year Smart suffered a severe relapse and was confined to a madhouse. Smart had short-term recoveries during the next seven years, but he did not fully return to society until 1763.

When Smart emerged from what was latterly a self-imposed isolation the poetry was different. Later as we examine two of his major works of that period, 'A Song to David' and 'Jubilate Agno', it might be possible to note an altered demeanour and a significant change to his previous religious stances. In his remaining years Smart produced: a *Translation of the Psalms of David* and wrote the words for the Oratorios, *Hannah* and *Abimilech* (1764); *The Hymns and Spiritual Songs for the Fasts and Festivals of the Church of England* (1765), which was bound up with his *Translations of the Psalms* and the second edition of 'A Song to David'; and two works for children, *The Parables of Our Lord and Saviour* (1768) and *Hymns for the Amusement of Children* (1770).[19]

Smart's wife, taking her two daughters with her, had left him shortly before his period of confinement and never returned to him. His inability to cope with the economics of living had not improved, and seven years after he had made his return to something resembling normality he again fell into debt, and died in the King's Bench Debtor's Prison in May 1771.

In the Seatonian Poems Smart submitted over the years from 1750 to 1755 there is expressed a fairly orthodox Christian faith.[20] It is communicated in terms that are obviously reflecting the scientific findings of Isaac Newton and the *Astro-* and *Physico-Theology* of William Derham.[21] Yet there are also indications within Smart's work of his attempts to break out from the restraints of Christian orthodoxy and to go further than the views of Derham. Within Smart's poems of this time there is evidence of his uneasy relationship with the God in whom he professes to believe and signs too of his own inner insecurity. The tensions in which he was living, and that eventually led to his mental breakdown in 1756, are beginning to show.

In the first of his prize-winning Seatonian Poems, 'On the Eternity of the Supreme Being', Smart reflects the contemporary orthodox Christian theology of the mid-eighteenth century Church. God is the creator of the universe in the biblical understanding of the phrase, and is described in similar terms to those used by Derham in his *Astro-Theology: or a Demonstration of the Being and Attributes of God from a Survey of the Heavens*: 'It appears that a wise and careful architect was the contriver and order of it all.' Smart writes:

> Before this earthly planet wound her course
> Round Light's perennial fountain, before Light
> Herself 'gan to shine, and at th' inspiring word
> Shot to existence in blaze of day
> Before "the morning stars together sang"
> And hail'd thee Architect of countless worlds
> Thou art – all glorious, all beneficent
> All wisdom and omnipotence thou art.[22]

Smart's 'morning stars' reference is his tribute to one of his poetic heroes, Milton, and here he is in accord with many of his fellow poets of the eighteenth century, but he is breaking from orthodoxy in his assertion that God is the 'Architect of countless worlds'. After making a very bold statement of the immediacy and timeless nature of God, with his repeated 'Thou art', he goes on to use the traditional language for his attributes. But at the very end, Smart adds two lines that show him again breaking with tradition as he poses the question, 'But is the era of creation fix'd / As when these worlds began?' In many of the Bibles of Smart's time, and indeed to this day in some of the editions of the King James Bible, there is an editorial dating offered as a guide as to when certain events took place. It became traditional to give the year of the Creation as 4004 BC.[23] Smart questions this with the two lines quoted above. He is even then beginning to question the orthodox views of the Church. In this same poem Smart projects his poetic imagination as to what will happen at the end of the world, and within the verse gives an indication of his own insecurity, as he calls upon the dead:

> "Ye sons of Adam and ye heirs of Heav'n
> Arise ye tenants of the grave
> Awake incorruptable and arise."
> 'Tis then, nor sooner, that the restless mind
> Shall find itself at home; and like the ark
> Fix'd on the mountain-top shall look aloft
> O'er the vague passage of precarious life
> And winds, and waves and rocks and tempests past
> Enjoy the everlasting calm of Heav'n.[24]

For Smart there is to be no peace of mind in this life; only after death will that become a possibility for him. The poem goes on to say that we should praise God, although all our praise, no matter how earnestly it is offered, is in a sense in vain: 'Yet all were vain to speak to him as he is, who is INEFFABLE'. The poet conveys a sense of both the necessity yet the futility of praising this God who is ineffable (writing the word in capitals seems to further distance God), the one who is unutterable, too great for description in words. Yet the poet still wants us to look towards this God: 'Yet still let reason thro' the eye of faith / View him with fearful love'. It is as though the poet wants a relationship with God, but is denied that relationship by the very nature of the unapproachability of God. He can only stand before him 'with fearful love'. In twice using 'Thou art' in a sentence talking about the distant past, Smart is emphazising the immediacy of God. He does this in another way in his 1753 Seatonian Poem on 'The Power of the Supreme Being'. God's power is demonstrated directly by Smart's allusion to an earthquake (probably two slight tremors that had shaken London):

Twice we have felt
Within Augusta's walls, twice we have felt
Thy threaten'd indignation.[25]

Whereas in Derham, earthquakes occur because God loosens his hold on nature's laws and lets them happen, in Smart, God is even more proactive and immediate. He is in the power of the earthquake and through it he is expressing his wrath. For Smart, God is more immediately involved in his creation. Moira Dearnley writes, 'Derham allows that God controls physical law. Smart implies that God is physical law, a more immediate version of God.'[26] Whereas Derham can say that gravity illustrates the wisdom and care of God, Smart would claim that God is that physical law.

After referring to the London earth tremors, the poem continues:

For at thy righteous power whole systems shake
For at thy nod tremble 10,000 worlds
Wherefore ye objects terrible and great
Ye thunders, earthquakes, and ye fire-fraught wombs
Of fell volcanoes, whirlwinds, hurricanes
And boiling billows hail! in chorus join
To celebrate and magnify your maker.

These phenomena are not things that have gone wrong and out of control when God has let go his hold upon them; rather, Smart's God has made them. They are the deliberately constructed instruments of his power. But yet there is an even greater sign of the power of God in Smart's vision, and that is the demonstration of the power of God by his act of redemption in the life and death of Jesus Christ. Smart writes:

But O Supreme, unutterable mercy!

Love unequall'd mystery immense,
Which angels long t'unfold! tis man's redemption
That crowns thy glory, and thy pow'r confirms.[27]

Smart's theology is in accord with the orthodoxy of the time, but occasionally he betrays a tendency to want to break away from its confines. Sometimes his own lack of conviction as to its being a sufficiently strong enough vehicle upon which to embark towards his own salvation is held up to question, as in the Seatonian Poem of 1752, which exhorts people to live in gratitude to God even if the door to Paradise is closed to them because of Adam's sin:

Yet murmur not, but praise – for tho' we stand
Of many a Godlike privilege amerce'd
By Adam's dire transgression, tho' no more
Is Paradise our home, but o'er the portal
Hangs in terrific pomp the burning blade
Still with 10,000 beauties blooms the earth.[28]

It is difficult to believe that Smart thought that the beauty of the earth was a sufficient compensation for a Paradise denied. There is a mixed signal emanating from these lines. The God who has made this beautiful world is still the God who has placed a flaming, threatening barrier between his people and the Paradise he had once made for them. However fervently Smart proclaims these orthodox views, lurking in the background is a sense of a man not entirely at ease with his God. Although Smart's faith is proclaimed in traditional terms, using all the corroboration of the scientific findings of Isaac Newton and all the back-up of Derham's *Astro-* and *Physico-Theology*, it is still insecure. Within the expression of this faith there is a sense of it not being enough to satisfy an intellect that was growing, moving on and wanting to explore an even greater world. It is with these conceptions of God, held to amidst persistent doubts and fears, that Smart moves towards the mental breakdown of the years 1756–63.

In his selection of the Old Testament King David as a subject through which to engage in the poetic celebration of God in 'A Song to David', published a few months after his release in 1763, Smart is perhaps telling us something about the development of his religious thought in those years of his retirement from public view. Smart had had a conversion experience, according to his poetic account of it in 'A Hymn to the Supreme Being', but it had not saved him from a further nervous breakdown.[29] His seeming adoption of a personal faith in Jesus Christ as his Saviour, the one who had died for him and paid the penalty for the consequence of his sin, had not brought about his freedom from his inner self and his inner angst. As the time passed he may have come nearer to an acceptance of the divers parts of himself. He had, as we have seen, an awareness of his own physical defects, a hyper-sensitivity to criticism, an inability to cope with the social pressures of company and possibly a tendency to over-indulge a drinking habit. Perhaps he also thought himself lacking in the qualities that are required of a husband and father and later suffered feelings of guilt for the failure of his marriage. Then too is the personality that knew the wild swings from depression to manic activity, and the tension of a nature driven to perform as 'Mrs. Mary Midnight, The Male Midwife' at the same time as producing Miltonesque verses of religious poetry for the Seatonian Prize. If all these aspects of his life and personality had not been reconciled by his conversion experience, perhaps he saw a way forward in simply accepting himself, and in the story of David he might have found just the right kind of encouragement towards doing that, and thereby found the means of his own salvation. For although chosen by God, David had many flaws in his character, a man of violence who was celebrated as a killer of the enemies of his people. But David had an even nastier streak, contriving the death of the husband of the woman he wanted to have to himself. Yet according to the Old Testament story, ambitious, lustful, violent, even murderous as he was, David was used by God to lead his people and to create the economic atmosphere in which it would become possible for Solomon his son to build a Temple fit for worship.[30] If David could be accepted by God so could Christopher Smart. But his acceptance was not because of the theory of the substitutionary death of Jesus Christ making atonement, it was because God was far greater than men imagined him to be. In recognition of this, praise was the only response – God was there to be celebrated.

Significantly, David was a poet, but not only that a religious poet, the author (as was then thought) of a huge body of songs to God, the 150 'Psalms of David' that were part of the biblical canon. David, through his psalms, was the celebrant supreme of God, and this was what Smart was most aware of and sought to emulate and to celebrate. Michael Schmidt asserts of Smart, 'His poems exist to celebrate God, not to cajole or persuade us.'[31] I would agree with this assessment particularly in relation to the two poems 'A Song to David' and 'Jubilate Agno'. If these are thought of in terms of their being a celebration of God – rather than attempts at persuading us to believe, or explaining theology, or informing us of the nature of God – then their eccentricities, if not always understood, are not to be put down to madness but rather to the vivacity of an imagination filled with the desire to celebrate the God who accepts all of creation because he is its author and sustainer.

Smart's fixing on David as the focus of his attention and perhaps as the bridge to his own salvation might have been encouraged by a revived interest in David's life that started around the time of Smart's birth and continued right up to his death. Moira Dearnley gives an account of the books and sermons written in these years that took David as their subject, which I will briefly summarise. In 1710, Pierre Bayle's *Dictionary* held up David as a 'fine model for the edification of faithful souls' and in 1740 Patrick Delaney published *A Historical Account of the Life and Reign of David*, which was a book known to Smart. In 1760 Samuel Chandler's sermon on the death of King George II made a comparison of the deceased monarch with David in eulogistic and enthusiastic terms, in which the list of George II's good points very closely resemble Smart's later catalogue of David's cardinal virtues. Other voices, such as John Noorthouk (1761), pointed out David's faults including his delight in bloodshed, but the earlier view prevailed and David was commonly held up as a proto-saint. As Dearnley remarks, 'It is no coincidence that Smart wrote "A Song to David" in the midst of this controversy.'[32]

Moving towards a critique of 'A Song to David', Smart's admiration for Alexander Pope as his model for the critic should be kept in mind. Pope, referring to a poet's right to exercise his own licence over the rules, writes:

> Thus Pegasus, a nearer way to take,
> May boldly deviate from the common track;
> From vulgar bounds may brave disorder part
> And snatch a grace beyond the reach of art,
> Which without passing thro' the judgment, gains
> The heart, and all its end at once attains.[33]

As Moira Dearnley opines, 'If we are to appreciate "A Song to David", we should be willing to respond with the heart, rather than the head.'[34]

The poem opens with three verses asserting the worthiness of David to receive the poet's praise, for David is the very 'minister of Praise', the one charged by God to organize the praise of the heavenly host. The next verse lists 12 qualities of David's character, and is followed by 12 verses elaborating on each of these. According to Smart, David was: great, valiant, pious, good, clean, sublime, contemplative, serene, strong, constant, pleasant and wise. Now any rational assessment of David might at best give him three of these qualities – say, great, valiant and strong – but it would be difficult to ascribe the rest to him based on the evidence of the biblical story. It would seem that Smart is choosing to ignore the biographical details and the events in the life of David, and that he is not really praising the man of the biblical narrative, but rather the man as derived from the psalms that are attributed to his authorship. In verse XVII Smart praises David for:

> His muse, bright angel of his verse,
> Gives balm for all the thorns that pierce,
> For all the pangs that rage.[35]

Smart then goes on from verse XVIII to verse XXVI to list the subjects covered by David in the Psalms, saying that he sings: of God, angels, man, the world, trees, plants and flowers, fowl, fishes, beasts and gems. In his verse on God (XVIII), Smart calls God:

The mighty source
Of all things – the stupendous force
On which all strength depends.

God is still, as before, the source, the driving force and the resource of all our strength. Smart attributes to David the ability to keep Satan at bay with his music, but Smart's own music descends to bathos as he describes how David 'sent the godly sounds aloft, / Or in delight refrain'd.' Eight verses follow (XXX to XXXVII) that identify the seven pillars of knowledge with the seven days of creation. At the beginning of this section Smart asserts the God that who in:

His wisdom drew the plan;
His WORD accomplish'd the design,
From brightest gem to deepest mine,
From CHRIST enthron'd to man.

David and Christ are then placed side by side: David hailed as 'Scholar of the Lord' and in the next verse God sending Christ is described: 'He from himself his semblance sent'. This juxtaposing of David and Christ has the effect of enhancing David's role and elevating his significance. Next comes an exercise on the Decalogue (XL to XLIX) in which Smart frequently seems to transpose Christian teaching into an Old Testament setting. The verse that opens this section is indicative of Smart's understanding of all nature being in response to God:

Tell them I am, JEHOVA said
To MOSES; while earth heard in dread,
And smitten to the heart,
At once above, beneath, around
All nature, without voice or sound,
Replied, O Lord, THOU ART.

Here Smart is asserting that all creation is in heartfelt response to God. In another verse (XLII), there is a clean break from the orthodox view of man defaced by sin, as Smart declares:

Open, and naked of offence,
Man's made of mercy, soul, and sense;

The completion of the verse follows, with a sudden change of reference to man in relation to the animals also made by God:

God arm'd the snail and wilk;
Be good to him that pulls thy plough;
Due food and care, due rest, allow
For her that yields thee milk.

So as God offers the snail and the wilk his protection in his very provision of their shells, he expects men to care for the horse that pulls the plough and the cows that provide the milk. Here are the practical implications of the Commandments. Then follows a further indication of Smart beginning to think in a new way about himself:

Use all thy passions! – love is thine,
And joy, and jealousy divine;
Thine hope's eternal fort.

In this verse Smart is acknowledging the fullness of his humanity, the variety and range of the modes of being, and urges that people should use all their passions, acknowledge that they are part of their nature, that they have the capacity to love, to know joy and a God given zeal for life and that in this realization of their true humanity, they will find the strengthening of their hope. A touch of existentialism comes in at verse XLV, as Smart counsels, 'Act simply, as occasion asks'. He is no longer governed by the fixed rules of life, either laid down by himself or set for him by others. He is free to improvise according to the occasion. It is noticeable that in this section, which purports to be about the Ten Commandments, Smart keeps introducing New Testament or Christian views. A new optimism is also evident as the reader is urged: 'By hope futurity pursue; / Look upwards to the past.' Gone is gloomy retrospective, a new age has begun in which the way to go is to look forward with hope. David is then praised as 'the highest in the list / Of worthies', and Praise itself is put forward as the best mode of existence. At this point a change is noted in the way that Smart is thinking about God. He is no longer the judge or the accuser, but 'the Lord [who] is great and glad'. Then follow 21 verses, 14 on the seasons and seven on the senses, in which the word 'ADORATION' (in capitals) is used in each verse. In verse LXIV, the last in the seasons section, Smart returns to the theme of the Psalms:

For ADORATION, DAVID'S psalms
Lift up the heart to deeds of alms;
And he who kneels and chants,
Prevails his passions to controul,

Finds meat and med'cine to the soul,
Which for translation pants.

In this verse there is almost a reversion to his former ways of thinking. We can almost see Smart justifying his earlier habit of dropping to his knees wherever he was to pray, in order that he might control his passions. In this section on 'ADORATION', the whole of creation – from the bullfinch and the robin to the constellations of stars and the winds and the waves, the perfumes of Arabia to the breath of the saints – all join in adoration of the Creator. The sensuous language is in contrast to the verses that conclude the section which seem to have a more functional flavour, but on further examination it is seen that all are different forms of the same adoration of God:

For ADORATION, all the paths
Of grace are open, all the baths of purity refresh;
And all the rays of glory beam
To deck the man of God's esteem,
Who triumphs o'er the flesh.

The poet is asserting that the way of adoration opens up the way to God, but there still seems to be a precondition to gaining the presence of God and that is winning the battle against the pull of the senses. Yet in the very next verse (LXXI), Smart seems to relax this condition, or provide a loophole for himself, by implying that all will find refuge within the Church:

For ADORATION, in the dome
Of Christ the sparrow's [*sic*] find an home;
And on his olives perch:
The swallow also dwells with thee,
O man of God's humility,
Within his Saviour's CHURCH.

In this verse Smart seems to be proclaiming a universal salvation. Righteousness through a conquering of the implied sinfulness of the flesh of the previous verse is no longer required, humility will suffice for admission to the protective dome of Christ's Church. Within the Church there is a place for all creation. This seems to be a departure from the theology that requires an individual response to Jesus Christ as Saviour. The place within the acceptance of God is won not by the acceptance of a standard form of words that make a confession of faith, but rather by the adoption of an attitude of humility and adoration.

The last 15 verses (LXXII to LXXXVI) are divided into five sections. In each section an adjective or its comparative, viz. Sweet, Strong, Beauteous, Precious, Glorious, are used three or four times in each verse. Each three-verse section builds up to a climax in its third verse which focuses on the human aspect of the subject. For example, in verses LXXV and LXXVI, after praising the strength of the horse, the glede (possibly a hunting dog), the ostrich, the swordfish, the lion, the eagle and the whale, Smart makes the comparison with the man of prayer whose strength, he claims, is even greater than these:

> But stronger still, in earth and air,
> And in the sea, the man of pray'r;
> And far beneath the tide;
> And in the seat to faith assign'd,
> Where ask is have, where seek is find,
> Where knock is open wide.

In this verse the poet is indicating that in the attitude of faith, there is the realization of what is being sought: asking is having, seeking is finding and in the act of attracting attention the door opens wide.

David again comes into prominence in verse LXXX, that is the climax of the verses on the theme of what is 'beauteous'. Having extolled the beauty of a fleet in full sail, an army, a garden, the moon, a virgin unveiled and a temple full of worshippers, Smart describes David as, 'Beauteous, yea beauteous more than these, / The shepherd king upon his knees'. When the detail of the things and the people that are being compared with David are examined, the extravagance of Smart's praise for the 'shepherd king' is seen to be extreme – the vigour and speed of the ships, the magnitude and extravagant decoration of the army, the variety and colour of the garden, the sensuous revelation of the virgin, the ornament of the temple and the sincerity of the worshipping people are all of less beauty and importance than David. This verse is a further indication of just how important David is to Smart, who believes him to be the one who is 'the man after God's own heart' despite all his sin, and therefore the one who gives the poet hope of his own acceptance. Like David, Smart prays upon his knees and is 'prostrate dust to dust', humble before God. Just as Smart never once mentions any of the acts of David that show him capable of wrongdoing, or what by Smart's own standards he would term wickedness or even sinfulness, neither does he give us any indication of his own activity which he in the past he has thought needed the forgiveness of God through the death of Christ. He now seems to have come round to an acceptance of himself as someone who will be as acceptable to God, as his hero David seems to be. Whereas before he could not bring himself to acknowledge his acceptance without the protection of the payment made to God by the sacrificial death of Christ, his Saviour, now it is enough for God to see the 'penitential tear' and to hear the 'sigh sincere' (LXXXII) for him to be acceptable to God. As Smart continues this section with another reference to David, he seems to have come to an understanding of a God who despite the failures of humans sees through to the intentions of the heart and accepts them as if they were actions:

More precious that diviner part
Of David, ev'n the Lord's own heart,
Great, beautiful, and new;
In all things where it was intent,
In all extreams, in each event,
Proof – answ'ring true to true. (LXXXIII)

Smart seems to see David as an example of the person who, despite all his obvious failures, nevertheless has been trying to acknowledge God; it has been the intent of his heart to do this, and God who recognizes this accepts such a man.

Smart comes to the conclusion of this 86-verse poem with three verses in which he includes the word 'glorious' 14 times. In the middle of this paean of praise comes the line, 'Glorious the song, when God's the theme'. This line says so much about Smart's now more joyous and confident attitude. In the last verse he focuses entirely on Jesus Christ as the one who has 'brought salvation down' and dramatically praises the accomplishment of Christ:

Glorious – more glorious is the crown
Of Him that brought salvation down
By meekness call'd thy Son;
Thou at stupendous truth believ'd,
And now the matchless deed's atchieved, [*sic*]
DETERMINED, DARED, and DONE.[36]

Yet there is perhaps a deliberate ambiguity built into the line 'By meekness call'd thy Son'. It can be read as referring to Jesus as being descended from David. The following line might also be an oblique reference to David's belief, thereby implying that David was a type of Christ achieving an earlier form of salvation. Whether or not the ambiguity is intended it makes the reader aware of the connection between David and Christ, and in this is a compliment to David.

The language of 'A Song to David' is at a quite different level from that of the Seatonian Poems. It is exultant and above all celebratory. Within it is discovered a personal experience, as against the earlier poems' listing of the tenets of faith. There is a new life breathing through it, compared with the stilted formality of the previous religious poems. Smart appears to be alive in a different way, more his own man than before. He is the one of whom it might also have been said that he had 'DETERMINED, DARED, and DONE'. He had determined what he really believed, he had dared to declare it and he had resolved something of the conflict that had been within him and had done with it.

The poem that I now propose to examine in some detail is 'Jubilate Agno', which was composed between 1759 and 1763 while Smart was confined following his nervous breakdown. The poem was omitted from his *Collected Poems* of 1791 and later collections, because it was deemed to have been composed in and reflected Smart's madness. It was not published until 1939, when W.F. Stead brought its remaining fragments to the public attention.[37] I hope to show that during the time of the writing of this poem, Smart was undergoing a change in his thinking about religion and how it might be expressed. In a sense, 'Jubilate Agno' had to be written almost as a purgative, a clearing of the mind, before the writing of 'A Song to David' could begin. In my writing about Smart so far, I have been very conscious of the powerful effect of his story and of how it can become almost more important than his writing. Michael Schmidt's comments warn of this:

> Biography obscures his [Smart's] achievement because it seems to apologise for it. He is regarded for his madness (so much more colourful than Cowper's or Collins') at the expense of his poems ... . We readily assume that he wrote in madness, that what he wrote, in its forms and themes, partakes of his derangement. Or we divide his work into 'sane' and 'insane' and judge the parts by distinct criteria. But his madness can be seen not so much as disorder as *alternative* order, his religious vision is not as eccentric but as direct, comprehensive.[38]

Schmidt has, I think, accurately assessed those who first judged Smart's work, especially 'Jubilate Agno'. I shall be looking at that poem not only in the light of his suggestion of an alternative order being put forward, but also as an assertion of an alternative religious view.

Smart was familiar with the work of Bishop Robert Lowth, who had produced a seminal book on the nature of the sacred poetry of the Hebrews, *De Sacra Poesi Hebrarorum*, which was published in 1753.[39] Lowth had illustrated that a distinctive feature of Hebrew poetry is that much of it is antiphonal or responsive in character. It is designed to be spoken or chanted by two groups. One choir might sing a single verse to the other, which would respond with a corresponding verse. Smart makes use of this idea in the structure of 'Jubilate Agno'. This idea was also in accord with one of Smart's known ambitions to reform the Anglican liturgy. A sign of Smart's interest in the reform of the Church of England's liturgy was his later production of a metrical version of the Psalms, with a view to their being used in church services. W.H. Bond, who re-edited the original manuscript of 'Jubilate Agno', claims that 'The poem was intended as a responsive reading', and adds, 'that is why the *Let* and *For* sections are physically distinct while corresponding verse for verse.'[40] In Bond's edition of the fragments of 'Jubilate Agno', the *Let* and *For* lines are printed on facing pages of the book. It is significant that when Smart published his metrical version of the Psalms in 1765, *A Translation of the Psalms of David, Attempted in the Spirit of Christianity, and Adapted to the Divine Service*, he reprinted in the book 'A Song to David', perhaps hoping that it might also be used liturgically. It is therefore not unreasonable to suggest that when Smart began the composition of 'Jubilate Agno', which was constructed immediately preceding 'A Song to David', in its initial stage it had also been intended as a liturgical piece. When the *Let* verses are examined, they are found to be of a more general nature than the *For* verses, which are in many cases clearly the personal response of, and intended to be spoken by, Smart himself as the reader or responder.

From Bond's examination of the remaining fragments of the manuscript, some of which are dated, it would seem that the poem was composed over the four-year period from August 1759 to January 1763. The sections of the manuscript have been labelled alphabetically and chronologically from A to D. The earliest fragments sustain the original design, but there is a departure from it in fragment C, when the precision and accuracy of the biblical references deteriorate and the personal references intrude more frequently than before. When fragment D is examined, it would appear that the original structure has been abandoned, and in great contrast to what has gone before there are signs of a more haphazard construction. Whether this was brought on by boredom or a further, if temporary, worsening of Smart's mental condition is not known. Bond has checked out many of Smart's seemingly oscure references and asserts that, 'research has provided authorities for many of the wildest of Smart's flights, with the result that the burden of proof now rests with those who would claim that a given passage represents pure fancy or the ravings of a madman.'[41] I have checked a large number of the biblical references in the *Let* sections and have found them to be accurate and pertinent in terms of the association of ideas that Smart was employing. I also discovered that the corresponding *For* line always had within it an appropriate and relevant reflection upon the figure featured in the *Let* line. Bond concludes:

> But this strange poem, compounded of wisdom and madness and innocence, arid wastes and flashes of startling beauty, is not an object to be studied in isolation. It provides the entree into the amazing, crowded lumber-room of Christopher Smart's mind at the moment when that mind was in crisis.

My one qualification of that would be in relation to his use of the word 'madness'. I think that I would be more comfortable with any term that might denote a temporary disturbance of the mind such as can be experienced by a highly sensitive human being. But Bond's description of the poem is helpful as we go on to explore that 'lumber-room' of Christopher Smart's mind that had within it many thoughts on religion that required to be sorted out.

In fragment A of 'Jubilate Agno' only the *Let* passages remain. It must be assumed that the opening pages of the *For* section have been lost. Its opening verse, after an initial salutation, begins a genealogy of praise:

> Rejoice in God, O ye Tongues; give the glory to the Lord, and to the Lamb.
> Nations, and languages, and every Creature, in which is the breath of Life.
> Let man and beast appear before him, and magnify his name together.
> Let Noah and his company approach the throne of Grace,
> and do homage to the Ark of their Salvation.[42]

In this opening verse there is evidence of Smart's conviction that his way forward to freedom from all that holds him imprisoned in mind and in body is to live in an attitude of gratitude and praise towards God. The praise is for God and for Jesus Christ who is typified as the Lamb. It is a praise in which he invites all to join; not just human beings, but every creature in which is the breath of life. He then goes on to list, in chronological order, the biblical characters who should praise, often linking them significantly and accurately with some incident or aspect of their lives. Occasionally, something of his own nature shapes the words to reveal what he holds to be valuable: 'Let Ahitub humble himself with an Ape before Almighty God, who is the maker of variety and pleasantry.' (A23)[43]

Ahitub was the father of Zadoc the High Priest in the time of David. Smart is here hinting at the pride of a father needing to be curbed by his associating with one of the lower species in his approach to God. Humility is asked of the proud. Also in this single line, something of Smart's sociable disposition shines through as he praises God as the maker of variety and pleasantry. Smart enjoyed conversation and mixing with people in congenial surroundings; incidentally, the gentleness of these comments is hardly commensurate with the ravings of a madman. A few lines later, Smart again reveals what he values as an offering to God: 'Let Moses, the Man of God, bless with a Lizard, in the sweet majesty of good-nature, and the magnanimity of meekness.' (A25)[44]

The only reference to the lizard in the Bible is in Leviticus 11:30, the book that contains the extension of the laws of Moses. In the King James Bible it is subtitled 'The Third Book of Moses'. The lizard is listed along with the ferret, the chameleon, the snail and the mole as 'unclean to you'. So Moses, the Man of God and the great leader of God's people, is invited to go to praise God in company with an unclean lizard and to display the valuable qualities of magnanimity and meekness.

It is often only when a concordance is checked that the full significance of a verse is discovered. While this might not be great poetry, it is not a sign of madness. When Smart writes 'Let Chalcol praise with the Beetle, whose life is precious in the sight of God, tho' his appearance is against him' (A38)[45] he is referring to 1 Kings 4:31, where Chalcol is on a list of wise men to whom

Solomon is being compared and to whom he was deemed to be superior in wisdom. The wise Chalcol is invited to share the company of the Beetle, whose appearance is off-putting but who nevertheless is precious to God. Smart is perhaps making a personal reference to his own appearance, both physical and mental, and signalling to those who judge him that they might be letting appearances deceive them. He is perhaps wiser than people think he is. Many more examples of Smart's apparently wild or seeming incongruous statements within the poem, when further examined, turn out to be perfectly sane and often wise observations.

Another thing that emerges is Smart's fascination for the period of Old Testament history that relates to the story of David and Solomon, for example Zadoc and Chalcol are both of that period. David himself features in the longest verse in this section, as if Smart was just itching to get to the bit of the poem in which he could introduce his great hero: 'Let David bless with the Bear – The beginning of the victory to the Lord – to the Lord the perfection of excellence – Hallelujah from the heart of God, and from the hand of the artist inimitable, and from the echo of the heavenly harp in sweetness magnifical and mighty, ...'. (A41)[46] This verse clearly indicates where Smart's muse is going to take him, as it later did, into the composition of 'A Song to David', and later still to produce his own version of the Psalms in metrical form. He sees David as the one who should praise the Lord for the beginning of the Lord's victory. It is not clear whether the 'Lord' is Jesus Christ or God himself. It can also be interpreted that it is through David as a proto-Christ that the beginnings of the Lord's victory have become apparent. God is said to offer a Hallelujah from his own heart, which joins with the efforts of David's hand and is echoed by David's harp. David, in Smart's mind, offers a way to victory through the kind of person he was and seeing that kind of person as having been acceptable to God.

Jesus Christ makes his official entrance into the poem a few verses later: 'Let Esdras bless Jesus Christ with the Rose and his people which is a nation of living sweetness.' (A 47)[47] Esdras, a book within the *Apocrypha*, deals with the exile and return of the Israelites from their Babylonian captivity.[48] Under the leadership of Zerubbabel, who was significantly of the House of David, and later, under Ezra, the people were led back to begin the task of rebuilding Jerusalem and most importantly to the rebuilding of the Temple. Esdras is to 'bless Jesus with the Rose', the symbol of the new life that shall bloom in 'the wilderness and the solitary place' (Isaiah 35:1). The Rose is also the name taken from 'The Song of Solomon' that was often given to Jesus in Christian devotion. Esdras and Jesus are joined in praise and have been followed by a nation of living sweetness. Here the Church is seen as a people from whose living emanates sweetness, a pleasing taste and in which pleasure is to be found. Here is a new vision of the nature of the Church as a living embodiment of the flavour of Jesus Christ. Smart was to later develop the theme of sweetness in verses LXXII to LXXIV of 'A Song to David'. Over and over again in this early part of 'Jubilate Agno' one discovers the well thought out and well researched significances of the images used by Smart, confirmation, if it was needed, that his mind was functioning lucidly.

Fragment B1 is the first part of the poem that fully reveals its structure and design. On the left hand page is the *Let* sentences and on the right the *For* sentences, or responses. The *Let* side lists names of people linked with names of birds and selects a characteristic of the latter, which then provides a metaphor for the *For* side's response, for example:

> Let Elizur rejoice with the Partridge, who is a prisoner of state and is proud of his keepers.
> For I am not without authority in my jeopardy, which I derive inevitably from the glory of the name of the Lord. (B1.3)[49]

Elizur, whose name means 'God is a rock', was a captain of the children of Reuben who assisted Moses in the taking of the census of the people. It is also noted that he made a very substantial peace offering of silver, incense and livestock (Numbers 7:30–35). But here he approaches the altar with only a small partridge. Enigmatically Smart adds, 'who is a prisoner of state', which might be an oblique reference to Smart's fable, 'The English Bulldog, the Dutch Mastiff and the Quail' (says Stead's annotation). This line is picked up on the opposite page where the response reveals Smart, remembering Elizur's authority, claiming that he too is 'not without authority', even in his present circumstances of confinement. But he claims that his authority comes from the fact that he benefits from the radiance shed into his life by God, the God who can give authority even to prisoners. Smart is asserting that even in his present state, his life is authentic and is sustained by God. When the rest of the responses of B1 are examined, many of them reflect Smart's state of mind, and are often in contrast to the more liturgically framed but also more fantastical *Let* sentences, for example: 'Let Shedeur rejoice with Pyrausta, who dwelleth in a medium of fire, which God hath adapted for him.' (B1.4)

Shedeur was Elizur's father and shared his role in counting the people. Pyrausta was a winged insect said to dwell in the fire. In the *Let* side it is interesting to again note the number counting element, for no doubt there would be a daily counting of the patients in Smart's place of confinement. Also on the *Let* side, it is noted that God has made a special provision for the insect that lives within the fire. Perhaps Smart is claiming that in the midst of his trial by fire, his mental illness, God has made special provision for him. When we turn to the *For* side of this verse it is clear that the God who is providing for Smart is not the traditional God who would consign some to hell, but one who has a zeal to provide a means of escape from the flames that threaten. Smart's

God, whose name is Jealous, still has the same name as the fiery Old Testament God of vengeance, but to Smart the meaning of his name is one who has a zeal to save. Here is a different sort of God beginning to emerge: this God holds no terror for Smart. God is on his side. Other responses bear out this new found confidence in God: 'For the word of God is a sword on my side – no matter what other weapon a stick or a straw.' (B1.20)[50] This is followed in the Hebrew poetic style with another verse that is dependent upon its predecessor, 'For I have adventured myself in the name of the Lord, and he hath mark'd me for his own.' (B1.21)

Here is a sign that a new Smart is beginning to emerge, one who despite the threat of illness is beginning to have confidence in the support of God and in his own self. Other verses such as the following confirm this:

> For the nightly Visitor is at the window of the impenitent, while I sing a psalm of my own composing.
> For there is a note added to the scale, which the Lord hath made fuller, stronger & more glorious. (B1.32,33)[51]

A few verses later, a telling new understanding of himself is revealed: 'For they have separated [*sic*] me and my bosom, whereas right comes by setting us together.' (B1.59)[52]

Who are 'they'? Family, doctors, friends, outside influences, convention, religion, anything or anyone who has attempted to enforce the isolation of heart from mind, body from soul, feelings from thought, emotions from spirit? All that would cause their separation are in error, for all these things have to be within the one person if that person is to be whole. Smart seems to have come to realize that his way to healing and wholeness is to accept and allow for all these aspects of his personality to have their due place within his life, for that is what will make him whole. Near the end of this section of the poem there is what I believe to be a confirmation of Smart's new-found faith in God and confidence in himself, when he writes:

> Let Mary Magdalen rejoice with the Place, whose goodness & purity are of the Lord's making. (*Let* B1.155)
> For I pray to be accepted as a dog without offence, which is best of all. (*For* B1.155)[53]

Here is Smart, placid, unworried and expectant of the approval of God as God would approve of an inoffensive dog. No longer, at this point at least, is he a man burdened with his sin. He stands before God unafraid and hopeful.

Following this section the poem begins to deteriorate in the quality of the variety of imagery, and the structure loses its previously strictly antiphonal plan. Fragment B2 contains only *For* verses and so it cannot properly be judged, but fragment C sees a departure from the original structure and includes an exercise on the alphabet that seems devoid of any real purpose. What then follows, says Bond, 'include some of his most fantastic and least intelligible speculations', and concludes that 'by fragment D the deterioration is complete'.[54] Either Smart has grown tired of the exercise or he may have suffered a further, if temporary, mental disturbance. But the breakthrough to a new understanding, referred to in the previous paragraph, had been made. When Smart emerged from confinement in 1763, the development of his thought that can be seen in fragment B.1 was remembered, retained and helped form the basis of his later work.

Smart had not been the first to have his work mistaken for the ravings of a lunatic. In fact, Smart himself recalled what had been said about Jesus Christ and took comfort from it: 'For I am under the same accusation with my Saviour, – for they said, he is besides himself.' (B1.151)[55]

William Blake had also been accused of madness and his writings written off as betraying his delusion, and that too occurred at a time when dissatisfied with orthodox Christian belief, he had tried to find a way of expressing his own faith. In 'The Marriage of Heaven and Hell', Blake postulates a new understanding of religion. In one section of the work, 'The Voice of the Devil', he sets out his religious tenets:

> All Bibles or sacred codes have been the causes of the following errors:
> 1. That Man has two real existing principles; viz: a Body & a Soul.
> 2. That Energy, call'd Evil, is alone from the Body; & that Reason, call'd Good, is alone from the Soul.
> 3. That God will torment Man in Eternity for following his Energies.
> But the following Contraries to these are True:
> 1. Man has no Body distinct from his Soul, for that call'd Body is a portion of Soul discerned by the five Senses, the chief inlets of Soul in this age.
> 2. Energy is the only life, and is from the Body; and Reason is the bound or outward circumference of Energy.
> 3. Energy is Eternal Delight.[56]

In making this brave challenge to orthodox Christianity, Blake might well have been brought up on a charge of heresy but was more kindly treated and dismissed as 'poor mad Blake'. But he knew that he was not suffering from madness and wrote in response to such a reaction, 'there are probably men shut up as mad in Bedlam who are not so: that possibly the madmen outside have shut up the sane people'.[57] Blake had turned away even from the non-conformist congregation to which he had been attached because it was becoming more like the established Church of England as it gradually formalized its ministry and ecclesiastical organization and practice. Blake believed that the congregation to which he had belonged was departing from the original independent spirit of the church that had above its door in Great Eastcheap the words 'Now it is Allowable' and was losing its radical nature.[58] In 'The Marriage of Heaven and Hell' Blake is putting forward an alternative view of humanity and challenging the metaphysical understanding that has been perpetrated by orthodox Christianity and now even by those more deviant and independent offshoots of it. In another passage Blake asserts that John Milton's *Paradise Lost* has got it wrong and claims that in trying to work within the framework of orthodox Christian belief, Milton has created a tyrranical God and an attractive Satan. Peter Ackroyd, in his biography of Blake, writes: 'He wanted to rewrite *Paradise Lost* … . He wished to change the epic of the Fall into the prophecy of Man's faculties restored, and in so doing allow Milton to re-enter the world where he might reclaim Satan as part of his own self.'[59]

Smart, writing between Milton and Blake, was struggling towards the same kind of understanding as Blake displayed in the 'Contraries' of 'The Marriage of Heaven and Hell'.[60] He was beginning to see that it was false to separate the body from the soul, that it was wrong to think of energy as only coming from the body and reason only from the mind, and that it was wrong to condemn the energies of the passions when in fact they were a source of delight. Smart is going through the same struggle as Milton, Blake and Burns. Milton had sought to justify the unjustifiable. Blake rebelled against the framework of understanding that had been set by the Church. Burns, though not delving as deeply into the psychological and philosophical aspects of the subject, nevertheless had expressed his puzzlement as to why the light that led astray was light from heaven. Smart was feeling his way, in his period of exclusion from society, towards a new understanding of himself that would enable him to live more at ease with himself in the world. It involved him in a complete re-think and resulted in his seeing himself, all of himself, as God-made. Not just the 'good' or the 'spiritual' parts, but the parts of himself that led him astray, for they were also parts that had been made by God and therefore not to be apologized for or to be thought of as causes for his condemnation.

Jacob Boehme, writing in the seventeenth century and drawing upon what he believed were the teachings of 'wise heathens', was one who had influenced William Blake in his search for an alternative set of beliefs such as he expounded in 'The Marriage of Heaven and Hell'. Boehme writes:

> Our whole doctrine is nothing else but an instruction to show how man may create a kingdom of light within himself … . He in whom this spring of divine power flows, carries within himself the divine image and the celestial substantiality. In him is Jesus born from the Virgin, and he will not die in eternity.[61]

I do not know if Smart knew of Boehme's work, but there is, as I think I have shown, sufficient evidence, even from the passages quoted from 'Jubilate

Agno', to substantiate the claim that a change was at work in the mind of Smart that is akin to Boehme's understanding. Whatever it was that prompted the change, it is obvious that he emerged from his years of confinement better equipped to face the world and enabled to live more at ease with others and, most importantly, with himself.

In making this relatively brief foray into the life and work of Christopher Smart, I have become aware of my increasing conviction that there are depths to this man that have not yet been reached by the various biographers and those (including myself) who have sought to interpret his poetry. Due to the nature of this study of Smart as a sub-contemporary of Robert Burns and from a particular interest in his religious poetry, I am aware that I am only making a partial assessment of his work. It seems a little unfair to make judgements only on his religious pieces, as it would also be unfair to do the same with Burns's work. Yet for the purpose of this study that is what I am doing and thereby not assessing the full nature of the man as might happen if all his secular poetry were to be included. Even from my cursory knowledge of Smart's work, I think the time is surely right for a fuller assessment of the work of a poet that I am sure is worthy of re-evaluation.

The two poets, Christopher Smart (1722–71) and Robert Burns (1759–96), whose lives only overlapped for a few years, are vastly different in character and in the work that they produced. Smart was comfortably brought up, versed in Latin and Greek and benefitted from a University education, connected with the minor aristocracy at an early age and made his way in literary circles from the very beginning of his working life. This contrasts sharply with the experience of Burns, who was born into the home of a cotter, briefly schooled and thereafter largely self taught, and who had to endure heavy manual work from childhood, and even in the last years of his life as an exciseman often having to ride many miles a day in all kinds of weather. But although their physical worlds are far apart and their social lives and cultural milieu are very different, there are common areas of experience that are worth looking at, for their reactions to these experiences are not the same.

Smart and Burns had read many of the same books: William Derham's twin volumes on *Physico-Theology* and *Astro-Theology*, James Hervey's *Meditations*, John Milton's *Paradise Lost*, and the poets Dryden, Pope, Thomson and Gray. Both were well versed in the Bible and both related to the Church that was the Established Church in their respective countries. Yet while Smart makes use of Derham in his argument for the existence of Deity in the very variety of creation, Burns does not seem to make any use of Derham's argument from nature that it posits a loving Creator. For Burns, nature is a source of wonder that leads to a speculation as to what it is all about, but it is never a proof of God's existence. James Hervey's work provides for Burns a source to meditate upon, but he diverges entirely from Hervey's speculations of judgement involving a heaven and a hell.[62] Smart, however, is haunted by the thought of what might happen to him after death and seeks salvation through the acceptance of the evangelical theology of Christ's sacrificial death. Burns is never attracted to that theology at all and sees no need for it, for he does not believe in the Doctrine of Original Sin; in fact, he severely mocks it in his poem 'Holy Willie's Prayer' and in his letter to Alexander Cunningham.[63] Familiar too with the work of John Goldie he could not bring himself to believe in a God who could so organize the life of the world that man would have a built-in sin factor that would result in his death followed by torments in hell, unless certain theological hoops were jumped through and his salvation thereby achieved.[64]

Smart's knowledge of the Bible is beyond dispute, but it seems to be like that of an encyclopaedist. He knows about it in an entirely passive way. He repeats it as factual and treats it as if it were beyond all questioning. He is strong on biblical narrative but weak in its analysis. It is as if he is too willing to accept what has been told to him about it by those whom he deems to be authorities. His lifetime attitude of deference bordering on obsequiousness towards those whom he thinks are on a higher plain, socially or in terms of their achievement, seems to have crept in to his thinking about the Bible. Burns, on the other hand, says: 'I am a very sincere believer in the Bible; but I am drawn to it by the conviction of a Man, not the halter of an Ass.'[65] Burns will not defer to ecclesiastical or clerical authority, but prefers, as a man, to make his own common-sense judgement of the Bible.

Smart and Burns share an appreciation of John Milton but whereas Smart emulates Milton's style, Burns picks up on Milton's content. Controversially for the times, Burns expresses himself as an admirer of Milton's figure of Satan in *Paradise Lost* in a letter to his friend William Nicol in 1787: 'I have bought a pocket Milton which I carry perpetually about with me, in order to study the sentiments – the dauntless magnanimity; the intrepid unyielding independance; the desperate daring, and the noble defiance of hardship, in that great Personage, Satan.'[66] Burns is the more radical thinker when it comes to making use of what he has read, whilst Smart, especially prior to his major illness, had always thought along orthodox lines in relation to theology.

In the case that I have put forward, I claim that during his confinement and especially in the years between 1759 and 1763, Smart began to think more for himself. The conclusions to which he seems to have come, as he selected from within the Christian framework of belief the things that he thought were truly significant, and rejected, or at least put into a lower category of importance, the things that were not, were sufficient to at least stabilize his life and bring him to a more comfortable way of being, indeed of being himself. Burns did not have to make such adjustments to his thinking. Although Burns had a life long connection with the Church, and also a life long fascination for religion, it was always, I think, born of a curiosity and a fascination for ideas. As a young man he had said that he wanted to 'study, men, their manners and their ways',[67] and the Church was one of the institutions to which he had ready access that gave him that opportunity. The interest in the ideas about which he heard in church caused him as he said 'to puzzle Calvinism' and to engage in debate. But an early introduction to the philosophy of John Locke, supplemented by the probing ideas of Adam Smith, the down-to-earthness of Thomas Reid and the very influential John Goldie, all contributed to an attitude of questioning and testing by observation and experience. This produced an almost natural and certainly healthy scepticism that seems to have been lacking from the much more willing to accept nature of Christopher Smart.

Christopher Smart's secular poetry prior to 1756 often shows a coquettishness and a sensuality that he had to keep under wraps, or chose to keep under control while writing his religious poetry, while Burns saw no incongruity in including sensuality within the context of a poem about religious matters. In 'The Holy Fair', an open air gathering of congregations for the celebration of Holy Communion, Burns writes:

> Here, some are thinkan on their sins,
> An' some upo' their claes;
> Ane curses feet that fyl'd his shins,
> Anither sighs an' prays:
> On this hand sits a Chosen swatch,
> Wi' screw'd-up, grace-proud faces;
> On that, a set o' chaps, at watch,
> Thrang winkan on the lasses[68]

Burns very openly criticizes the defects of the Church in his poetry and offers even stronger opinions of it in his letters. Smart is always deferential in his poetry when writing on religious subjects, but allowed himself to criticize the Church when, almost writing under another persona, he contributes a letter to 'The Student' in September 1750, in an article on the corruption within the Church titled 'A New System of Castle Building': 'Let well fed pluralists ... reflect on the miseries and hardships of the inferior clergy, on their sons who are reduced to begging to avoid theft, and on their daughters who must submit to prostitution to keep themselves from starving.'[69] It is likely that in his reference to the daughters, Smart was perhaps 'going over the top', but at least he was making a point about an abuse within the Church.

For Christopher Smart, religion was much more of a life and death issue than it was for Robert Burns. This is especially true in the years immediately prior to and the early period of his illness. It is as if during the years 1759–63 there is a working out of a set of beliefs that enabled him to accept his own imperfections and see them as of less significance in the wider scheme of things. Nevertheless his beliefs to the end of his life were more in keeping with orthodoxy than those of Burns. Smart's beliefs were more well defined than those of Burns. Jesus Christ continues to feature in Smart's belief and he continues to use traditional Christian terminology, such as 'the Gospel of Christ' and 'the Lord Jesus'. He displays his willingness to be called 'a fool for Christ's sake'. He uses Jesus in an extended way when he writes, 'For flowers are the peculiar poetry of Christ'.[70] Smart is much more overtly religious in Christian terms than Burns ever is. Burns confines his comments on Jesus Christ to his letters and never ever mentions him in his poetry. Yet while Smart's religion was part of his problem, it was never a problem for Burns. For Smart, religion often seems to have taken prime place in his life, while for Burns it was always only a part of it. For Smart, religion posed real problems and became one of the threats to his sanity. For Burns, religion was always, right to the end of his life, a fascination; the issues that it raised were important, but the God it proclaimed, although Burns related to him, it was never a very personal relationship. Burns's God remained the 'Great Unknown' even if the poet did add, 'whose creature I am'.[71]

The last words of this chapter must be from Christopher Smart, some of whose troubles and tragedies have been recorded, and which to a certain extent might be thought to have been brought about because of the extremes of awareness that made him a poet. I have listened with a great deal of sympathy for the man who once said in explanation of himself, 'I have a greater compass both of mirth and melancholy than another.'[72]

Chapter 9

The Ministers of 'The Kirk of Scotland's Garland – a New Song'

ORTHODOX, ORTHODOX, who believe in John Knox,
Let me sound an alarm to your conscience;
A heretic blast has been blawn i' the West –
That what is not Sense must be Nonsense, Orthodox,
That what is not Sense must be Nonsense. –

One of the fashion fads of Burns's time was the miniature portrait. In the poem 'The Church of Scotland's Garland – a new Song', often known as 'The Kirk's Alarm', Burns rivals the greatest of the miniaturists of his day in his beautifully drawn sketches of some of the ministers involved in the prosecution or defence in the pursuit of a heresy charge against the Reverend Dr William McGill of the Auld Kirk of Ayr. In the space of a five-line stanza some of the essential characteristics are revealed, but as with all good portraits there is the hint of a life outwith the part of the life on show. In some of these portraits strong colours are used, but when one looks further into the background of the sitter the poet's treatment is justified, both in terms of the delineation of character and his knowledge of their background. These pen portraits should help towards a better understanding when the characters are mentioned in the poems. They also serve the purpose of adding to our knowledge of the nature of some of the clergymen who through their ministry had a considerable input into the local culture amidst which the poet formed his views on religion.

William Peebles

The most explicitly abusive stanza in 'The Kirk's Alarm' is addressed to the Reverend William Peebles, Minister of Newton upon Ayr Parish Church and Clerk to the Presbytery of Ayr:

Poet Willie, Poet Willie, gie the Doctor a volley
Wi' your 'liberty's chain' and your wit:
O'er Pegasus' side ye ne'er laid a stride,
Ye only stood by where he sh—, &c.[1]

In the same volume containing the sermon criticizing McGill that had been preached on 5 November 1788 to commemorate the 100th anniversary of the 'glorious revolution', Peebles's poem 'Ode to Liberty' was published. The first and last verses of the ten in the poem give a flavour of the quality of the poetry:

Hail, liberty celestial maid!
To ev'ry free-born Briton dear,
In beauteous robes of light array'd,
With all thy radiant train appear:
To thee, on this auspicious day
We raise the votive, solemn lay;
Smit with thy charms – thy energy divine,
The wond'ring nations 'round in one vast chorus join.

Britain thy winding shores along
Let the glad voice of praise arise;
Thy verdant vales repeat the sound
Thy cities waft it to the skies.
May sons unborn prolong the lay,
And oft proclaim this glorious day
And, bound in LIBERTY'S endearing chain,
May latest ages hail RELIGION's blessful reign![2]

Burns might have said more about the stilted, clichéd, lifeless verses but he contents himself with mocking the paradoxical, inept and incongruous metaphor 'LIBERTY'S endearing chain', and slyly attributes 'wit' to one whose work seems devoid of it. In one of Peebles's sermons he says, 'True joy is a serious thing'.[3] His writing in sermons, Kirk Session and Presbytery Minutes and especially in his later book *Burnomania*,[4] reveals a man who seems to have no appreciation of the lighter, more playful use of language and a man who presented life as an unremitting struggle.

Burns had singled out Peebles for criticism in his earlier poem written in 1785, 'The Holy Tulzie', that took up the subject of the quarrel between the Reverend Alexander Moodie and the Reverend John Russel. As Burns relates the tale, he calls upon the minister to bring the quarrelling pair together and names Peebles second in the list of 11 ministers:

O ye wha tent the Gospel-fauld,
Thee, Duncan deep, and Peebles shaul,
And chiefly great Apostle Auld,
We trust in thee,
That thou wilt work them het and cauld
To gar them gree.[5]

Even in 1785 Burns rated Peebles as shallow. This judgement is borne out by an examination of his exegetical methods, for example in a sermon on Psalm 45:2, 'Thou art fairer than the children of men', he claims that these words apply to Jesus. He does this on the basis that the author of Hebrews, whom he claims to be Paul, 'applies a part of this psalm to our Lord Jesus Christ in order to prove his infinite superiority to angels' (a reference to Hebrews I:7,8). This simplistic, unexamined, uncontextual use of words shows a cleverness with words, but betrays a naive and literalist attitude to scripture.[6]

Again, in Sermon V, 'A man of sorrows and acquainted with grief', he accepts unquestioningly the 'suffering servant' passage (Isaiah:53) as being a prophecy concerning the person of Jesus, ignoring completely the relevance of the prophetic statement as it was made to the people of Isaiah's time. This sermon again shows that tendency to a literalism that takes no account of the figurative use of language. As the sermon develops, the darkness at the crucifixion is described as having been caused because, 'the sun turns away from beholding it, darkens his glory and hides his face. The earth trembles with the impiety of men, and while their hearts are hardened in guilt, the flinty rocks are rent in pieces.'[7] As a piece of fine writing it is impressive, but it is hardly an honest treatment of Matthew's version of the events. But the greatest flaw in the work of any exegete is to make the text fit the preconceived theological theory, and this is Peebles's basic fault. In that same sermon when he turns to the sufferings of Jesus he makes no reference to the human circumstances that brought them about but sees them caused 'by the heavy hand which was laid upon him by the law and justice of his Father, as the righteous governor of the universe ... for all that he endured was to satisfy Divine justice for his offending people.'[8]

Peebles could and regularly did express himself eloquently, for example, in a sermon on 'The Fall' he writes:

> When man by disobedience fell from the station originally assigned him, a new spectacle was exhibited in this fair and beautiful world. Sin, that alluring but poisonous foe, erected his awful standard on the ruins of rational existence, withered the glory of our creation, and overspread the regions of animation with a sable cloud, portentous of the bursting storm of mortality. Darkness more awful far than what invests our midnight hours, involved the perceptions and faculties of men, and through the dreadful gloom, death in all his terrific horrors was discovered, seizing his lawful prey, and leading under his banners, the whole rational world. Sin for his reception had previously opened a wide passage to every heart.[9]

Such a theology is not derived by a mind that seeks openly to discover what the Old and New Testaments are trying to say about God, but from a mind that is already made up as to what they are saying, and that has been helped to that understanding by the acceptance of man-made credal statements that predetermine what is to be found in scripture. I am sure that Burns had listened to Peebles and had detected, for all their eloquence, the words of a shallow thinker. The descriptions of the preaching characteristics of the other ministers mentioned in 'The Holy Tulzie' give ample evidence that Burns was a 'sermon taster'. The very words that he uses are the kind that would be used by the listener rather than the reader.

Duncan is referred to as 'deep'. This is a typical remark of the person who has listened and although finding the reasoning of the preacher hard to follow, nevertheless acknowledges that the fault probably lies with themselves and not the preacher, who really does have something worthwhile to say. The brothers Shaw and Dr Dalrymple were styled 'eloquent', a word that is more often used of spoken than of written language. McGill's description seems to fit well with his writing, which is at times closely reasoned and with his character that withstood a huge amount of pressure and personal abuse, yet ever maintained a standard of excellence and integrity. His reference to 'McQuhae's pathetic manly sense' is another observation made of a preacher at work. The sympathy and the humanity of a preacher are easily detected from the pew. The same words spoken by different people will not always convey the same things. Similarly Burns's reference to George Smith of Galston is the result of observation. He has seen in Smith someone who wavers from the hard-line Calvinism of the Auld Lights and who has the ability to see deeply into the human heart. With Smith, Burns has had that experience of having his own heart revealed to him. That is the art of the preacher, but the knowledge of the experience is that of the listener. Burns's final comment on this list of those to whom he had undoubtedly listened is just to refer to the man to whom he was later to send a copy of 'Holy Willie's Prayer' with an accompanying verse epistle as 'guid McMath'. Sometimes the experience of a preacher results in people saying 'Oh, he's good'. It is a total judgement. It is an expression of satisfaction in the experience of the person. These comments of Burns are not the considered judgements of someone who has made a detailed study of the work of the people to whom he is referring: they all bear the mark of experience of the person, and carry the value of the impression that each has made upon him. That was the kind of judgement that Burns made on the preachers.[10]

Burns's judgement of Peebles is by comparison with the others a harsh one. Yet Burns always chooses his words with great care, and that makes the second half of the verse about Peebles something to consider in detail:

> O'er Pegasus's side ye ne'er laid a stride
> Ye only stood by where he sh—, &c.

Pegasus was Burns's favourite horse, named after the legendary winged horse that enabled its rider to perform many great and heroic deeds. It was also the horse of the poetic Muses.[11] In using the Pegasus metaphor Burns was mocking

Peebles's lack of ability as a poet, but the vehemence of his language seems to indicate that he was doing more than offering his criticism of Peebles's poetry. Was Burns saying to Peebles, 'you have never ventured out into life. You have never done anything valiant. On the contrary, you have been left behind, only capable of detecting the unpleasant smells of life, your feet stuck in the mire'? Was it a way of saying, 'you and your kind with your view of God and Man are missing the point. You have been left behind. Life has moved on and all you are left with is a view of the life that you might have had'?

The precise nature of Burns's abuse of Peebles leads me to believe that it was based on more than just a knowledge of him as a preacher or as a poet. His friendship with Dr McGill and his interest in the local religious controversies probably gave him a greater understanding of Peebles than most of the others, particularly because Peebles, as Clerk to the Presbytery of Ayr, played a very active part in the local church scene.

Peebles had become minister of Newton upon Ayr when the congregation was a Chapel of Ease in 1778. In 1780 it was raised to full status as a parish church.[12] Peebles pursued an active ministry from the beginning, and must have become well known in the community for some of the methods he employed. He was soon known as a rigorist. A Minute of the Kirk Session of 23 July 1780 dealing with a case of fornication describes the act not as a sin, but as a crime.[13] On 27 October 1780 the Kirk Session showed concern:

> that many of the inhabitants in this place ... absent themselves from the House of God on the Lord's Day and either spend that holy day by entertaining idle and immoral people in their houses during the time of divine service or by employing themselves in visiting their neighbours and in irreligious conversations.[14]

The Kirk Session decided that:

> it is their firm purpose to cause every house suspected of such ungodly practice to be visited in time of publick worship, especially in the forenoon. And whoever is found at home without any proper sufficient excuse; or entertaining idle and licentious people in their Houses shall be cited first opportunity fore the Session, and if they will not appear to account for their conduct, they shall be proceeded against according to the rules of the Church, and if these prove ineffectual to be brought before the civil magistrate.

This resolution was indeed implemented and a case is on record of a man 'found in the street during the time of publick worship' being cited and appearing before the Session where he submitted to their rebuke.[15]

The Kirk Session records also reveal Peebles behaving in a manner that is consistent with his behaviour in Presbytery, further justifying the harshness of Burns's comments. On 6 November 1783 the appointment of the Session Clerk,

John Ramsay, came under review. The Kirk Session voted to continue the appointment for a trial period of six months, passing the motion by one vote. William Peebles formally dissented from the decision. At the next meeting of the Kirk Session on 13 November 1783, he presented his reasons for dissent. He declared that John Ramsay, 'was not qualified for being Clerk to any ecclesiastical court for how can it be seeing that he has never got any education for that purpose.'[16] He asserted that Ramsay's behaviour had 'all along such as has given great offence to any serious person'. But the most damaging reason he gives is that one vote was cast by an elder, John Young:

> who publickly declared before the Session that this was no matter of conscience with them. The dissenter is therefore of opinion that his vote by this free acknowledgement was rendered null and void, and that the person who said so and voted, as it was under the invocation of the Divine presence by prayer is liable to a rebuke from the session. If the Dissenter is seconded he moves that it be tried whether the vote of John Young can be of any avail when it was given in an affair which he declared was a matter of no conscience with them.

The outcome was that Peebles's motion was seconded and carried. John Young admitted what he had said. The session declared his vote null and void and the matter was left to the casting vote of the Moderator, William Peebles. The Minute continues, 'Upon which the Moderator instead of giving his casting vote either one way or other proposed for the sake of peace, that this affair should be delayed for a few weeks till the publick school of this parish be examined by the Presbytery.' John Ramsay was also the schoolmaster and by that appointment automatically Session Clerk. Mr Young tendered his resignation, but demanded that it be recorded according to his dictation. The Minute records it in a way that reveals the atmosphere of the meetings:

> That I John Young in presence of the session of Newton freely resign my office as being a member of that session for several reasons best known to myself. That I have been a member of said session since the commencement of said session has seldom seen much love or unity in it but often of different opinions of what was done there as in a private session was commonly reported in publick, therefore finding it unconvenient for me to attend.

The Minute adds: '(N.B. This is copied word for word from the minute written by the Clerk)'.[17] John Young's resignation statement seems to indicate an atmosphere within the Kirk Session's meetings, over which Peebles presides, that is lacking in oneness of purpose, in trust and in love.

On 25 December 1783 a report is sent from the Kirk Session meeting to the Magistrates asking that they dismiss the schoolmaster, as there is only one pupil attending the school and he is supported by the Poor Fund. On 5 January 1784 it is duly reported at the Kirk Session that the Magistrates had dismissed

John Ramsay from his post as schoolmaster at Newton, and Peebles has thereby effected the dismissal of his Session Clerk.[18] Such scheming and manipulation, not to say deviousness, could hardly go unnoticed in the small community that Ayr then was. It is unlikely that Burns would be unaware of such events and therefore points to his remarks about Peebles being far from gratuitous abuse, and much more a judgement on a well-known local character.

A more temperate but nonetheless telling judgement of Peebles is made by Sir John Sinclair in *The Statistical Account*. Mr Peebles gives an account of the burgh of Newton, boasting of its ancient nature and telling of how 'all its privileges formerly given to the borough were reviewed by James VI of Scotland and I of England by a charter dated 24 September 1595.'[19] He goes on to describe its constitution in some detail. Unusually, Sir John Sinclair writes an appendix to the report that is highly critical of its content. He comments:

> The constitution of the Burgh of Newton upon Ayr, is certainly *in theory* the purest and the best republican system, anywhere to be met with. Nothing, at first sight, can yield more satisfaction, to a mind capable of feeling for the happiness of the species, than to find, that a community actually exists, whose government is founded on the generous principles of equality and independence. In the whole course of this investigation, nothing gave me more satisfaction than the account of this district, as returned by the minister – Upon farther inquiry, from various quarters in the neighbourhood, I learnt, however, with regret, that beautiful theories do not always answer in practice; and, in particular, that no beneficial consequences could be traced from this constitution; – that the freemen were, in no respect, superior to the inhabitants of other little boroughs; – that, in general, little attention was paid to their education, and that some of them could not read; that no funds were allotted for the maintenance of the poor brethren; that the place was reckoned almost a century behind other towns in point of improvement. In regard to their property, that a considerable tract of ground, belonging to them, remained in common; and, that no favourable presage could be drawn, from the manner in which their small possessions were cultivated; for, that in a much inclosed country, their acres remained open, were kept constantly in tillage, and consequently, in a state greatly inferior to the lands of those who held a larger extent of ground in their possession and whose rights were not liable to the same system of restrictions.[20]

Sinclair had rather pointedly laid the blame for a misleading report squarely on the shoulders of Peebles. He had shown that Peebles's beautiful theories of the state of the secular world bore little relation to the facts, just as Burns had endeavoured to criticize the theological theories of Peebles 'frae the water-fit' by indicating that when they are voiced from the 'holy rostrum':

> COMMON-SENSE has taen the road,
> An' aff, an' up the COWGATE
>   Fast, fast that day.[21]

It would be interesting to discover who the people were that Sinclair says he consulted as to the real situation in Newton upon Ayr. Did they include Dalrymple, McGill or Burns, all of whom were contributers to *The Statistical Account*?[22] Was someone getting back at Peebles?

Dr McGill certainly made a most interesting contribution to *The Statistical Account* in his supplementary report for the Parish of Ayr. His report was submitted in 1791 but was too late for inclusion in the first printing and was not finally published until 1799. In a section on 'Learned Men' he pays this daring tribute to Robert Burns:

> History has recorded but few men, natives of this place, who were distinguished in the republic of letters. Only in the 9th century it produced the famous John Scot, sirnamed *Erigena*, or born in Ayr, to distinguish him from a former born at Melrose, and from another born in the 13th century in the town of Dunse. Erigena is said to have excelled all the men of his time, in the knowledge of languages and philosophy, as also in acuteness of judgement, readiness of wit, and fluency of elocution. He studied at Athens, lived in great favour with Charles the Bald of France, and wrote many books upon different points of philosophy and theology, of which some remain at this day. To him may be added Andrew Ramsay, better known by the name of *Chevalier Ramsay*, the author of *Cyrus's Travels*, and other works. And lastly, Robert Burns, the poet, born in the country part of the parish of Ayr, and by his genius at least, as much distinguished as either of the former authors.[23]

McGill is writing this in the immediate aftermath of the dismissal of the charge of heresy at the General Assembly of 1791. His tribute to Burns defied the conventions of the time. I am sure he carefully selected the two literary figures to accompany Burns in his pantheon of 'Learned Men'. Many of the qualities of Erigena could be applied to Burns: knowledge of languages, acuteness of judgement, readiness of wit and fluency of elocution. When Andrew Ramsay's life is examined there are parallels of sympathy with the sentiments of Burns. Ramsay was a friend and student of Fenelon, Archbishop of Cambrai, a man much embroiled in the religious and philosophical controversies of the time. (Ramsay was later to write the *Life of Fenelon*.) Burns was given Fenelon's *The Adventures of Telemachus*, when he studied French under John Murdoch. Ramsay was to become tutor to the young Prince Charles Edward Stewart (1724–26).[24] Burns had a nostalgia for the exiled House of Stuart and was possibly a repressed Jacobin. And as if McGill was thumbing his nose at the establishment he chose in Ramsay a man who had converted to Roman Catholicism. This recognition of this anti-establishment figure and the placing of Burns alongside him is stretching coincidence too far. McGill is making a statement here in adopting these three men as his 'Learned Men'. In that statement he is generously acknowledging his appreciation of the stature of Robert Burns, poet.

Yet Peebles had the last word. Outliving both Burns and McGill, in 1811 he published a work called *Burnomania: the Celebrity of Robert Burns considered in a Discourse Addressed to All Real Christians of Every Denomination. To which are added Epistles in Verse, respecting Peter Pindar, Burns &c.* The frontispiece contains a verse which sets the tone for the whole book:

> A whole family of Bards
> Corruptive, illegitimate and base
> A spurious breed of wickedness and wit
> A muse's genius with a demon's heart.
>
> Cumberland[25]

Peebles proceeds to cut, slash and mutilate both the work and the character of Burns. It is a vicious, vindictive and intemperate work that says far more about Peebles than the subject he sets out to deal with. Not surprisingly, and perhaps characteristically, it was printed anonymously, but it was later acknowledged as the work of Peebles.

Peebles sees his role as that of one who has to administer an antidote to the poisonous writings and attitudes of his time, a time in which the work of Burns is being lauded and the cult of the celebration of Burns is beginning to develop. However he sets out to write on a broader field and indicates this in the *Advertisement*:

> I am a Scotsman. I am fully persuaded that much danger arises to the interests of morals and religion, the present and the future happiness of the age, in this part of the world, from the writings and characters of Scotsmen, or two of our countrymen in particularly, of Mr David Hume, of the ploughman Burns ... Much have I been surprised and indeed I have often been shocked to hear the names of Hume and Burns mentioned with warmth of applause by those who are Christians, the one a determined infidel, living and dying, the other an irreligious profligate. Much do I regret the countenance they have received and the currency of their writings which soothe and vindicate vice and condemn religion! ... In life, in death and after death Hume labours to shake and overturn the faith of Christians, to overturn Christianity; that is, in the language of scripture, and of everyone who believes that the Gospel is true, he fights against God. Burns deliberately, repeatedly, exultingly glories in vice, ridicules religion, makes the truths of God the subject of merriment and exhibits himself as biographers and panegyrists do, as a prophane blackguard.

His opening barrage closes:

> Which of these characters is most criminal, most to be abhorred, and most dangerous, it is perhaps difficult to determine ... hereafter I may employ myself in exhibiting Hume an object of abhorrence and detestation. I regret exceedingly, and

> would reprove sharply the adulation paid to this leader of infidelity and irreligion by those who call themselves Christians.

But after taking this one swipe at Hume, Peebles continues: 'Burns has been encouraged and extolled, Burns was spoilt and ruined by the imprudent and excessive attention paid to him, his popularity and celebrity, of a sort such as it is, are of poisonous and destructive quality and influence. To Burns I shall confine myself at present'.[26] That very last line confirms Burns's judgement of Peebles as shallow. He lacked the intellect for a proper critique of Hume. Burns was an easier target.

He begins his onslaught on Burns with a protestation that need never have been made had he been innocent of the things that he disclaims:

> Need I to preface my remarks and complaints and epostulations by disclaiming all malevolence or envy or censoriousness toward the character or fame of the man? He is no more. I never saw him. I have and can have no interest in bringing him from that eminence to which some have foolishly exalted him. My only concern and motive is checking, depressing and preventing what is injurious to morals, to religion, to philosophy.[27]

Peebles's criticism of Burns's poetry is minimal. Whenever he attempts to deal with a poem he seems to become distracted by the subject matter and appears to have little understanding of what is being attempted by the poet. He approaches poetry in the same way as he does the Bible, refusing to acknowledge the figurative use of language and applying a literalist interpretation that totally misses the point. After referring to Burns's swearing, he criticizes 'Green Grow the Rashes O':

> There are however many instances I suspect of grosser impiety and irreligion in these books of Burns. Such as, Woman is a masterpiece. Man was made by an apprentice. Nature in forming his idol did the best she could, she could do no more. This is a flight of genius! so some may say, and he himself seems to be fond of it, and in this manner compliments more than one, but I believe that Christians with me will exclaim first, shocking impiety! and then shocking sycophancy and will reckon the idolized lady and gentleman rather disgraced than honoured.[28]

This humourless, ill-informed approach is one of the few ventures into detailed criticism of the poetry. But he cannot concentrate on the poetry; he seems compelled to judge the poet. Even when he seems to be trying to be fair he quickly resorts to abuse:

> But can it be denied that he was clever, that his genius is justly admired? I have no wish in the smallest degree to deny him the least particle of what is his due. At the same time, I must regret the currency and the popularity of his trash. I must consider

> anything that endangers or injures morals, decency, and piety as detestable and to be detested. I must add that some of the pieces that are held up and celebrated as peculiarly excellent, appear to me very exceptionable or rather I should say infamous. I shall mention two "The Holy Fair" and "Tom o' Shanter". [*sic*] I trust that I am not singular in saying the immoral tendency of both is such that they ought not to remain in the principal volume his critics pronounce so invaluable.

One line of praise follows, the only one I detected in the whole book: 'Be it so that superstition and hypocrasy [*sic*] and fun are well described, that blackguardism and profanity are naturally exhibited.'[29] But then follows the rhetorical question, 'Will all this atone for the levity with which he exhibits himself a Sabbath-breaker, devoted to fun, ridiculing the ministers of religion?'

'Aye there's the rub', it could be said. Peebles's self-image was being mocked by Burns's treatment of the ministers of religion and that was something that this humourless man could not bear. In common with some other ministers of the time Peebles was ready to interpret any mockery of establishment figures such as ministers as indicative of a disrespect that could lead to impiety and even treason. He saw a clear line running from impiety to treason and in his thinking Burns was guilty of both.

In 1798, one of Peebles's ministerial colleagues in the nearby parish of Maybole, James Wright, had written *A Treatise on the Causes of Sedition* in which he expounded the connections between religion and the state: 'Religion unites men to the State as well as to the Church of God. Therefore by destroying the power of religious principle the civil magistrate loses his respect.'[30] Wright sees the threatened loss of religion as something that would result in anarchy: 'If we could suppose a whole nation of people without any religion they would be no better than an assemblage of wild beasts.'[31] He then turns his attention to the factors that he judges could well bring about the destruction of society as he knows it: 'There are several other powerful causes of disaffection and sedition such as Jacobin Newspapers, speeches in opposition to the measures of government, and the doctrines of certain religious sectaries.'[32]

Wright was writing amidst rumours of French invasion but the near paranoia that he shows against any outspokenness against the establishment of Church or State was a feeling that was still abroad at the time of Peebles's writing. Peebles is critical of Burns's attachment to the Stuart family which 'was strong, was avowed and gloried in'. He reveals that in his view orthodoxy and patriotism are closely linked as he declaims: 'A Christian is a patriot, a lover of peace and good order.'[33]

Peebles criticizes the poem 'Scotch Drink' in these terms: '[Burns] reprobates the measures of Mr Pitt, he stirs up, as he can, tumults and mobs, he threatens rebellion, if his petition respecting Scots drink is not granted – all without effect, 'tis true, but the spirit and character are the same and equally blameable whether successful or unsuccessful.'[34]

Here again the literalism that plagued Peebles is in evidence, and his rating of spirit and act as equally blameable shows the illogicality of his thinking. Almost immediately following this outburst he engages in yet another innuendo against Burns: 'When his pen was so employed [against the establishment] what was his tongue doing? In these days of turbulence and sedition, of Tom Paine's blasphemies.'[35] Again note the equation of impiety and sedition. Tom Paine he had earlier described as 'the lowest of the low, the vilest of the vile';[36] Burns by the process of guilt by association is placed in the same category as Paine.

In the Appendix to *Burnomania*, Peebles's 'Epistle Second' concludes:

To the great Bard erect a Bust
Nor is this all, from age to age
As for a monarch, hero, sage
Let anniversaries repeat
His glories, celebrate a fete
Imbibe his spirit, sing his songs
Extol his name, lament his wrongs
His death deplore, accuse his fate
And raise him far above the great.

What call you this? Is it Insania
I'll coin a word, 'tis Burnomania.
His Greenock friends we therefore dub
The Annual Burnomanian Club.[37]

These were the last published words of William Peebles on the subject. His attempt at setting the record straight, or giving the 'right-thinking' Christian a proper perspective on Burns, was a failure for the reason that it says more about William Peebles than it does of Robert Burns. Peebles was a failed polemicist as well as a failed poet. Despite the near paranoia of his attack on Burns he had unwittingly paid him one of the greatest compliments and witnessed to his true stature by linking his name, even in reprobation, with one who has become acknowledged as the greatest philosopher of the Enlightenment, David Hume.

William Dalrymple

If Peebles was one of the principal players in the drama of the 'Kirk's Alarm', Burns's comments on some of the other members of the cast are not without interest, and also indicate his familiarity with their theology as well as their character. His affection for and sympathy with the Reverend Dr William Dalrymple (1723–1814) is clear:

D'rmple mild, D'rymple mild, tho' your heart's like a child,
And your life like the new-driven snaw;
Yet that winna save ye, auld Satan maun have ye,
For preaching that three's ane and twa, &c.[38]

Dr William Dalrymple of the Auld Kirk of Ayr had baptised Burns as an infant and was the family's minister in the years at the cottage at Alloway and at Mount Oliphant Farm. This scholarly man, by his preaching and writing, nurtured the faith of William Burnes and must have contributed to the understanding that in time helped William to produce his little handbook *A Manual of Religious Belief in a Dialogue between Father and Son for the religious instruction of his family*.[39] That book's milder form of Calvinism is in keeping with the tone of Dr Dalrymple's writings. Several works of biblical exposition, Christian education and sermons were published during his long ministry at Ayr.[40] Throughout the controversy over McGill's book he remained steadfast in his support of his colleague. Just as the criticism was getting under way Dr Dalrymple paid tribute to Dr McGill in the preface to his (Dalrymple's) book *A History of Christ, for the use of the Unlearned* (1787). Referring to McGill's *A Practical Essay on the Death of Christ* (1786) he writes:

I will not with-hold the pleasure I likewise found from my worthy colleague, Dr William McGill, his having carried out at the same time and without either of our designs being made known to one another, a similar good work, founded upon the most important branch of our sacred gospel-history, the Sufferings and Death of Christ considered by way of a practical essay; which there is little doubt, from its piously condescending manner, the simple elegance of its composition, exactness of method, and whole tendency to excite and cherish the best affections will prove universally acceptable.[41]

Dalrymple, already aware of the criticisms that have been levelled at McGill, seems to go out of his way to emphasize that his tribute is from a full understanding of the *Essay* by adding:

He [McGill] will pardon me, after perusing the whole in manuscript, to have cast in this mite of tribute without his knowledge; less could not be said, and more might have been liable to misconstruction, besides doing hurt where modesty wishes to be spared. If in any particular we may seem to differ they will not be such as affect either Love or Duty; and upon lesser points all will have right to judge for themselves.

Addressing the parishioners to whom the Preface had been directed, he concludes:

> My trust and hope in the Divine mercy is, that you may yet long continue to enjoy and value his [McGill's] sacred ministration, and to set a special mark of regard, as you now do, upon the unremitting accuracy with which the truths of scripture are explained and applied by lectures.

Dalrymple and McGill sat comfortably with each other's theology, so much so that at a later stage in the controversy there were those like James Ramsay who also wanted to prosecute Dalrymple with the same charge of heresy as had been laid against McGill.[42]

Both Dalrymple and McGill were judged by their contemporaries to be in the New Light or Moderate party of the Church of Scotland. An examination of their written work shows that both asserted the authority of scripture over the *The Westminster Confession*. Both rejected any argument that required blind faith and acknowledged the need to apply the use of their God-given reasoning powers and common sense in the interpretation of scripture and its resultant theology. In addition to their being of a similar theological persuasion, they also were on the same side of another issue that deeply divided the Church of Scotland – patronage. Both accepted patronage and indeed were in charges whose patronage lay, in the case of Dalrymple with the Crown and in the case of McGill with the Town Council. These were the bodies who had presented them to the first and second charges of the Auld Kirk of Ayr (John the Baptist).[43]

An examination of Dalrymple's writing confirms the accuracy of Burns's comments. In *A History of Christ* (1787), Dalrymple concentrates on explaining the meaning of the Gospel texts, giving background information to provide a better context for understanding them. He adopts a simple style and offers an unobtrusive commentary that does not take over from or obscure the original text. The tone is that of a mild-mannered, courteous and gentle person offering his opinion with a certain diffidence, yet every now and again declaring a firmly held opinion, but never in polemical terms. The book was produced with the hope that it would be of use to parents and schoolteachers in the religious education of children, which could partly account for its lack of polemic.[44] A subsequent book, *A Sequel to the Life of Christ* (1791), was equally free of that type of writing although its format, as described on its title page as 'containing Practical Reflexions', ideally provided a platform for the author's opinions. These opinions, although bearing traces of the controversy over the McGill case, are expressed in mild language. Were those intent on judically punishing Dr McGill in mind when he writes, 'There can be no right of punishing in a church but that which is spiritual'.[45] Again there is a gentle tilting at his opponents in the debate in his comment: 'Hypocrites of all others are most apt to condemn those who differ from them.'[46] Another of his comments in this same section both reflects the recent experience and gives a hint to the reason for Burns's admiration and respect for Dalrymple. He writes: 'Religion often serves for a cloak to hard-heartedness, one of the worst kinds of impiety.'[47] Burns himself had earlier (in 1785) written to the Reverend John McMath on that same theme:

God knows, I'm no the thing I shou'd be,
Nor am I even the thing I cou'd be,
But twenty times, I rather wou'd be
An atheist clean,
Than under gospel colours hid be
Just for a screen.

An honest man may like a glass,
An honest man may like a lass,
But mean revenge, an' malice fause
He'll still disdain,
An' then cry zeal for gospel laws,
Like some we ken.[48]

Burns had detected in Dalrymple someone who appreciated the religion of the heart and this is borne out by Dalrymple's writing. In a section on 'Which is the greatest commandment', Dalrymple writes: 'Those who boast of their profession are often greatly defective in obedience, and even in solid learning. We must follow from the heart what we perceive to be best ... the heart ought to be sincerely wholly and constantly devoted to God .... '[49]

In that same section Dalrymple reveals another aspect of his belief that would have brought Burns into sympathy with his sentiments, when he writes of God and our human nature: 'To love him, is to gain him; to make him our supreme good. Such love is as old as the creation and engraven in our very nature ... it is necessary and of eternal duration.' Such sentiments are in opposition to the then more frequently preached views of the utter corruption of man by his fall, views which Burns heartily disputed. Dalrymple regularly returns to the theme, writing in later sections of the same book: 'A heart without love is a lamp without oil ... warm love attends not always to necessary prudent circumstances ... the most intimate of all conjunctions is that of the mind and heart. Love can do nothing against the beloved.'[50]

Dalrymple's warm and gentle expressions of his faith in this book are typical of the sermons that he preached and that Burns on many occasions must have heard. But apart from there being this bridge of sentiment between the two men, Burns also would have had cause to appreciate Dalrymple's common-sense approach to religion. It is significant that in the Preface to *A Sequel to the Life of Christ* Dalrymple actually quotes Thomas Reid's book, which he calls

Principles of Common Sense, in support of his own endeavour 'to accomplish a real triumph of truth over error'.[51] Burns had already linked Dr Dalrymple with common sense in the general use of that term in his lines in 'The Twa Herds or The Holy Tulzie' when he portrayed Dalrymple as the foe of the orthodox who wished that:

> that curst cur ca'd Common Sense
> Wha bites sae sair,
> Be banish'd o'er the seas to France.[52]

It could be argued that because of the capital letters given to 'Common Sense' in that poem Burns was also making a reference to the philosophical use of the term. If this is so, then he is even more aware of Dalrymple's philosophical and theological stance than I have so far argued. Burns defended this fair-minded, generous man with whom he found himself in sympathy at many points, and by that defence attacked those who seemed to condemn him. But Dalrymple in his own gentle way makes several comments that reveal a man well able to defend himself, a man who is capable of exercising a judgement upon those whose religion he deems inconsistent with that advocated by Jesus Christ. In *A Sequel to the Life of Christ* I suspect he is writing of some of the protagonists in the McGill case. He writes of those who have closed their minds to evidence that is contrary to their preconceived ideas, 'evidence comes too late when the mind is violently prepossessed', and of those who bring grave charges against another, 'calumny is the blackest and most irreparable of crimes. The more weighty an accusation is, the more clear ought the proofs to be.'[53]

Dalrymple hits out at the kind of religion that is just a matter of principles and that is as simple as ABC: 'In an evil age something more is wanted than first principles or mere alphabet religion. That which does not sanctify a man's mind or make him better, doth not subserve religion. Truth is better manifested by holiness than by argument'.[54]

He displays a breadth of vision of the Church that is in contrast to those who want to narrow it down to a much more select band: the chosen few – the elect. He writes, I suspect, remembering the acrimonious and contentious debate:

> The true church comprehends all who love the Lord Jesus in sincerity. "His reign is in the hearts of man" (S.C.) [He quotes Samuel Charteris in approval]. Besides being brethren, they are fellow travellers to a land where strife and contention, anger and debate, pride and hypocrisy shall prevail no more.[55]

Saddened by his recent experiences he writes: 'How many there are who seem to interrogate truth only to dishonour and persecute it? Before we inquire, let us hearken to our hearts whether as of God and as of truth we mean to profit.'[56] As if to indicate that he has seen through some of the people involved in the prosecution of Dr McGill, he concludes: 'zeal counterfeited is a most atrocious crime.'[57]

Even this fairly brief excursion into some of the writings of Dr Dalrymple bears out the accuracy of the judgement made of him by Burns, a judgement that is corroborated by Mrs Dunlop's letter of 1 August 1789 in response to Burns sending her a copy of the first draft of 'The Kirk's Alarm'. She advises against publishing it and writes:

> I cannot help being afraid that, instead of relieving the Dr.[McGill], and putting his enemies to shame, you may be blowing the horn for a new chase against one of his friends, and a man who rivals him in innocent simplicity and goodness of heart. But I need not tell you what D–r Mild is when you have painted him so strongly and in his true natural colours, as like a picture as ever was sketched by Sir Joshua Reynolds. Yet should your ballad lead the puppies' full cry a heretic-hunting, you'll wish you had bit your tongue rather than given the view-hollo, and cast off a whole pack of blood-hounds against a poor little white rabbit.[58]

Mrs Dunlop's use of language here in describing Dr Dalrymple as 'a poor little white rabbit' reflects and reinforces the accuracy of Burns's description of Dalrymple's life as being 'like the new-driven snaw',[59] and is another tribute to the purity, innocence and lovable nature of the man. But just as the writings quoted above show, she acknowledges here that he was also a man who could express his opinions strongly:

> Should this happen, I verily think it would be the blackest sin you ever committed, and I'm sure I would sympathize with your penitential pangs which could not fail of being very acute, were you to hurt one whom all mankind ought to love, for he loves them all, and if he sometimes scolds them in the pulpit, he means it all for their own good.[60]

In 'The Twa Herds or The Holy Tulzie', Burns makes reference to 'D'rmple's eloquence'.[61] Why Burns should use that particular word to describe Dalrymple's language is perhaps revealed by something that Dalrymple himself writes in *A Sequel to the Life of Christ*: 'What does not touch the heart cannot gain attention. On the knowledge of the heart, all true eloquence is founded.'[62] I suspect that Dalrymple had first gained Burns's attention by words that touched the heart, and that in this eloquence he recognized one who had a knowledge of the heart. 'D'rymple Mild' may even have been the one to inspire the words that sum up so much of the poet's aspiration: 'My Muse, tho hamely in attire / May touch the heart.'[63]

But whether or not he inspired the lines, Dalrymple had certainly won the affectionate respect of the poet who painted his portrait with the accuracy of the artist who knows his subject well.

James Mackinlay

Simper James, Simper James, leave the fair Killie dames,
There's a holier chase in your view:
I'll lay on your head that the PACK ye'll soon lead,
For PUPPIES like you there's but few, &c.[64]

This stanza refers to the Reverend James Mackinlay (1756–1841), Minister of the Laigh Kirk, Kilmarnock. Mackinlay's presentation to the charge of the Laigh Kirk by James Cunningham, Earl of Glencairn in December 1785 was opposed by the Moderates of Kilmarnock Presbytery, and he was not inducted and ordained until 6 April 1786.[65]

The epithet 'Simper James' seems to refer to a preaching mannerism observed. It is being linked to a reference to the women of his parish, implying that Burns saw him as one who set out to please with the refinement of his language and, being at that time unmarried, engaged in pursuit of a wife. He did not marry until 1815. Burns wagers that as an ardent evangelical he will soon be the leader of a group, whom he likens to dogs, that are out to get McGill. His final insult is to call Mackinlay a pup, indicating that he has not even matured to a dog.

Mackinlay was an Auld Light evangelical with a theology that could result in this interpretation of an accident that occurred in the Laigh Kirk during a Sunday Service in which 31 people were killed: 'This calamity has been brought upon us on account of sin – not the sin of one individual, or of a few, but the sins of ignorance, the unthankfulness, the injustice and immorality of many.'[66] Preaching that on the Sunday following the accident betrays not only a simplistic theology, but a massive insensitivity to the feelings of the people in his congregation.

In 'The Ordination', which Burns's letter of 17 February 1786 to John Richmond reveals was written before Mackinlay was finally ordained on 6 April 1786,[67] Burns portrays Mackinlay as one who takes a flail to 'Common-sense' (stanza 2) and then links his name with the Reverend John Russel, writing: 'M' ******* and R ***** are the boys / That Heresy can torture' (stanza 13)[68]

Mackinlay had been licensed by the Presbytery of Ayr on 3 July 1782 and had become tutor in the family of Sir William Cunningham of Windyhill, a relative of James Cunningham who became the 14th Earl of Glencairn in 1775 and who presented him to the second charge of the Laigh Kirk in 1785.[69] Burns was also to receive Glencairn's patronage when he was introduced to him in Edinburgh through the good offices of Dalrymple of Orangefield in 1786.[70] Through this mutual friendship, but also because Mackinlay had been part of the local clergy, Burns had the opportunity to learn of Mackinlay at close hand. His fixing on the epithet 'Simper James' certainly smacks of a very personal awareness of his manner of speech, but Burns's opinion of Mackinlay's theology must have been formed from listening to what he had to say and corroborated to a certain extent by those with whom he associated.

Burns writes from Edinburgh to James Dalrymple of Orangefield in February 1787 in appreciation of the Earl of Glencairn, who, he says:

> took me by the hand today, and interested himself in my concerns with a goodness like that benevolent Being whose image he so richly bears. "*Oubliez moi, grand Dieu, si jamais je l'oublie*". He is a stronger proof of the immortality of the Soul than any that Philosophy has ever produced. A Mind like his can never die.[71]

But then he goes on to make a comparison of this goodness with what he discerns in two other acquaintances, Hugh Logan, and James Mackinlay: 'Let the Wp.full Squire Hugh Logan or Mass James McKindlay, [*sic*] go into their primitive nothing. At best they are but ill digested lumps of Chaos, only one of them strongly tinged with bituminous particles and sulphureous effluvia.' The powerful metaphors Burns uses create an impression of someone primitive, crude and bearing traces of a hellish origin, but because of the ambiguous nature of the language it seems to refer not only to Mackinlay's personality but to his theology, for example not only is Mackinlay ill digested, that is 'hard to take', but so is his theology. Burns clearly puts him into the same category as 'H–ll-mouthing John Russell' [*sic*] whom he has mentioned earlier in the same letter to Dalrymple.

Certainly Mackinlay and Russel were close associates and continued to be so. In 1796 Russel preached a sermon before the Missionary Society of Kilmarnock. When it was published it was Mackinlay, as Secretary, who wrote the preface:

> Kilmarnock, August 18 1796. At a General Meeting of the Missionary Society of this place, resolved unanimously, that the thanks of the Society be given to the Rev Mr Russel for his excellent sermon preached this day before them and that he be requested to permit the same to be printed for the benefit of the Society.[72]

If, as he says, this was an 'excellent sermon', then he is identifying himself with a theology that could happily produce words such as these:

> Adam who was by divine constitution the federal head or representative of all his posterity, being by the influence of Satan, seduced from his allegiance to the great Creator, every one lineally descending from him by ordinary generation is actually involved in the guilt of his first sin and consequently is liable to all the tremendous effects of his ungrateful apostacy.[73]

Sharing such beliefs as Russel's, Mackinlay was an obvious target for Burns, who never could see himself as responsible for Adam's sin. It is clear that Burns's words relating to Mackinlay were not randomly chosen but related to a knowledge of his person and his theology.

Mackinlay himself was an able man and in 1791 wrote the first part of the account of the parish of Kilmarnock for *The Statistical Account*. He gathers statistics on population, church affiliation, birth and death. He enlists the help of 'the most intelligent manufacturers in the town' to draw up an analysis of the moneys raised by them in the different types of manufactures. He writes compassionately of the plight of the poor of the parish and urges greater help be given by the absent landowners. He expresses concern about the number of wine and ale houses in the town, 50, exclusive of spirit shops, besides three or four in the country. This, he claims, must have a pernicious effect upon the morals of the people. Yet showing a loyalty to the people of the community he writes: 'In justice, however to the inhabitants of Kilmarnock ... in general they are as sober and industrious as the people of any town of its size in Scotland.'[74] However, he seems to gloss over the religious controversies in which he has been involved, writing: 'ecclesiastical rancour, has fortunately given place to the milder disportions of forebearance, benevolence and charity'. Mackinlay is not one of the villains of the piece, but nevertheless one weak enough to be carried along unresisting by stronger parties such as Russel and Peebles. In 1810 he was awarded a doctorate by Aberdeen University and died in 1841.[75]

Andrew Mitchell

> Andrew Gowk, Andrew Gowk, ye may slander the BOOK,
> And the BOOK nought the waur, let me tell ye:
> Ye're rich and look big, but lay by hat and wig –
> And ye'll hae a CALF'S-HEAD o' sma' value, &c.[76]

Anecdotal accounts of the Reverend Andrew Mitchell (1725–1811), Minister of Monkton and Prestwick, quoted by Chambers-Wallace and taken up by Maurice Lindsay and James Kinsley, have picked up on Mitchell's 'extreme love of money, and a strange confusion of ideas and language'. Kinsley and Lindsay both quote as evidence of this his once having prayed for '*her* Majesty the Prince of Wales'.[77] This last quote would seem very weak evidence to bring to the charge that Mitchell was a 'Gowk' or a fool. It may not have been that meaning of the word that Burns intended – 'Gowk' was also the common word for a cuckoo, a bird with a reputation for laying its eggs in other birds' nests. Was Andrew Mitchell making use of the Church to nurture his own interests? Burns seems to be criticizing a certain foppishness in referring to 'hat and wig', which may have been worn as an ostentatious display of his riches. He is very much cutting Mitchell down to size by his use of a herdsman's evaluation of a calf's worth by the size of its head. The final criticism is akin to the plucking of the feathers off an exotic bird.

In fairness to Andrew Mitchell, who was awarded a D.D. by Edinburgh University in 1784,[78] his account of the 'Parish of Monktown and Prestwick' in *The Statistical Account* is well written, displaying none of the 'strange confusion of ideas and language' of which he has been accused, and although a careful description of his own stipend is given, there is an equally careful and detailed description of the wages of the tradesmen and day labourers and servants of the Parish that gives no indication of its being the work of a fool. On the contrary it seems a well-balanced account of the parish given by a man who displays an interest in many of its aspects – soil, agriculture, trades, school, wages, history, constitution and church.[79]

That Burns did not deal with Andrew Mitchell in much more than a superficial way is perhaps indicative of a view that the criticisms of Mitchell, who had a reputation for other interests, would have little effect in any case on the issues raised by Dr McGill's book.

Stephen Young

Barr Steenie, Barr Steenie, what mean ye, what mean ye?
If ye'll meddle nae mair wi' the matter,
Ye may hae some pretence, man, to havins and sense, man, –
Wi' people that ken you nae better, &c[80]

This stanza refers to the Reverend Stephen Young (1745–1819), Minister of the Parish of Barr from 1780, prior to which he had been assistant at Ochiltree.[81] Since he had been in the area for some time Burns might have learned something of his character. That Burns seems surprised that he should take part in the process against McGill is hinted at in the advice he gives to him to 'meddle nae mair wi' the matter'. It is as if Burns was of the opinion that Stephen Young did not have any contribution to make to the local religious controversy. Was it because Burns suspected that the minister was much more interested in farming than in religion? An examination of Stephen Young's contribution to *The Statistical Account* would certainly give that impression. Written in 1793 the *Account* reveals the writer as someone who was greatly interested in farming.[82] Young seems to have forgotten that although *The Statistical Account* was intended to enable the government to assess the current state of the country it was also concerned with 'ascertaining the quantum of happiness enjoyed by its inhabitants and the means of its future improvement.'[83] Young's account of the population is entirely statistical, totally devoid of comment as to the well-being or otherwise of the people. He spends three sentences on describing the creation of the parish church and its stipend, one paragraph on a ruin, 'an old Popist chapel', and thereafter the account deals with minerals, climate, agriculture and black cattle, with a concluding section on cheviot sheep to which he devotes no less than four pages.[84]

Young's account makes no assessment of the 'quantum of happiness'. It is devoid of any expression of concern for the people, for example making the statement 'consumptions prevail most in this place', without linking it in any way to the lifestyle or conditions in which people live, or even offering any suggestions as to what might be done to enable them to enjoy better health. 'Barr Steenie' was curtly dismissed by Burns as one who would be better not to meddle with people about whom he knew but little, for if he did he would only be found out.

James Young

> Jamie Goose, Jamie Goose, ye hae made but toom roose
> O' hunting the wicked Lieutenant;
> But the Doctor's your mark, for the L—d's holy ark
> He has couper'd and ca'd a wrang pin in, &c[85]

The Reverend James Young was minister of New Cumnock. As he twice tells us in *The Statistical Account*, 'the present incumbent was settled about 1757'.[86] He had been in the area for a considerable number of years before Burns wrote about him in 1789, and perhaps in the very brief three-page account it shows. In that year he was appointed to serve on the committee that was formed on 15 July to investigate the writings of Dr McGill. The initial meeting of the committee on 11 August 1789 was attended by Dr Auld, Dr Mitchell, Mr Stephen Young, Mr William Peebles, Mr David Grant and Mr James Young, Ministers, and Messrs W. Fisher, R. Wilson, D. Boyd, J. Tannoch, R. Wilson and J. McGeachan, Elders. The known supporters of Dr McGill were deliberately absent on that occasion; although appointed members of the committee, they believed that the procedure adopted by the Presbytery was illegal and so they refused to be part of it. These supporters were Dr Wodrow, Dr Dalrymple, Dr Shaw and Mr Wright. Less is known of the attitudes of the other members who were absent, Mr Thomson and Mr Ramsay, but Mr John Shepherd who was absent at the first meeting took part in the second meeting on 29 September 1789. Dr McGill had sent his letter in protest against the committee proceeding by means of a bearer who read it out, but the committee still went ahead under its convener Reverend David Grant. It was no doubt assisted by the presence of James Young (Jamie Goose) who at the time was also Moderator of the Presbytery.[87]

The stanza shows that Burns was not just well aware of the local gossip in his reference to the 'toom roose', the bad bargain Young had made with 'the Lieutenant' whom he had unsuccessfully attempted to prosecute at the church courts, but that he was aware of Young's background as the son of a cooper.[88] This stanza is further evidence that the words Burns used in connection with the Ministers who appear in 'The Kirk's Alarm', were well chosen and reveal a more than passing acquaintance with the people concerned.

George Smith

> Cessnock side, Cessnock side, wi' your turkey-cock pride,
> O' manhood but sma' is your share
> Ye've the figure, it's true, even your faes maun allow,
> And your friends dare na say ye hae mair, &c.[89]

This is a puzzling inclusion in a poem that started out as an attack upon those who were pursuing Dr McGill for his alleged heresy. George Smith, minister of Galston, being from the neigbouring Presbytery of Kilmarnock was not involved in the inquiry set up by the Presbytery of Ayr.[90] He had featured already in two of Burns's poems. In 'The Holy Tulzie' he is referred to as one of the 'Turn-coats', the word being used in this instance to refer to one who had been orthodox but who had turned in favour of the moderates like Dalrymple and McGill.[91] In 'The Holy Fair' Smith is referred to in terms that could be construed as criticism. Whilst Burns is adopting the voice of the observer of the scene, an element of personal criticism seems to enter when he describes the style of the preacher:

> ***** opens out his cauld harangues,
> on *practice* and on *morals*;
> An' aff the godly pour in thrangs,
> To gie the jars an' barrels
> A lift that day.
>
> What signifies his barren shine,
> of *moral pow'rs*, an' *reason*;
> His English style, an' gesture fine,
> Are a' clean out o' season.
> Like SOCRATES or ANTONINE,
> Or some auld pagan heathen,
> The *moral man* he does define
> But ne'er a word o' *faith* in
> That's right that day.[92]

Burns has italicized the words 'practice', 'morals', 'moral pow'rs', 'reason', 'moral man' and 'faith' to emphasize the thrust of Smith's sermon. But running through it all there is evidence of a personal contempt for the manner in which Smith presented himself to the audience. The italicizing of the words almost allows us to hear the emphatic manner of the preacher, and it was one that Burns more forthrightly criticized in 'The Kirk's Alarm' where he sums it up as 'turkey-cock pride'.

No immediate incident is referred to in the stanza referring to Smith and it would appear that he just came to Burns's mind as one who might well join the critics of McGill perhaps because of the proud and judgemental stance that he adopted. In *The Statistical Account* of 1791 Smith concludes his account of the parish:

> the inhabitants of Galston are, in general sober industrious and charitable to the distressed. It is to be regretted, however, that instead of the wholesome beverage of ale, they are now compelled by the high duties on that article, to betake themselves to the use of whisky, which is equally destructive to the health, and to the morals of the people.[93]

These words show a readiness to make a judgement and perhaps not a very balanced judgement at that, and perhaps that was what Burns had in earlier years detected in George Smith.

John Shepherd

> Muirland Jock, Muirland Jock, whom the L—d made a rock
> To crush Common sense for her sins;
> If ill-manners were Wit, there's no mortal so fit
> To confound the poor Doctor at ance, &c.[94]

The Reverend John Shepherd (1741–99) was inducted to the moorland parish of Muirkirk in 1775. According to Chambers-Wallace he had 'an unfortunate habit of saying rude things, which he mistook for wit'.[95] An examination of Shepherd's account of the parish in *The Statistical Account* does seem to indicate that Burns's judgement was well founded, in that in the course of this account Shepherd displays his wit several times. Talking of local poachers who use nets, he writes: '[they] at once pillage the rivers and destroy the more moderate sport of the *angler*, who seldom fails to pour forth blessings liberally on them, as he returns home with his basket much lighter than usual.'[96] He relates a humorous anecdote in a description of the bird life of the area. An Englishman asks a visiting Scotsman what he thinks of the nightingale to whose song he has been listening. The Scotsman replies, 'It's a' very gude, But I wadna gie the wheeple of a whaup for a' the nightingales that ever sang.' His humour intrudes into an account of the glebe:

> In many places it is wet and in others runs into the opposite extreme being light and gravelly. Draining has been attempted for the former and in many places with success. Indeed this mode never almost misses [*sic*] its aim, for it seldom fails to drain either the ground or the pocket.

His humour too could be of the grim variety. After telling of the martyrdom of a covenanter of the parish, John Brown, he writes ironically: 'Such are the blessed effects of enforcing or attempting to enforce uniformity in religion.'

Perhaps Muirland Jock's only fault was that in trying to be funny he more often than not put his foot in it. Even from an examination of this one piece of his writing, it can be seen how an infelicity or clumsiness of style or the occasional choosing of an inappropriate word might have given him a reputation for rudeness. One example of this has already been noted in the phrase 'never almost misses its aim'. Another is to be found in Shepherd's account of the poor.

> None of the poor are allowed to stroll into other parishes ... and there is seldom an instance of one begging within the bounds of the parish itself, yet the country in general, and this parish in particular is much visited or rather infested by strolling poor from other quarters.

He sees the problem caused by the cities banishing the poor from their bounds and concludes: 'Because the worthless behave ill in one part of the kingdom seems no good reason for sending them over the country at large and allowing them a wider range for their depredations.' In that passage the use of the words 'stroll', 'strolling poor', 'infested', 'the worthless' and 'depredations' could be legitimate causes for offence.

The insensitivity of the man is clear, and if he could write like that for the formal purpose of *The Statistical Account* it is reasonable to surmise that his other pronouncements on more informal occasions would be even more likely to give offence. Burns again has picked up on the characteristics of the person about whom he is writing and deems him to be one who would be an ideal instrument with which 'to crush Common sense'.

William Auld

Daddie Auld, Daddie Auld, there's a tod i' the fauld,
A tod meikle waur than the CLERK:

> Tho' ye do little skaith, ye'll be in at the death,
> For if ye canna bite ye can bark, &c.[97]

When Burns moved from Lochlie to Mossgiel in March 1784, he came to live in the parish of Mauchline where the Reverend William Auld (1709–91) had been minister since 1742 and would go on to hold that office until his death on 12 December 1791.[98]

Auld was one of the Auld Lights, a strict Calvinist, yet despite the severity of some of his judgements there seems to have been an element within his nature that held him back from applying the full rigour of the law, as Burns's first recorded personal encounter with him on the matter of Jean Armour's pregnancy reveals.[99]

Auld, for all that he had remained in a rural parish all his ordained ministry among a people whose lives were largely restricted by lack of education, was very well qualified academically. After graduating in Arts at the University of Edinburgh in 1733, he had gone on to theological studies at the Universities of Glasgow and Leyden.[100] It is possible that Auld's breadth of experience both at home and at Leyden might have been a factor that softened his attitude to Burns and Jean.

Auld betrayed a similar reluctance to assert his rights to the full in the latter stages of the case of alleged contumacy against Gavin Hamilton. On 19 September 1787 the Presbytery of Ayr failed to uphold the Mauchline Kirk Session's censure of Hamilton, and Mr Auld appealed to the Synod of Glasgow and Ayr. But at the next meeting of the Presbytery it was reported that Mr Auld's appeal on behalf of the Kirk Session had not been pursued. Auld, although making his protest, had not followed it up with the action that would have left his resolution unquestioned.[101]

Burns again reveals in his stanza on Auld a personal knowledge of the character of the person of whom he is writing. He describes Auld as someone whose bark is worse than his bite, and as one who by long years of applying the discipline of the Church automatically begins its process, but who does not any longer have the will to see it through to the very end. Burns's words are softened by the epithet 'Daddie'. In this there is an underlying affection and respect being expressed, especially when it is remembered that Auld remained unmarried all his life. A certain playfulness is here in this portrayal of a fatherly old man who has spent a lifetime expressing a father's concern for the people of his parish, who even now that he is toothless still has the power to bark a warning to those whom he wants to save. Burns does not see Auld as a threat to the 'tod i' the fauld' (McGill) who is much more to be worried about than 'the CLERK' (Gavin Hamilton), but nevertheless like the old toothless watchdog, he (Auld) will be in at the death gathering around the quarry.[102]

David Grant

Davie Rant, Davie Rant, wi' a face like a saunt,
And a heart that wad poison a hog;
Raise an impudent roar, like a breaker lee-shore,
Or the Kirk will be tint in a bog, &c.[103]

The Reverend David Grant (1750–91) was only translated from Ettrick to Ochiltree the estate owned by the Countess of Glencairn in 1786,[104] yet Burns claimed to know him well, for in his letter to Lady Elizabeth Cunningham enclosing 'The Kirk's Alarm' he writes, 'You must not read Lady Glencairn the stanza about the Priest of Ochiltree – Though I know him to be a designing rotten-hearted Puritan. Yet perhaps her Ladyship has a different idea of him.'[105]

It is quite clear from the manuscript variations quoted by Kinsley that Burns had a very low opinion of Grant:

Davie Bluster, Davie Bluster, for a Saunt if ye muster,
It's a sign they're no' nice o' RECRUITS:
Yet to WORTH let's be just, Royal blood ye might boast,
If the Ass were the king o' the BRUTES, &c.[106]

or, as another version has it:

Pauky Clark to George Gordon – gi'e the Doctor a Cord-on,
And to grape for witch marks – gi'e it o'er;
If ye pass for a Saint, it's a sign we maun grant,
That there's a few gentlemen i' the cor'.

David Grant was appointed convener of the committee set up by the Presbytery of Ayr on 15 July 1789, 'to enquire whether there be anything in Dr McGill's publications erroneous or inconsistent with the purity of the doctrines and the authority of the standards of this church.'[107] Almost certainly this would have been with the help of William Peebles, the prime mover of the case against McGill, who would have been out to ensure that the committee would be convened by someone sympathetic to his (Peebles's) own opinion.[108] Grant would be known by Burns as one who would be likely to be in opposition to McGill, if Grant's previous activities were anything to go by.

On 7 December 1778 a 'Rev Mr David Grant was appointed to serve on the 'Committee of Correspondence', formed in Edinburgh. This committee was appointed at a public meeting and was charged with keeping a watching brief on the Government's intentions to try to pass a bill equivalent to the English bill that had been passed earlier that year, which gave greater freedom to

Roman Catholics in England. That it is the same David Grant is very likely, as immediately after recording the election of the committee it is noted that 'The Right Honourable Lord George Gordon was afterwards elected a member of the Committee'.[109] Burns's description of Grant as 'Clark to George Gordon' is now seen to have a much greater connection with reality than has been ascribed to it by Kinsley, who sees it as 'apparently a satiric association of Grant, who came from the north-east, with Lord George Gordon, the mad anti-papist who was behind the protestant riots of 1780.'[110] It is quite possible that Grant became secretary of the committee that was virtually headed up by Gordon.

Grant's extreme views on Roman Catholics were probably well known to Burns, who could not have avoided hearing of the 'No Popery' disturbances in Edinburgh in 1778. Richard B. Sher asserts that these were 'the model for the Gordon Riots that ravaged London in June 1780', news of which spread throughout the United Kingdom.[111] Far from being mere gratuitous abuse, Burns's words attacking the character of David Grant are based on his knowledge of the person and the activities in which he engaged.

Alexander Moodie

> Singet Sawnie, Singet Sawnie, are ye herding the PENNIE,
> Unconscious what danger awaits?
> With a jump, yell and howl, alarm ev'ry soul,
> For Hannibal's just at your gates, &c[112]

This stanza relates to the Reverend Alexander Moodie, Minister of Riccarton, a village outside Kilmarnock. Burns had previously dealt at some length with Moodie in 'The Holy Tulzie' and in 'The Holy Fair'. On both occasions he adopted a tone of mockery. In 'The Holy Tulzie' he expresses shock that two ministers, Moodie and Russel, cast in the same theological mould should disagree:

> Sic twa— O, do I live to see 't,
> Sic famous twa, sud disagree 't!
> And names like, 'Villain, Hypocrite',
> Each other giein;
> While enemies wi' laughin spite
> Say, 'Neither's liein'.[113]

In 'The Holy Fair' Burns casts Moodie in the role of the hellfire and damnation preacher:

Now a' the congregation o'er,
Is silent expectation;
For ****** speels the holy door,
Wi' tidings o' d–mn–t—–n:[114]

But Burns does not just mock his theology, he mocks his appearance that seems to be as dark and threatening as the hellfire he preaches:

Should *Hornie*, as in ancient days,
'Mang sons o' G—present him,
The vera sight o' ******'s face,
To's ain *het hame* had sent him,
Wi' fright that day.

The stanza in 'The Kirk's Alarm' seems to hark back to the idea of hellfire with the nickname 'Singet', which can mean 'singed' or 'shrivelled'. Alexander too is reduced to 'Sawnie', not the name of a conqueror but one of the commonest Scottish names. There seems to be a hint that Moodie was fond of looking after his money and that he was so preoccupied by that pastime that he was unaware of the threatening 'Hannibal' (McGill) that was at the gates. Burns seems to content himself with these comments as if he had already told his readers enough about Moodie, or perhaps because any mention of Moodie would make people almost automatically expect him to be one of those opposed to the writings of McGill. For whatever reasons, the stanza is lacking in any new insight into the character of Moodie, unless there is substance in Burns's charge of his being more interested in money than anything else, but for this I can find no positive evidence. However an examination of *The Statistical Account* written by Moodie in 1791 reveals someone who hardly seems to offer any strong opinion in any of the matters relating to the parish. It is a very bland account for someone who had the reputation of being a fiery creature. He permits himself this comment on the poor: 'The poor in this parish are, at present, but slenderly supported. Almost the only fund for maintaining them arises from the voluntary contributions of the people at church.'[115] There is no passion in evidence, no expression of concern. Yet when the figures are given they reveal that the church collections for the poor yield only £24 per annum and that this has to be shared among 15 people; so the poor were expected to survive on £1 12/- per annum or about 8d a week. A comparison with the payment to the poor at Mauchline at that same time shows that Mauchline's poor received a distribution of 2/- a week to such as are unable to work, and 3/- to such as are confined to bed.[116] Moodie was not apparently concerned with other people's lack of money. Was Burns hinting that he was more concerned with his own?

John Russel

Rumble John, Rumble John, mount the steps with a groan,
Cry, the Book is with heresy cramm'd;
Then lug out your ladle, deal brimstone like aidle,
And roar ev'ry note o' the D–MN'D, &c.[117]

In this reference to the Reverend John Russel of Kilmarnock Burns emphasizes the serious demeanour of Russel. I detect the words of an observer, not a poet looking for a rhyme. Russel was, as some preachers are, burdened and almost overburdened with the weight of the message that they feel called to bear. As he climbs the pulpit steps he groans at the task he has to perform, but once there, like the thunder that has been rumbling in the distance, his voice breaks out with the cry, 'the Book is with heresy cramm'd'. From his opening nickname 'Rumble John' Burns makes every word add to the picture. Russel is pictured as violently dishing out his message of hellish substance but Burns even pokes fun at that, reductive as ever, likening the brimstone to cattle's urine. Russel's loudness is stressed both by the use of the word 'roar' and by the capital letters used for the final word 'D–MN'D'.

Along with William Peebles, John Russel was probably one of Burns's main targets in this poem. Russel was the first to openly preach against Dr McGill's book[118] and was a close associate of William Peebles. This was signalled early by Peebles's invitation to Russel to preach both at the Evening Service and the Thanksgiving Service at the first Communion Season in the newly established parish church at Newton upon Ayr at the beginning of Peebles's ministry there. Assisting Mr Russel that day was his later opponent in 'The Holy Tulzie', Alexander Moodie. By a strange double irony the first preacher appointed by the Presbytery to preach at Peebles's admission service was Dr Dalrymple, and the preacher who began the first Communion Season at the Day of Fasting and Humiliation was Dr William McGill. Also taking part in the service that day was the Reverend William Auld of Mauchline.[119] These facts should remind us of how well known to each other were the protagonists and allies in this relatively small community of Ayr that provides a microcosm of the theological and ecclesiastical conflicts of the period.

Even at a distance of two centuries it is difficult to remain objective in a critique of the theological writings of John Russel, minister of the High Kirk parish, Kilmarnock, from 1774 to 1800 and an ardent participant in what Burns described as 'controversial divinity'.[120] He features in 'The Holy Tulzie', 'The Holy Fair', 'The Ordination' and 'The Kirk's Alarm'.[121] While in Burns's letters there are oblique allusions to him as one of the group of ministers engaged in heresy hunting, there is one very specific and dismissive reference in a letter of February 1787 to James Dalrymple of Orangefield. Burns lightheartedly telling of his 'foreboding ideas', envisages the granting of 'St Peter's keys to the h–ll–mouthing John Russell [*sic*]'.[122]

Russel was a firm believer in the Doctrine of Original Sin, which declared that all mankind had been affected by Adam's sin, and he writes with a supreme confidence and a fearless logic:

> Adam who was by divine constitution the federal head or representative of all his posterity, being by the influence of Satan seduced from his allegiance to the great Creator, every one, lineally descending from him by ordinary generation is actually involved in the guilt of his first sin, and consequently liable to all the tremendous affects of his ungrateful apostacy.[123]

In holding to such beliefs he was no different from many of his Calvinist colleagues of the Auld Light persuasion, but it is in the conclusion that follows this statement that something of the attitude and the character of Russel is revealed and with it the reasons for Burns's criticism of him: 'This is the fundamental principle upon which divine revelation proceeds and therefore the secret or open disavowal of it must have a direct tendency to lead men into the gloomy regions of infedility [*sic*].'[124] Hugely confident that he has discovered the 'fundamental principle upon which divine revelation proceeds', Russel sees those who do not accept that principle as those who will lead others astray, and notice they will do this even if they hold these views in secret.

This sort of all-embracing conclusion is arrived at by the faulty, although not intentionally dishonest, exegetical method of making the biblical text suit the theological premise, for example he asserts without any apparent reason that the first people to hear the Gospel were Adam and Eve and says that the one who preached to them was Jesus. He tries to gain credence for this by saying: 'It hath been conceived by earnest and judicious divines that the illustrious preacher on this occasion was God the Son.'[125] He carefully avoids telling his audience who the 'earnest and judicious divines' were. No one taking a common-sense view of the story of Genesis could possibly come to the conclusion that the words spoken to Adam and Eve were spoken by the pre-existent Jesus, the Son of God. Here is a clear case of the theological premise determining the exegesis. Again as an ardent believer in the substitutionary theory of the atonement, he latches on to the legal phrase 'in the room of'[126] and applies it to the action of Jesus in standing in place of the sinner, that is *instead* of the sinner, 'dying for' not 'dying on account of' us as McGill preferred to say and was accused of heresy for so saying.[127]

Russel is not always honest in his use of biblical texts. He quotes from Psalm 40:7–8 putting these words into the mouth of Jesus: 'Then, said I, lo I come: I delight to do thy will yea thy law', but then he interjects his own words, 'to be fulfilled in the room of my people', before completing the quote from the Psalm with the words, 'is within my heart'.[128] By interjecting his own words, thereby splitting the quotation, Russel is not being entirely honest. It is unlikely that a listening congregation would be able to discern that only part of the sentence was from the Bible, while the rest and loaded part of it was the preacher's. This phrase, beloved by Russel, is used again in the subsequent section to pad out and to slant the scriptural text towards the substitutionary theory of the atonement.

If there is a doctrine at stake Russel is none too particular in how he uses scripture, for example he believed in the doctrine of Election whereby God had elected that some should be saved (we will not go into the corollary of that in the meantime). His use of scripture in support of that doctrine is just that, usage, to suit the purpose of promoting a pet doctrine at every opportunity. Russel takes the incident from the Gospel according to Luke where it is recorded that Jesus was taken outside the city to be executed, adds to it with a text from Hebrews that Jesus, 'suffered without the gate' and uses both to support his claim that Jesus' death was for those outside Jerusalem (that is, outside the Jewish nation).[129] But instead of drawing the conclusion (if any could be drawn) that this was an indication that Jesus died for all, not just those enclosed within a religious group, he says: 'It was not his (Jesus Christ) intention to confine the inestimable blessings of his death unto the Jews but to extend them to all *elect* sinners.'[130] He never misses a trick! But in this instance we have a clear example of a theological premise determining the scriptural exegesis.

The least attractive side of Russel emerges when he begins to talk of people, and especially his fellow ministers. When talking to his congregation he takes refuge behind the mystery of the incomprehensible, by implication, indicating that inferior minds must submit to superior ones (like his?). 'The more sublime and mysterious the truths are, the more are they fitted by the unsearchable wisdom of God for promoting holiness in the souls of true believers.'[131] In other words, even if you cannot understand it, it will do your soul good. But he then uses this to go on to conclude that those who oppose such doctrines as 'speculative opinions' are deeply ignorant, for he says: 'There is no speculative opinion in Christianity. Every doctrine, even that which rises most above the comprehension of finite minds hath *a practical tendency* and is found in fact to produce the *most glorious effects* on the souls of those who *cordially* embrace it.'[132] Note the copious use of italics. It reminds me of the anecdote from George McLeod of the preacher who used to mark in the margin of his sermons 'shout here, argument weak'.

Russel's own nature is revealed in a passage in which he asserts that it is not uncharitable to condemn heretics. He links heresy with immorality, speaking of it as if the one led to the other, or at least as if the one was as bad as the other. He writes: 'For false doctrine is as really fatal to the soul as poison is to the body. Let no man insinuate that it is highly uncharitable not to entertain favourable sentiments of those who avow a different belief of the *peculiar doctrines* of the gospel.' He says that the word charity is used in the Bible only when it describes love to God as Father, Son or Holy Spirit, and it is urged to be given only to those 'who are members of Christ's spiritual body and our brethren in the faith'.[133] He chooses to ignore Jesus's injunction 'love your enemies' and Paul's great discourse on love in I Corinthians 13 where he is quite unspecific as to those to whom such love is to be directed.

Russel's sermon concludes with the assertion that it is the combination of the lack of sound principles and exemplary lives that has 'contributed exceedingly to the progress of that infidelity and immorality which now threatens to inundate our land'.[134] These are the attitudes that prevailed among some of the Auld Light ministers in the Ayrshire of Burns's time. The sermon from which I have been quoting was preached on 18 August 1796, that is, within a month of the poet's death. But Russel had been criticized by Burns for these attitudes long before that, and features adversely in several poems from 1785 onwards.

On the 17 July 1789 Burns wrote to Mrs Dunlop: 'You will be well acquainted with the persecutions that my worthy friend, Dr Mcgill, [*sic*] is undergoing among your Divines. Several of these reverend lads, his opponents, have come thro' my hands before; but I have some thoughts of serving them up again in a different dish.'[135] John Russel was one of these 'reverend lads' and Burns had referred to him some five years before in 'The Holy Tulzie', which had been written about a parish border dispute between Russel and the Reverend Alexander Moodie of Riccarton, which had deteriorated into a slanging match in Presbytery. Both were of the Auld Light faction and Burns obviously relished having a go at them:

O Moodie, man an wordy Russel,
How could you breed sae vile a bustle?

Concentrating on Russel, Burns writes:

And wha like Russel tell'd his tale;
His voice was heard o'er moor and dale:
He kend the L—d's sheep, ilka tail,
O'er a' the height;
And tell'd gin they were sick or hale
At the first sight.

He fine a maingie sheep could scrub,
Or nobly swing the Gospel-club;
Or New-Light herds could nicely drub,
And pay their skin;
Or hing them o'er the burning dub,
Or shute them in.[136]

In this first judgement of Russel, Burns sees him as long winded, loud mouthed, quick in judgement from appearances, anxious to keep his flock scrupulously clean even if he had to seize them violently to do it, one who was willing to strike out in the name of the Gospel and who was not averse to mud slinging or of exacting his pound of flesh even to the point of torture or of finally consigning his opponents to hell.

If Russel the Pastor had featured in 'The Holy Tulzie', it is Russel the Preacher who is portrayed in 'The Holy Fair':

But now the L—'s ain trumpet touts.
Till a' the hills are rairan,
An' echos back return the shouts,
Black******'s na spairan:
His piercin words, like highlan swords,
Divide the joints an' marrow;
His talk o' H–ll, whare devils dwell,
Our vera 'Sauls does harrow'
Wi' fright that day.[137]

Burns gives us an impression of a proud, confident, self-assured man whose preaching style relies on shouting and loudly haranguing his audience. This reference to his appearance and style ties in with a description given by Hugh Miller, the geologist and writer, who was one of Russel's pupils at Cromarty: 'a large robust, dark complexioned man – imperturbably grave and with a sullen expression seated in the deep folds of his forehead.'[138]

But if Burns paints an accurate physical picture by the deft use of words he also conveys the theological stance in an equally skilful way. One of the theological controversies of the earlier part of the eighteenth century had centred on an old Puritan book first published in 1646 and reprinted in 1718, *The Marrow of Modern Divinity* by Edward Fisher of Oxford. Thomas Boston of Ettrick was one of its defenders, but in 1720 the General Assembly of the Church of Scotland forbade ministers to use or commend the book and enjoined them to warn their parishioners against it.[139] It was said to contain heresies and in particular to encourage an antinomian stance. This heresy was attached to the strongly held belief that some were of the elect regardless of their conduct, that because they were of the elect they would be saved regardless of whether they continued to sin. In using the word 'marrow' Burns is hinting that Russel's theology bordered on Antinomianism, which was the heresy into which those who were so secure in their faith and in their own salvation could easily fall.

In 'The Ordination' it is Russel's lack of common sense that comes in for criticism:

Curst Common-sense, that imp o' h–ll,
Cam in wi Maggie Lauder;
But O******* aft made her yell,
An R***** sair misca'd her.[140]

Burns found it hard to understand how quite well-educated men could leave aside their common sense out of respect for the authority of the Bible. According to Burns, not only did Russel not apply his common sense, but he even abused those who did.

It was this very issue of the lack of common sense in dealing with the Bible that was one of the main reasons for Burns entering into the defence of Dr McGill in the summer of 1789. He wrote to Mr Robert Graham of Fintry on 9 December of that year:

> You must have heard of Dr Mcgill ... and his heretical book – God help him poor man! though he is one of the worthiest as well as one of the ablest in the whole priesthood of the Kirk of Scotland ... yet for the blasphemous heresies of squaring Religion by the rules of Common Sense, and attempting to give a decent character to Almighty God and a rational account of his proceedings with the Sons of Men, the poor Doctor and his numerous family are in imminent danger of being thrown to the mercy of the winter winds. The inclosed Ballad (The Kirk's Alarm) on that business is I confess too local, but I laughed at some conceits in it myself though I am convinced in my conscience that there are several heavy stanzas in it too.[141]

The first one certainly is:

ORTHODOX, ORTHODOX, who believe in John Knox,
Let me sound an alarm to your conscience;
A heretic blast has been blawn i' the West –
That what is not Sense must be Nonsense, Orthodox,
That what is not Sense must be Nonsense. –[142]

Burns saw McGill accused of heresy for speaking truthfully and in a common-sense way about the Bible. Russel had been one of those who had attempted to have Dr McGill tried for heresy because of his book *A Practical Essay on the Death of Christ*, published in 1786. But, according to Burns, what to Russel was heresy was to others common sense. Undoubtedly, as far as Burns is concerned, Russel fits into the category once described in a letter of 24 November 1787 to Mrs Dunlop, 'I ever could ill endure those surly cubs of "Chaos and old Night"; these ghostly beasts of prey, who foul the hallow'd ground of Religion with their nocturnal prowlings.'[143] Burns went on to promise that if they tried to harm his 'learned and truly worthy friend, Dr McGill' he would, 'fly at them with the faulcons of Ridicule, or run them down with the bloodhounds of Satire as lawful game'. As far as Russel is concerned he certainly did just that.

Chapter 10

Poems Reflecting the Recurrent Themes of a Benevolent God, Life After Death and Accountability

'A Prayer in Prospect of Death'[1]

In this very early poem, noted in Burns's *First Commonplace Book* as having been composed in August 1784, Burns's belief in a benevolent God seems to be something that the poet wishes to use to his own advantage. The model for this poem is Alexander Pope's 'The Universal Prayer', which begins with the assertion that God is good and that man has been created with an understanding of this. Pope writes:

Thou Great First Cause, least understood:
Who all my Sense confin'd
To know but this, that Thou art Good,
And that myself am blind,[2]

Pope goes on to portray man as having been created by this God, bound by his human nature, yet allowed to be free to assert his will. He writes of this paradox of determination by nature yet freedom of the will:

Yet give me in this dark Estate,
To see the Good from Ill;
And binding Nature fast in Fate,
Left free the Human Will.

Then, according to Warburton, Pope's literary executor, in a stanza that originally had been written to follow, Pope continues:

Can sins of moments claim the rod
Of everlasting fires?
And that offend great Nature's God
Which Nature's self inspires?

Burns clearly reflects Pope's themes in 'A Prayer in Prospect of Death':

Thou unknown, Almighty Cause
Of all my hope and fear!
In whose dread Presence, ere an hour,
Perhaps I must appear!

then goes on to assert that this God has created him with a nature that is bound to lead to trouble:

Thou know'st that Thou hast formed me,
With Passions wild and strong;
And list'ning to their witching
Has often led me wrong.

Burns, with almost indecent haste, then makes excuses for his human weakness and frailty, seeming almost to blame God because of the nature that he had bestowed upon him. It is as if in this poem Burns is adopting the attitude that he so mocks in the later 'Holy Willie's Prayer'.[3] There seems to be a naivety or a trotting out of the conventional complacencies or platitudes that is different from his later reflections on the same subject. This would of course be in keeping with what we have already charted of the development of his thought.

The poem ends rather abjectly with a stanza in which, even although the subject admits his intention to do wrong, he relies on his knowledge of God as good and who delights to forgive as the thing that will save him. The attitude displayed by the poet here is a kind of perversion of Antinomianism. It is as if this belief in the benevolence of God allows the subject to think that because of his goodness God has no option but to forgive. As a later cynic, sure of his forgiveness, was to exclaim, *'C'est son métier!'*[4]

It could be said that there is something unhealthy in this first poetic expression of Burns's belief in a benevolent God. Kinsley notes that although the poem is dated by the *First Commonplace Book* entry of 1784, it is more likely that it stems from the period in Irvine, when the young Burns was very despondent at the lack of success in the flax manufacturing business, and on 27 December 1781 had written to his father, 'the weakness of my nerves has so debilitated my mind'.[5] The poem might well have been an expression of a young man, under the stress of a depressing period in his life, trying to reconcile his conflicting beliefs. On the one hand he has been led to accept that God is his creator, yet God has given him a nature that leads him on to do what he knows to be wrong. Therefore, the young man reasoned, if God had known what he was doing, knowing that it would lead to wrong-doing, then he must also be prepared to forgive that wrong-doing.

In this poem we see all three of the recurring themes that I have previously identified in Burns's religious thinking: a belief in a benevolent God, a speculation on an existence beyond the grave and an acknowledgement of his own accountablity. Two of these are warring with each other: a benevolent God and the inescapable sense of accountability. Burns will return to this theme, and indeed to Pope's same verses on other occasions, as we shall later see. In this first attempt at sorting out these potentially conflicting beliefs about God and his own human nature, Burns does not quite manage to resolve the problem, and the resulting poem has a lameness about it, as if the poet was ill at ease with the conclusions to which he has come.

Another two poems from that same period, 'Stanzas on the same Occasion' and 'A Prayer, Under the Pressure of violent Anguish', reinforce the impression of a person living in a depressed state, not seeing much in life as it has hitherto been experienced or in its prospects as they present themselves to have any hope of enjoying it. The poet is pessimistic of his own ability to escape the round of wrong-doing that will prevent him from acting in such a way as to, 'exalt the rule and sink the man', nevertheless he makes a plea to God for mercy, even if it comes from one, 'Who sin so oft have mourn'd, yet to temptation ran?' Yet even the first verse of 'Stanzas' speaks of God's benevolence, if in a wistful way. Although the poet's actions are in direct opposition to, and undeserving of it, he says: 'Then how should I for Heavenly Mercy pray, / Who act so counter Heavenly Mercy's plan?'[6]

Here in this poem, a very tentative belief in the benevolence of God begins to come through by the third verse. But it is held to by a very uncertain faith, and set against it are an almost overwhelming dread of the consequences of a life in which 'furious passions' seem to rule and a fear of what might lie beyond in 'Death's unlovely, dreary, dark abode'. The God of this poem is not a loving, caring being, but more the mechanical 'Great Governor' and impersonal 'Omnipotence Divine' of the Deists. The plea for help is to a power not to a person, and it is made by someone who seems sceptical of being able to be helped. But the impersonal manner of addressing God is perhaps indicative of a state of mind that feels the isolation of a world in which nobody seems to care.

'A Prayer, Under the Pressure of violent Anguish' addresses God in a more personal way, and yet acknowledges that God is beyond human understanding: 'Thou great Being! what Thou art, / Surpasses me to know'.[7] Yet the poet feels sure that although he does not know God, God knows him as his creature. In the third verse, the lines from Pope's 'The Universal Prayer':

Can sins of moments claim the rod
Of everlasting fires?
And that offend great Nature's God
Which Nature's self inspires?[8]

again come to mind when Burns writes: 'Sure Thou, Almighty, canst not act / From cruelty or wrath!'[9] This conviction of the goodness of God being sufficient to cope with the unruliness of man comes through to the comfort of the poet. And at the end of the poem there is at least a resignation to rest on the providence of a God who is of greater benevolence than can be conceived by the meaner minds of men.

These early poems reveal a poet struggling to break through the restricting walls of his earliest beliefs, gained in an environment much influenced by Calvinist theology. The poem that is generally known by the title 'Remorse' is dated by the *First Commonplace Book* as having been written in September 1783. Burns had been impressed by Adam Smith's *The Theory of Moral Sentiments,* which he had read in an edition owned by his father. In a preface to the poem he alludes to 'that judicious Philosopher Mr. Smith'.[10] Smith had written, 'Such is the nature of that sentiment which is properly called remorse; of all the sentiments which can enter the human heart the most dreadful.'[11] Burns's opening lines parallel those of Smith, and later in the poem he muses on the effect of remorse, the inescapable sense of responsibility for the wrong we have done. But Burns probes the wound even further, alleging that even after an attempt has been made to make recompense for the offence, the one who has caused the hurt still cannot rest easy:

> Lives there a man so firm who, while his heart
> Feels all the bitter horrors of his crime,
> Can reason down its agonizing throbs,
> And, after proper purpose of amendment,
> Can firmly force his jarring thoughts to peace?

The poetry may be melodramatic, but there is no mistaking the experiental language. Here is someone tortured by a sense of being accountable. He does not project a judge, either human or eternal, but leaves the reader with a sense of a mind that cannot be at peace. 'Remorse' signals that for Burns, at this time in his life, there can be no squaring of the accounts. He will be forever held responsible for his actions. The poem does not offer any balm for a hurt mind. It does not let the poet off the hook and leaves the reader sharing his anguish. It displays the darker side of Burns's beliefs, at least at this stage of his life. For him there is no 'cheap grace', no easy acceptance of the efficacy of repentance and no escape from conscience. Ultimately, he is a responsible creature.

'Address to the Unco Guid, or the Rigidly Righteous'[12]

The epigraph to the poem takes up the theme of Ecclesiastes 7:16, which in the King James Bible reads: 'Be not righteous overmuch; neither make thyself over wise: why shouldest thou destroy thyself?' Burns not only refers us to this text as a preface to the poem, but as it develops he clearly demonstrates that he has not only grasped the text, but that he is aware of the whole thrust of the chapter. The worldly-wise writer of Ecclesiastes writes in verse ten, 'Be not hasty in thy spirit to be angry: for anger resteth only in the bosom of fools', and this is taken up by Burns. There is a measured, temperate tone being exercised by the poet as he advises a compassionate understanding of human conduct. He augments the counsel of Ecclesiastes with a pleading for the ethic derived from the words of Jesus as they are found in St Matthew's Gospel 7:1, 'Judge not that ye be not judged' and the ensuing parable that culminates with the words, 'Thou hypocrite, first cast out the beam out of your own eye; and then thou shalt see clearly to cast out the mote out of your brother's eye.' In this poem Burns is pleading for a non-judgemental attitude towards those who 'gang a kennin wrang'. He makes the point that it is likely that righteousness and wrong-doing are products of circumstances more than anything else. In his *First Commonplace Book* in March 1784 he had written:

> Let any of the strictest character for regularity of conduct among us, examine impartially how many of his virtues are owing to constitution and education; how many vices he has never been guilty of, not from any care or vigilance, but from want of opportunity, or some accidental circumstance intervening; how many of the weaknesses of mankind he has escaped because he was out of the line of such temptation; and what often, if not always, weighs more than all the rest; how much he is indebted to the world's good, because the world does not know all; I say, any man who can thus think, will scan the failings, nay the faults and crimes of mankind around him, with a brother's eye.[13]

In the poem Burns suggests that as those who are quick to offer condemnation had better be more circumspect, as given similar circumstances to those whom they condemn they might well have found themselves acting similarly. At the end of the day, the judgement is best left to the God who is the creator, who knows the inner workings of mankind and who sees the whole picture. Underlying Burns's words is a belief in a God who is at least sufficiently benevolent to take everything into account – even the things that have been resisted – before coming to a judgement. The impression is left that God is likely to be more forgiving than those who have rushed to the judgement of their fellow men and women. Again, there is a sense conveyed that there will indeed be an accounting, a balancing exercise at the end of life as we know it, and a hint that there might be eternal consequences of what we do in the here and now. But the poet still manages to convey that there is hope for those,' … poor mortals / That frequent pass douce Wisdom's door / For glaikit Folly's portals'[14] and that the compassionate attitude that he displays within the poem is a reflection of the kind of judgement that will be made by a benevolent God.

Burns's ethical attitude within the poem bears traces not just of the attitudes of Ecclesiastes and Jesus, but of the sentiments he imbibed from the works of Adam Smith and Alexander Pope, who between them may well have provided models from which he built the concluding stanzas of his 'Address to the Unco Guid, or the Rigidly Righteous'. Adam Smith, in *The Theory of Moral Sentiments*, writes of God and Judgement: 'Sentiments, designs, affections, though it is from these that according to cool reason human actions derive their whole merit or demerit, are placed by the great Judge of hearts beyond the limits of every human jurisdiction, and are reserved for the cognizance of his own unerring tribunal.'[15] Burns is echoing this in his description of God as the one 'who made the heart', and in his evaluation of the imperfect judgements of which human beings are capable because they do not know the whole story. Alexander Pope's, 'Essay on Man', may also have contributed to Burns's thought as he neared the end of the poem, and remembered Pope's lines:

> Virtuous and vicious ev'ry Man must be,
> Few in th' extreme, but all in the degree;
> The rogue and fool by fits is fair and wise;
> And ev'n the best, by fits, what they despise.
> 'Tis but by parts we follow good or ill;
> For, Vice or Virtue, Self directs it still;
> Each individual seeks a sev'ral goal;
> But HEAV'N'S great view is One, and that the Whole.[16]

Burn's theological views in this poem are an amalgam of ideas influenced both by the secular writers like Smith and Pope and by the teachings of Ecclesiastes and Jesus Christ. These combine on this occasion to give substance to the recurring themes in his religious thought – a benevolent God, life after death and human accountability.

'The Holy Tulzie'[17]

'The Holy Tulzie' does not display the specifics of Burns's theological understanding, but it does give clear indications as to where his sympathies lay in relation to the ecclesiastical divisions within the Church of Scotland. The major causes of disagreement, and eventually of schisms, were the Patronage Act of 1712 and the Burgher's Oath of 1747.

The Patronage Act of 1712 restored the right of the heritors to present a minister to a vacant parish, and was a revocation of the hard won right of a congregation to be able to choose a minister needing only the approval of the local Presbytery. This right had been established by law in 1690 and ratified in the Act of Union in 1707. The Act of 1690 had restored the system of church government, whereby the Church had the freedom to govern itself by means of kirk sessions, presbyteries, provincial synods and general assemblies, a system that had been in place since 1592, but that had been threatened and in part denied to the Church during the Restoration period from 1660 to 1690. The Patronage Act of 1712 was seen by many in the Church not only to have violated the Act of 1690, but to have infringed the Act of Union of 1707, which had ratified the earlier Act and in which the rights and presbyterian polity of the Church had been enshrined and assured.[18]

Two factions within the Church of Scotland began to emerge as the implications of the Patronage Act began to set in. The Moderates, who were accepting of patronage and what came to be known as the Popular Party, were opposed to patronage. The Moderates were commonly called the 'New Lights', and their opponents the 'Auld Lights', principally because the Moderates seemed to be more open to new ideas and more influenced by the secular thinking of the enlightenment period. The Popular Party, or 'Auld Lights', clung to what they thought of as the more orthodox beliefs and practices of the past.

Care has to be taken to guard against thinking that these labels signal well-defined and organized parties within the Church. John R. McIntosh, in his *Church and Theology in Enlightenment Scotland*, urges caution in the use of the terms Moderate and Popular, because of the variations of theology and ecclesiastical commitment that can be seen in individual members associated with either party. He cites as a seminal work I.D.L. Clark's *Moderatism and the Moderate Party in the Church of Scotland 1752–1805*, and summarizes the respective theology of the two parties: 'Clark categorised Popular theology as reacting against Moderate theology which gave too great a place to the role of Reason as a source of faith and which erected it into a standard of right and wrong through the role of conscience.'[19]

The controversy that later developed between the Reverend John Russel of Kilmarnock and the Reverend Doctor William McGill of Ayr over McGill's book *A Practical Essay on the Death of Jesus Christ* (1786) exemplifies the respective approaches of 'Auld Light' (Popular) and 'New Light' (Moderate) theology. Russel criticizes McGill for over emphasizing the humanity of Jesus Christ and neglecting the divine aspect of his being, and of concentrating on the human example that he gives as against his God-directed mission of dying as a substitute for the death that human beings were by justice required to meet because of their sin.[20]

However, McIntosh concludes that the term Popular Party has limited use as a concept to denote the doctrinal or ideological positions of those who opposed the patronage system in the later half of the eighteenth century. For simplicity's sake, here I shall use the terms New Lights and Auld Lights to denote the

Moderates as supporters of patronage and the Popular Party as the opponents of patronage.

The New Lights favoured a less rigorous form of Calvinism and were influenced by the growing spirit of enquiry, the questioning nature of investigation and the reliance upon the findings of observation that were evident in so many aspects of philosophical, literary, theological and scientific studies. The absorption of these attitudes naturally led to a more open-minded consideration of the Bible, and a greater willingness to be as critical of it, as with any other text of the secular world. As the eighteenth century progressed, the Bible and *The Westminster Confession of Faith* came under ever more rigorous scrutiny, and as scholars in secular fields grew bolder, so did theologians and parish ministers. Even a self-educated layman like John Goldie of Kilmarnock was, in 1779, bold enough to publish his theological opinions in pleading for a more rational interpretation of the Bible.[21]

While New Lights called in question such doctrines as Original Sin, Predestination and Election and challenged the authority of *The Westminster Confession of Faith*, these very things were strongly upheld by their Auld Light opponents. While the New Lights sat easily under patronage, often it seems because many patrons quietly did not exercise their legal rights but left it to the local congregation and Presbytery to sort out matters for themselves, the Auld Lights took the patronage issue much more seriously and eventually so seriously that it led to the first secession from the Church of Scotland in 1733.[22]

In the intervening years from the passing of the Act in 1712, there had been a number of cases where the presentee of the patron had been opposed by a congregation and a Presbytery. J.H.S. Burleigh, in *A Church History of Scotland*, writes of how the General Assembly protested within months of the passing of the Act, deploring the recent legislation as 'grievous and prejudicial to the Church' and announcing that they had instructed their Commission to use all proper and dutiful means to have the Patronage Act repealed.[23]

Matters came to a head in 1731, when because of such variations in the practice throughout the Church, an Overture was sent down by the General Assembly to Presbyteries seeking their agreement to a uniformity of procedures during a vacancy and the filling of it. The Presbyteries were divided in their opinion and the 1732 General Assembly legislated according to the Overture, disregarding the inconclusiveness of the votes cast by the Presbyteries. Protest against the legislation was expressed both at the General Assembly and later in the year from Ebenezer Erskine, a minister at Stirling. The following General Assembly, in 1733, demanded that Erskine withdraw his protest or face suspension. He did not withdraw his protest and in August that year he was suspended, along with three of his fellow ministers. He seceded with them from the Church of Scotland and on the 5 December 1733 they formed The Associate Presbytery (later The Associate Synod). The main body of the Church that they had left, at later General Assemblies, attempted to heal the breach, even in 1734 annulling the offending Act of 1732 and continuing the dialogue with the seceders, until, after eight years when they had continued to be in possession of their churches, manses and stipends, they were deposed in 1740.[24] The fact that the legislation that had ostensibly been the cause of the breach had been repealed yet the seceders remained out, indicates that issues other than patronage lay at the heart of their protest. G.D. Henderson, in *The Church of Scotland, A Short History*, points out that the underlying causes of separation, apart from patronage, were the trend of theology, Church and State and finally the relation of the Church's authority to the individual conscience.[25]

In time, The Associate Presbytery, as others joined the seceders, became The Associate Synod, but although their zeal for the Church's distinctiveness maintained its witness, it also at times indulged in what Henderson calls, 'an exaggerated idea of the importance of small differences'.[26] An example of this is the dispute over the Burgher Oath in 1747. The stricter members of the Synod disapproved of the terms of the oath to which the burgesses of certain towns had to declare their allegiance to 'the true religion presently professed within this realm'. Perceiving that the established Church was not representative of 'true religion', many of the seceders baulked at the Burgher Oath. The resulting split in the secession brought about a division into two factions, the Burghers and the Anti-Burghers. By the end of the century, the Church was displaying the fragmented, not to say undignified, pattern in which four separate groupings could be discerned: Auld Light Burghers, Auld Light Anti-Burghers, New Light Burghers and New Light Anti-Burghers. It is into this theological and ecclesiastical melee that Burns enters and, not surprisingly, has something whimsical and ironic to say.

In one of the manuscript copies of 'The Holie Tulzie', Burns writes of what prompted the poem, 'The occasion was a bitter and shameless quarrel between two Revd. Gentlemen – Mr. Moodie of Riccarton and Mr. Russel of Kilmarnock. It was at the time when the hue and cry against Patronage was at its worst.'[27] Alexander Moodie and John Russel had engaged in a dispute in the Presbytery of Irvine and Kilmarnock over the matter of parish boundaries. Burns seems to relish poking fun at these two Auld Light ministers from the same side of the theological fence nevertheless quarrelling over the physical division of the areas for which they were responsible. Both of these ministers adopted an anti-Patronage stance, and had been themselves chosen by their congregations without the say-so of any Patron. Further, they represented the very quintessence of pure Calvinist orthodoxy. These facts emerge in the verses that follow the relating of the dispute between the two ministers. Burns writes:

You wha was ne'er by Lairds respeckit,
To wear the Plaid;
But by the vera Brutes eleckit
To be their Guide.[28]

Here, Burns rather coarsely refers to the people of the congregations as 'Brutes', and in the next verse continues the animal metaphor by likening them to a 'Flock'. In the following verse, he again makes sure his readers get the point, by calling Russel's congregation 'sheep'. Burns's awareness of the theological issues is evident as he refers to Moodie's congregation not being given, 'poison'd Arminian stank', but instead being provided with refreshment from 'Calvin's fountain-head'. The Auld Lights, Moodie and Russel gave their congregations what they conceived as the purest Christian doctrine, drawn from the great fountainhead of Protestant theology, John Calvin. They would never have offered their people what they considered the stagnant, adulterated brew that came from Jacobus Arminius, one-time Professor at the University of Leyden, from 1603 to 1609. Owen Chadwick writes:

> Arminius began to contend that the New Testament revealed a loving God and that this was incompatible with the interpretation which consigned many mortals to hell without regard to their conduct ... [shortly after his death] ... his followers assented to a document called the "Remonstrance". This declared that election to eternal life is conditional upon good works in this life, that grace can be resisted and lost, that Christ died for all men.[29]

By the time of Burns, the word Arminian was used almost as a term of abuse by the strict Calvinists. In their eyes, Arminians were those who did not recognize the demands of the Justice of a Sovereign God, the arbitrary nature of election, predestination and judgement. The term was often used loosely alongside Socinianism and Pelagianism, implying that like these other heresies, it denied the divinity of Jesus Christ, or overemphasized his humanity to such an extent as to detract from his Divine origins and did not fully recognize the significance of his sacrificial death.

Gerald R. Cragg, in *The Church and the Age of Reason 1648–1789*, contrasts Calvinism and Arminianism:

> Whitefield was a Calvinist, Wesley was not. Calvinism which exalts the absalute sovereignty of God, claims that in his inscruitable wisdom he has ordained to salvation only those whom he selects. Arminianism on the other hand, leaves far more scope for man's free will. [John] Wesley was a convinced Arminian. He held firmly to the belief that "God willeth all men to be saved". Whitefield ... claimed that because Wesley had misunderstood the doctrine of election he had fallen into the heresy of universal redemption. To Whitefield it was clear that Arminianism dulled the all important sense of sin; it made men complacent, whereas election tended to "rouse the soul out of its carnal security".[30]

These opinions were being voiced in the mid-eighteenth century, and were still being held by the likes of Moodie and Russel in its last quarter.

The context into which Burns introduces the subject of Arminianism shows his grasp of the issues that lay behind the term, when he portrays the vigour with which Moodie engages in the hunt for 'Fulmart, Wil-cat, Brock and Tod'. Burns is implying that Moodie is just as vigorous in pursuing the members of his congregation in order to confront them with their sin. Russel, too, is depicted as someone who knows every aspect of his peoples' lives; haranguing them, closely examining them to discern whether they were 'sick or hale'. Then turning from his congregation, Russel applies these same methods to the 'New-light Herds', ministers who would be attacked and threatened and hung over the burning lake of hell, or even cast into it like sheep into a dip.

The poem then moves on to tell of how Moodie and Russel called each other names like 'Villain, Hypocrite', while their enemies, 'wi' laughin' spite / Say, Neither's liein'. Burns then displays his first-hand knowledge of a number of local ministers. (See Chapter 9 for further details.) Listing first the Auld Lights – Duncan, Peebles and Auld, who look after those within the 'Gospel Fauld' (note the exclusiveness of the phrase) – he then goes on to list the New Lights, revealing in the passing that they outnumber the Auld Lights: Dalrymple, McGill, McQuhae, the Shaws, Wodrow and his colleague and successor [McMath] and Smith, who had once been in the Auld Light camp. Incidentally, in so listing these ministers Burns might be indicating that the majority in the Presbytery were of the Moderate persuasion. But perhaps, as seems to me more likely, he is only signalling that these are the ministers whose company he has sought because their theology was more congenial and compatible with his own. The poem ends with a return to the theme of Patronage, and to a comment on what categorizes the theology of the New Lights. First, there is a verse that purports to be an exhortation to the congregations scattered throughout the land, to unite in opposition to the Lairds, that is the Patrons, that the people might be allowed to choose their minister themselves:

> O a' ye flocks o'er a' the hills,
> By mosses, meadows, moors and fells,
> Come join your counsels and your skills
> To cowe the Lairds,
> And get the Brutes the power themsels
> To chuse their Herds.

Burns's own sympathy for Patronage might be showing through in the less than complimentary language he uses in this appeal to the people made by the Auld Lights. It is almost as if in choosing the term 'Brutes' he is mocking the ability of the ordinary members of a congregation to make a wise choice of a minister. In repeating the word 'Herds' in relation to ministers, it could be that he is saying that the people are no better than sheep who need a shepherd. Burns associated more with New Light ministers who supported Patronage than with Auld Lights who opposed it, while he himself, at a later stage in his life, worked the then system of Patronage quite unashamedly when seeking to further his career in the Excise. Added to this was the natural affinity he felt for the Moderates who shared a theology that was in many respects much nearer his own than that held to by the Auld Lights.

In closing, the poet singles out 'Common Sense' as the real enemy of the Auld Lights, who are made to rejoice at the prospect of:

> ... that curst cur ca'd Common Sense
> Wha bites sae sair,
> Be banish'd o'er the sea to France,
> Let him bark there.

Here, in this highly topical poem, Burns displays his grasp of the issues involved in the dispute between the Auld Lights and New Lights. He clearly indicates that his sympathy lies with the New Lights and what had been called their 'Arminian stank', which was, as Burns perceived it, their less orthodox, kindlier, more common sense and less dogmatic theology.

'Holy Willie's Prayer'[31]

The Doctrines of Election, Predestination and Original Sin, all of which underlie the understanding and attitude of the character of 'Holy Willie', have already been expounded in relation to the poem in Chapter 3. I do not propose to deal with them again here, but you may find it useful to refer back to the earlier passage. Nor will I deal with the poem verse by verse, as it would be difficult to add significantly to Kinsley's superb analysis, both of the structure of the poem and his delineation of the theology that it embodies. My observations will concentrate on attempting to view the poem from the point of view of Burns's own religious stance, and his adherence to the three main strands of it that I have been able to discern: a belief in a benevolent God, a sense of his own accountability and a fascination with the subject of a life after death. If the poem is viewed keeping in mind these three aspects of Burns's religion, and added to this his abhorrence of hypocrisy, some fresh insights might be gleaned from the well-worked field of, 'Holy Willie's Prayer'. I want to explore what might have been going on in Burns's head as he set out to write this description of one man's interpretation of certain commonly held beliefs, and of how they manifested themselves, however distortedly, in Holy Willie's life.

Many people held to, or at least gave 'lip-service' to, the same doctrines as 'Holy Willie' – election, predestination and original sin – as they were outlined in great detail in *The Westminster Confession of Faith*, which everyone who became a communicant member of the Church of Scotland had to acknowledge as representing their own faith.[32] But as people were under social pressures to conform to the convention of being part of the Church, most sat lightly to the detail of belief. Many people would have come to a knowledge of Christian doctrine through a classroom learning of the *Catechism* by rote, and so for them faith was more likely to be a matter of acceptance, even if only to win their teacher's approval, rather than a matter over which they had earnestly thought. I suspect that for many it was an unexamined faith, for some others, who took these doctrines seriously, it was of vital importance. 'Holy Willie's Prayer' contains a portrait of a man who ruthlessly follows the logic of these doctrines in relation to himself and others. Like a Francis Bacon painting, it shows a man on the edge of his sanity, in all his ugliness, pursued by his own fear and yet still with a capacity for vindictiveness. In creating this horrific picture, Burns was seeing a man who had gone overboard on some aspects of his belief and seemingly laid aside, or conveniently forgotten, other beliefs that were equally well known, prominent and important and at least just as biblically based.

Missing from Holy Willie's portrait of God are the aspects of God outlined by Jesus in his parables. In these, God is the father who wants only good things for his children, the father who welcomes home the wayward son and the impartial creator who sends the sun and the rain to the good and bad alike. Missing too is the God of St John's Gospel, where he is the one who loves the world so much that he sends it a Saviour in Jesus Christ. Nor is there any place in Holy Willie's thoughts of God for 'The Sermon on the Mount' in St Matthew's Gospel (Chapters 5–7), where, among other things, a new ethic is suggested, more kindly standards are offered and a daringly different, more charitable counsel on judgement is put forward. All of these things are missing from Holy Willie's 'important things to remember about God'. He does not have room in his theology for other aspects of God, even of what might be termed 'The Old Testament God', a Creator who looked upon his creation and 'saw that it was good'; or the long-suffering God who still loved his people in spite of their sins; or the God revealed through the prophet Micah (6:8) who spoke up for him saying, 'what doth the Lord require of thee, but to do justly, and to love mercy, and to walk humbly with thy God'. All of these things are missing from Holy Willie's perception of God. All of this would have been noted by Burns as he pondered upon the Doctrines, which if applied rigorously and driven without mercy to their conclusion, could result in the travesty of Christian faith as displayed by Holy Willie. It is precisely because Burns leaned towards all these aspects of religion that are never taken into account by the likes of Holy Willie and those whose thoughts are governed by such doctrines, that he sought in 'Holy Willie's Prayer' to ruthlessly expose them. Burns judged such doctrines as nonsense and, as he remarked on the subject to his friend

Alexander Cunningham, he was of the opinion that, 'of all Nonsense, Religious Nonsense is the most nonsensical'.[33]

Burns's concept of God as essentially good was in direct contradiction to the God of Holy Willie. His conviction of man being responsible for his own actions, and his openness of mind to the possibility of there being something beyond what are thought to be the boundaries of human life, were offended by the kind of attitudes that he saw emerging from those who held to such doctrines. When to these natural aversions is added his loathing of hypocrisy, the resultant explosion of condemnation that is evident in the poem is inevitable. For example, Willie makes excuses for his sexual misdemeanors by suggesting that God has designed his nature quite deliberately to provide him with a weakness to keep him humble. The twisted logic of Willie makes allowances for his conduct by suggesting that God is ultimately to blame because of the way he has made him. Even Willie's sinful actions are part of a predestined plan. As Willie is of the elect, who once having been chosen will never be able to fall from God's hands no matter what they do, he will be saved and will take his place in Heaven. Such reliance on a faith that seemed utterly beyond reason provoked Burns's poetic response, in a fierce mockery of its theology, in 'Holy Willie's Prayer'.

When the stated context of the birth of the poem is remembered, it is easy to see how Burns saw the act of the Mauchline Kirk Session, especially when it had among it men like Holy Willie, as being hypocritical in the extreme. Here were men who apparently believed that they were of the elect, condemning one of their fellow men, Gavin Hamilton, who in Burns's eyes was far more honourable than they were.[34]

In 'Holy Willie's Prayer', Burns focuses on all that is deliberately rejected by him as incompatible with the ideas that he has of God as benevolent, as one to whom he is accountable and as one who might possibly preside over a life after death. The first of these ideas derives, as much as from anything else, from his attitude that if there is a God, then that God must be much superior in nature to his creation, man. The second idea possibly comes from the background of the firmly moral attitude engendered in his home, where William Burnes, his father, was anxious to provide as well as he could for his children that they might grow up as understanding men and women. In his early schooling, too, Burns was confronted with the sense of accountability, in that the very examples of his *Spelling Book* were couched in terms that were darkly Calvinistic and designed to bring the child to an awareness that they should accept responsibility for their actions, or else face the eternal consequences.[35] As to what these eternal consequences were Burns was never sure. One thing, however, seemed to remain in his mind, and that was an image from 'The Vision of Mirza', an article in his first school reading book, *A Collection of Prose and Verse from the Best English Authors*.[36] 'The Vision' is partly concerned with life after death and Mirza tells of it as being like a huge ocean, divided into two parts by a rock of adamant. One half of the ocean has clouds still shrouding it, but the other half contains numerous fertile islands, in which he learns are, 'the mansions of good men after death'. However, when Mirza enquires as to what lies under the dark clouds that hover over the other half of the ocean, the vision vanishes. If Burns believed, or even half believed, in any life after death, it was one in which only a good could be envisaged. As for the rest, like 'The Vision of Mirza', it remained unknown. What he could not bring himself to believe was that a good God could contrive an eternal hell for those who, after all, were his own creation. Such beliefs then, as were criticized by Burns under the guise of 'Holy Willie's Prayer', were quite incompatible with his own religious understanding.

'Epistle to John Goldie in Kilmarnock, Author of The Gospel Recovered'[37]

Burns wrote this poem in 1785, the year in which the second edition of John Goldie's *Essays on various important subjects Moral and Divine*, was published. The opening lines of the poem allude to Goldie's already established reputation: 'O GOWDIE, terror o' the whigs, / Dread o' black coats and reverend wigs!' His reputation as an opponent of the Auld Light theology had been gained following the publication of the first edition of the *Essays* in 1779, when he emerged as a critic of some of the prized Doctrines, such as Election, Predestination and Original Sin, that were then being firmly adhered to, and vehemently promoted by his Kilmarnock neighbour, the Reverend John Russel of The High Kirk Parish of Kilmarnock.[38]

In this poem Burns praises Goldie for being such an able opponent of bigotry, superstition and enthusiasm – three elements of religion for which he had no sympathy. He alludes also to Goldie's attack on the orthodox view of scriptural interpretation. Goldie, like the earlier commentator Dr John Taylor of Norwich, had put forward what might be called a common-sense view of scriptural interpretation; whereby, if a scripture passage offended against common sense, it would be correct to interpret it figuratively rather than literally. He also wanted sometimes to interpret scripture with scripture, for example if one part of scripture seemed to be contrary to another part of scripture, then the text that was deemed to contradict the good character of God should be ignored.[39] All of this, of course, was in direct opposition to the orthodox view that all scripture was the word of God, and for many of the orthodox opinion a literal interpretation was the only one possible.

Both Goldie and Taylor had written at length on the Doctrine of Original Sin and were united in condemning it, Goldie castigating it as, 'a most horrid and shocking theology'.[40] In the poem Burns does not elaborate on his reasons for praising Goldie, but instead holds him up as a kind of champion of those who want to rid religion of its harmful elements, like bigotry, superstition and enthusiasm (that over-zealousness and near fanaticism that left common sense and reason behind, and whose first casualty was love).

As is so often the case in his poems that refer to religion, Burns merely signals by symbol-like words that lie innocently on the surface, but under which lie huge depths of understanding on his part. As a young man he had read his father's copy of John Taylor's *The Scripture Doctrine of Original Sin*, and by the time of his writing of this poem he had read Goldie's 1779 edition of the *Essays*, that contained a 220 page piece 'An Essay upon what is commonly called Original Sin'.[41] Again, hidden in the depths of apparently simple words of praise for the common-sense attitude of John Goldie in opposing bigotry, superstition and enthusiasm, lie an understanding of the nuances of the term 'common sense', both as used by Goldie in applying it to theology and in its use by Thomas Reid in his work of philosophy *An Inquiry into the Human Mind on the Principles of Common Sense*, which Burns had also read.[42]

As Burns read the words of such men as Taylor and Goldie, they seemed to confirm what he had discovered from his own observation and experience. He became more critical of the works of theologians like Thomas Boston, James Hervey and Thomas Watson, as can be seen from his letters to his bookseller Peter Hill.[43] Preachers such as John Russel and William Peebles who were so sure of the correctness of their beliefs and who had built elaborate theologies upon what, according to Goldie, would seem to be very doubtful premises, came under Burns's close scrutiny. The poem itself reflects something of this attitude. It is as if Burns is saying to Goldie: keep up the good work of harassing 'the whigs, black coats and reverend wigs'; continue your campaign against bigotry, superstition and enthusiasm, no matter what they say; in any case what does it matter what they say, it is a load of nonsense anyway; away and have a good dram.

The dismissive nature of the last four stanzas is Burns's attempt at getting a true perspective on the issues raised by Goldie's work. At the end of the day, all these mean little theological squabbles are of no significance in the larger affair of life itself. Burns is adopting the same attitude that he was to display some four years later in a letter to Mrs Frances Anna Dunlop on 22 June 1789. Burns writes:

> I have just heard [Mr Kirkpatrick] give a sermon. He is a man famous for his benevolence and I revere him; but from such ideas of my Creator, good Lord deliver me! Religion, my honoured friend, is surely a simple business, as it equally concerns the ignorant and the learned, the poor and the rich.[44]

Here in his 'Epistle to John Goldie', Burns is expressing his frustration at how complicated an essentially simple thing has become. The sudden breaking off from the subject of orthodoxy's quarrel with Goldie the mischief maker, to take up the theme of the comforting effects of a good whisky, is almost like a signal that Burns has become fed up with the whole totally unnecessary *stushie* over matters that would never have arisen had religion been kept as the simple thing that Burns believed it to be. Perhaps, in the odd ending given to this poem, there is a reminder being given to us by the poet, that he was content to believe but a few things, and to leave the rest to future revelation or later understanding, or even, just to let them be.

'Man was Made to Mourn, A Dirge'[45]

'Man was made to mourn' is dismissed rather summarily by most of the commentators that I have read, except for James Kinsley and Hans Hecht. The poem is placed in a group that are commonly acknowledged as having been written while Burns was in a state of depression. Maurice Lindsay suggests that, 'no time need be wasted on these pieces written in a foreign mode of which Burns was not the master'.[46] But despite how poorly the poem 'Man was made to mourn' was accomplished, or however formal its adopted style, nevertheless it is worth looking at for the sentiment that it contains.

Kinsley points out that Gilbert Burns had asserted that several poems were written to:

> bring forward some favourite sentiment of the author. He [Robert] used to remark to me, that he could not well conceive a more mortifying picture of human life, than a man seeking work. In casting about in his mind how this sentiment might be brought forward, the elegy *Man was made to mourn*, was composed.[47]

The poem is therefore worth examining as an expression of the sentiment it is seeking to expound. In the poem Burns takes up a theme that was to appear in many of his poems: an awareness of the plight of the ordinary labouring men who worked on the land; and in the discussion of their circumstances, Burns invariably expressed his sympathy and compassion for them. They are portrayed in this poem as living in a world that is uncaring of the consequences of their being unable to gain employment and of the effect this has upon their wives and children. Despite the egalitarian feelings expressed, there is no solution suggested as to how things might be bettered for them in this life. A fatalistic acceptance seems to be adopted by the 'rev'rend Sage', the voice of the poem, who just mourns that things should be the way that they are. But he does offer one consolation: that which is to be found in religious belief.

In this poem it is possible to discern an encouragement to believe in a life after death, a life in which there is a greater prospect of enjoyment than anything that had preceded it in any earthly life. Burns expresses a religious hope through the mouth of the old man in his eighties, who, having gone through the catalogue of woes that beset Man in this life, says:

Yet, let not this too much, my Son
Disturb thy youthful breast:
This partial view of human-kind
Is surely not the *last*!

Then having asserted that the description of man's fate that he has put forward is not the final word on the life of man, he goes on to posit the hope that there must be 'some recompence / To comfort those that mourn!' This was one of the arguments used by Burns as offering a ground for there being a life after death as a compensation for unrecognized worth in this life.[48]

Since 1647, when it was approved by the General Assembly, *The Westminster Confession of Faith*, had become the standard textbook from which the Christian faith was taught in the Church of Scotland. Only the Bible was acknowledged as more important, although in some of the theological issues that were debated during the eighteenth century, sometimes the *Confession* was used as if it were of equal authority. Burns, like many of his contemporaries, would have been familiar with the *Confession*'s section on 'The State of Man after Death', which says:

> The bodies of men after death return to dust, and see corruption; but their souls (which neither die nor sleep), having an immortal subsistence, immediately return to God who gave them. The souls of the righteous, being then made perfect in holiness, are received into the highest heavens, where they behold the face of God in light and glory, waiting for the full redemption of their bodies; and the souls of the wicked are cast into hell, where they remain in torments and utter darkness, reserved to the judgement of the great day.[49]

The latter part of the last sentence, however, should not have overly troubled those who had striven to live honestly, worked hard and observed the faith and practice of the Church. Their hope of a better life to come would have been helped by the sentiments of the *Confession* and, unless they had lived in a very determinedly evil way, they would have been likely to make the assumption that they would be going to a better place in the hereafter.

Heaven gets only one mention in the poem, but it is not as a metaphor for a benevolent God; it merely signals the pathetic nature of man who despite all his troubles, has a 'heav'n erected face / The smiles of love adorn'. Nevertheless it is this same man whose 'inhumanity to Man / Makes countless thousands mourn'. Any sense of a benevolent God is absent from this poem. Man is 'By Nature's law design'd', and his life is determined by 'Fate'. God is a '*Deus abscondita*', leaving man to his fate and only at the end is it hinted that he might have something else planned that will recompense man for all that he has been through in life. It is a very dark picture of life that has been painted and Burns does not lighten it with any details of a brighter future to be given by God. If Burns does offer anything, it is but the faintest glimmer of hope that what we see of life is not all that there is to it, but that perhaps, just perhaps, something better awaits us beyond the grave.

'To the Rev. John McMath, Inclosing a Copy of *Holy Willie's Prayer*, which he had Requested September 17th, 1785'[50]

As the title of the above poem states, this verse epistle was sent to the Reverend John McMath, enclosing a copy of 'Holy Willie's Prayer', which had been requested by the minister. John McMath had graduated M.A. from the University of Glasgow in 1772. He became assistant and successor to the Reverend Patrick Wodrow, Minister of Tarbolton, near Ayr, in 1782. Patrick Wodrow, born in 1713, had been minister there since 1738, and was the son of the ecclesiastical historian the Reverend Robert Wodrow (1679–1734). After graduating M.A. from the University of Glasgow, Robert Wodrow became its librarian from 1697 to 1701, before being ordained minister of Eastwood Parish Church, near Glasgow, in 1703, where he remained until his death in 1734. He had played a significant part in drafting the legislation for the General Assembly of the Church of Scotland in 1731 that upheld the compliance with the law of Patronage wherever it applied. He was known as the author of *History of the Sufferings of the Church of Scotland from Restoration to Revolution* (published 1721–2). His son, Patrick, therefore had been long nurtured in New Light theology and in the ethos of the Moderates, and was in his own right an accomplished and respected parish minister, having been awarded a Doctor of Divinity from the University of St Andrews in 1784.[51]

It is into this setting that John McMath had come to work as assistant to, and on the understanding of becoming successor to, Patrick Wodrow when he retired. Upon the appointment of a junior minister in such circumstances, he was commonly referred to as the senior minister's 'colleague and successor'. Already resident within the parish of Tarbolton was the poet's father William Burnes, who with his sons Gilbert and Robert worked the farm at Lochlie. Following the death of William Burnes in 1784, Gilbert and Robert moved to take the tenancy of the farm at Mossgiel, just about two and a half miles away but in the parish of Mauchline. This proximity helped promote the friendship and mutual respect between John McMath and Robert Burns.

Copies of 'Holy Willie's Prayer' had been circulating privately from early in 1785 following the January meeting of the Presbytery of Ayr, which had ordered the Mauchline Kirk Session to strike from its minutes the censure of

Gavin Hamilton. Matters were not finally settled until the Session's appeal against the Presbytery was turned down by the Synod, and the Session, reluctantly, had to grant Hamilton a certificate declaring that he was freed from any ecclesiastical censure. It was quite natural, in the circumstances of such a furore in a small community, that a New Light minister such as John McMath would want a copy of the poem that had dealt with the controversy, and that featured some of the characters that were the subject of local gossip.[52]

But quite apart from the topicality, and the immediacy given to it by its reference to the community in which he lived, John McMath would have found much to interest him in the poem 'Holy Willie's Prayer'. Even a quick scanning of James Kinsley's notes on the text of the poem reveals the depths of Burns's familiarity with the Bible. Burns alludes to, uses phrases based on or directly quotes from the Bible to the extent that Kinsley has traced no fewer than 43 biblical texts that substantiate, or that might have been drawn upon, to provide Burns's words.[53] In addition to this accurate knowledge of biblical material, Burns also displays an understanding of the theological Doctrines of Predestination, Election and Original Sin, as well as writing in familiar terms about the ecclesiastical scene in which the issues were then being debated.

In the verse epistle 'To the Rev. John McMath', Burns takes the opportunity to explain why he had written 'Holy Willie's Prayer' and extends the criticisms of the attitudes that he had so dramatically satirized in that poem. The poet begins his verse epistle in the same way as if he were writing a prose letter, telling of how he has taken the chance to write while the weather is wet and no work can be done about the farm. He explains that after he had written 'Holy Willie's Prayer', he was a bit apprehensive of the consequence of his actions, and poses in the role of being just, 'a simple, countra bardie' who feigns fear of the local ecclesiastical powers, who, 'can easy, wi' a single wordie, / Louse h–ll upon me'. But his anger at what he deems is their hypocritical conduct had overcome those fears, and he had therefore risen to the defence of the reputation of his friend Gavin Hamilton, who had been 'miska't waur than a beast'. Burns had also been angered by the religious poses they adopted and by their ostentatiously long prayers and graces, but even more by their 'raxan conscience', that is their self-accommodating conscience, which allowed them to live in the same way that they condemned in others. The poet wishes that he had as great a satirical power as Alexander Pope that he might more adequately deal with Hamilton's attackers. But, again, perhaps there is just a touch of false modesty coming through here, for his own satire seems to have been every bit as bitingly accurate as any by the earlier writer. Burns then confesses to McMath, in what I think is a moment of very honest self disclosure:

> God knows, I'm no the thing I shou'd be,
> Nor am I even the thing I cou'd be,

But twenty times, I rather wou'd be
An atheist clean,
Than under gospel colors hid be
Just for a screen.

Here again is evidence of Burns's sense of accountability – believing that his life should be better and admitting that his life could be better, but still saying that he would rather be considered to be an out and out atheist than try to justify very doubtful activity by claiming that it was done for the sake of the Gospel. He then goes on to detail the reasons for his criticism of those who had hounded Gavin Hamilton:

They take religion in their mouth;
They talk o' mercy, grace an' truth,
For what? – to gie their malice skouth
On some puir wight,
An' hunt him down, o'er right an' ruth,
To ruin streight.

There is real venom in these words. Burns's anger is not self-righteous anger but the anger of a man who sees right through the hypocrisy of those whose actions belie their claim to believe in a merciful God, to live in his grace and to seek to adhere to the truth that he reveals. The poet, however, is aware that when he rants on against religious people, he might be accused of attacking religion itself, and so, in the very next stanza, praises religion in unequivocal terms:

All hail, Religion! maid divine!
Pardon a muse sae mean as mine,
Who in her rough imperfect line
Thus daurs to name thee;
To stigmatize false friends of thine
Can ne'er defame thee.

Burns is distinguishing between religion and the unhealthy religiosity that merely takes religion in its mouth, but does not allow it to affect either the mind or the heart. Religion is addressed as the maid, the servant of the divine; it is not in control, but has a servant's role. Religion is there to serve mankind not to dominate it. Burns again apologizes that someone as unworthy as he should take up the defence of religion, and again he wants to ward off any accusation of attacking religion, and claims that to castigate those whom he sees as the 'false friends' of religion can do no harm to religion itself. Burns goes on to say that despite his life being 'blotch'd an' foul wi' mony a stain', he still wants to sing the praises of religion itself in company with those who would uphold it, in spite of others – yes even some within the ranks of the Church – who would undermine it with their parody of what religion really stands for. In his final condemnation of those whom he set out to criticize, he does not spare them, but lashes out at the 'scoundrels, even wi' holy robes / But hellish spirit'.

The poem concludes with a tribute to the Moderates, the New Lights within the Presbytery of Ayr:

> O Ayr, my dear, my native ground,
> Within thy presbytereal bound
> A candid lib'ral band is found
> Of public teachers,
> As men, as Christians too renown'd
> An' manly preachers.

Burns then singles out John McMath: 'Sir, in that circle you are nam'd; / Sir, in that circle you are fam'd;' and, taking a last swipe at those whom he has been criticizing, he reminds the minister that if his theology is criticized by some, he should take it as a compliment, nevertheless, to also remember that even some of those who criticize his beliefs still respect him as a person. The tone of unqualified respect that Burns conveys by the final words that he addresses to McMath is consistent with the manner in which Burns had already used in writing of him in 'The Holy Tulzie', in which he had hailed him as a worthy successor to the long lasting New Light ministry of Patrick Wodrow at Tarbolton. He portrayed McMath as being thought of by the Auld Lights with some trepidation as, 'A chap will soundly buff our beef'. Also in that poem, Burns refers to the minister in affectionate terms as, 'guid McMath'.

In the verse epistle, Burns does not overtly state his own theological position to McMath, but it is clear from all that he does say that he knows that McMath is aware of his sympathy for the theological and ecclesiastical stance of the liberal, Moderate, New Light ideas.

The later years of McMath's life are not well documented. McMath demitted his charge at Tarbolton in December 1791. The reasons for his demission are variously attributed to ill health or an alcohol problem. It seems that he did suffer from bouts of depression, and possibly therefore sought comfort from drinking. He eventually enlisted as a soldier, and the last records of him indicate that he died in relative obscurity on the Island of Mull in 1825.[54] Perhaps, even in this largely anecdotally based reconstruction of his last years and with a fair amount of conjecture, there is a hint as to one additional cause for the bond of sympathy that undoubtedly existed between Burns and McMath. Burns knew the depths of depression and he also knew the temptation of alcoholic overindulgence. Whatever the truth, the epithet 'guid' when applied to McMath, rings true – when it comes from the mouth of Burns.

'The Holy Fair'[55]

The falsity of the pose that Burns had adopted in calling himself 'a simple countra bardie' is fully exposed in 'The Holy Fair'.[56] In this poem Burns cannot hide the evidence of his understanding of the poetical techniques of a medieval genre, nor disguise his familiarity with more recent poets who had adopted it. 'The Holy Fair' follows in the tradition of the fifteenth century 'Peblis to the Play' and the sixteenth century 'Christ's Kirk on the Green', both of which had been republished in the eighteenth century. The former appeared in *Select Scotish Ballads* (1785) and the latter in Allan Ramsay's *Poems* (1721)[57] Both these anonymous poems are written in the medieval tradition of the peasant 'brawl'. A further encouragement to engage with the genre was provided by Robert Fergusson's 'Hallow Fair' and 'Leith Races'. Burns had become familiar with Fergusson's work by the time he was at Lochlie. Dr John Mackenzie who visited the poet's father, William Burnes, there during his last illness attests that Robert Burns had, 'a thorough acquaintance with many of our Scottish poets, and an enthusiastic admiration for Ramsay and Fergusson'.[58]

'Peblis to the Play' depicts the scene in the small Scottish border town of Peebles on the occasion of a Beltane, or May Day festival. The anonymous poet describes the people as they prepare to dress for the event: 'All the wenches of the west / War up or the cok crew.'[59] They had risen early and are pictured as they fuss over what to wear. As they go along the road to the town, the girls talk of who they will meet and of which lad they hope to get. There is broad humour when one of the young girls who falls with 'her taill up' is told to cover herself up, and is jokingly rebuked: 'Quhat neidis you maik it sua? / Yon man will not owrryd you.'

The narrative continues with descriptions of eating and drinking, a fight breaking out, people falling into the gutter and a peddler getting involved and falling off his horse into the mud. Then the dancing starts and the party grows more wild. Will Swane, who has been dancing to the pipes so long that his face has got sunburned, is taken away by the hand by Tisbe, who wants to have sex with him but is a little afraid as the door of her house has no latch. But she still leads him away, to the laughter of all the other men, 'as hir taill brynt'. The poem ends as the day ends with the lovers making their trysts and pledging that:

> "Thair sall be mirth at our meeting,"
> Yit,
> Of Peblis to the play.

'Christ's Kirk on the Green', which in its opening verse refers to the earlier 'Peblis to the Play', is more confined in its subject matter.[60] The first four stanzas tell of the preparations for the dance that is to be held at Christ's Kirk on the Green. The girls, freshly washed and clean, don 'thair new kirtillis of gray' and one, Gillie, tells of how she is only interested in one lad and of how she 'wold haif bot sweit Willie / Allone'. The dance starts, but a quarrel begins and soon a fight involving bows and arrows breaks out. The aim of the bowmen is so bad that no one at whom they are aiming gets hurt. Jokingly it is said of one shot:

> The bolt flew owr the byre.
> Ane cryit 'Fy! he had slane a preist
> A myll beyond ane myre'.[61]

The fight continues with cudgels and stones, but ends inconclusively when one man who is seeking revenge upon those who have assaulted his brother is told by his wife and his mother, 'Ga hame, gud glaikis!' (go home you silly fool), and so he hits them instead.

Such was the medieval genre of the peasant 'brawl'. Robert Fergusson took the same structure, but transformed it by making it the bearer of a more natural tale.[62] His 'Hallow-Fair' is full of believable characters going to a fair: 'trig-made maidens ... John in bonnet blue / An' eke his Sunday's claes on ... chapman billies ... cairds and tinklers ... ne'er-do-weel horse-coupers ... spae-wives ... army recruiters ... and the City Guard'. They are all there, brought vividly into being, the medieval rhyming scheme seeming to give added impetus to the turbulent currents of the city's life. The characters in the poem are seen as if they are part of a long procession of events. The awareness of this is heightened as the verses are ended and linked together by the clever device of the 'bob-wheel', whereby the last line or wheel provides a refrain that links it to the previous and the next verse.

Fergusson uses the same stanza in 'Leith Races'[63] and seems to have provided Burns with a model for the first scenes of 'The Holy Fair', with the narrator meeting up with a young lady early on a summer morning. Fergusson's young 'quean' is 'Mirth' while Burns's young 'hizzie' is 'Fun'. Mirth then offers to conduct the narrator to the races at Leith, promising, 'We'el reel an' ramble thro' the sands, / And jeer wi a' we meet.'

Mirth then goes on to list the people they will meet; 'servant maids ... mony ... a scraw'd and bare-ars'd loun ... the betting touts ... the barber ... the town guard ... the tinker billies ... the brewer wives ... the fish sellers.' The narrator then takes us on a journey in which all these and more are met. From the Lord Lyon King at Arms to the people in the chaises that pass, some 'that honest folk contain / And some hae mony a whure in.' All of life is there for the poet to comment on. Perhaps it was this aspect of the medieval genre, as brought to light by Ramsay and developed by Robert Fergusson, that so attracted Robert Burns. In January 1783 he had written to his former schoolteacher, John Murdoch, 'The joy of my heart is to "Study men, their manners, and their ways."'[64] The ancient poetic form was the ideal vehicle to carry his lively commentary on the people who gathered at 'The Holy Fair'.

The Kilmarnock MS indicates that the poem was composed in 1785, and the occasion that prompted it is likely to have been the annual celebration of Holy Communion that took place that year on the second Sunday of August. Part of the celebration involved an open air service, as this was often the only way in which the large numbers of people who attended could be accommodated. Several parishes would unite for the occasion, and their ministers would share in the preaching and in the administration of the bread and wine at the tables. The numbers meant people had to take it in turn to be served communion and the service might last several hours. James Kinsley records that in Mauchline in 1786, where there were only 400 communicant members, 1400 people received the Sacrament.[65] In Mauchline, these occasions were held in the ground adjacent to the parish church, which was in the very heart of that small town, which had its fair share of inns and ale-houses. Due to the crowds that attended, the time that it took for the services to be completed and the availability of nearby food and refreshment these occasions gathered about them an air of festivity, which caused them to become known as Holy Fairs. An account of one such fair, which confirms the accuracy of Burns's observation and commentary, is found in *Letter from a Blacksmith to the Ministers and Elders of the Church of Scotland.* Written at Inverary in 1758, it describes the scene at a Holy Fair:

> Allow me then to describe it as it really is: at first you find a great number of men and women lying together on the grass; here they are sleeping and snoring, some with their faces towards heaven, others with their faces turned downwards, or covered with their bonnets, there you find a knot of young fellows and girls making assignations to go home together in the evening, or to meet at some ale-house; in another place you see a pious circle sitting round an ale barrel, many of which stand ready on carts for the refreshment of the saints. The heat of the summer season, the heat of the travelling, the greatness of the crowd naturally dispose them to drink; which inclines some of them to sleep, works up the enthusiasm of others and contributes not a little to produce those miraculous conversions that sometimes happen on these occasions, in a word, in this sacred assembly there is an odd mixture of religion, sleep, drinking, courtship and a confusion of sexes, ages and characters. When you get a little nearer to the speaker so as to be within reach of the sound 'tho not of the sense of the words, for that can only reach a small circle; even when the preacher is favoured with a calm; and when there happens to be any wind stirring hardly one sentence can be heard distinctly at any considerable distance; in this second circle you will find some weeping and others laughing, some pressing to get nearer the tent or tub in which the parson is sweating, bawling, jumping and beating the desk; others fainting with the stifling heat or wrestling to extricate themselves from the crowd; one seems very devout and serious and the next moment is scolding

> and cursing his neighbour for squeezing or treading on him; in an instant after, his countenance is composed to the religious gloom, and he is groaning, sighing and weeping for his sins; in a word, there is such an absurd mixture of the serious and the comick that were we convened for any other purpose, than of worshipping the God and governor of nature, the scene would exceed all power of farce.[66]

The 'Blacksmith's' account of a Holy Fair confirms that Burns is not conjuring the events of his 'Holy Fair' out of his imagination, but that he is using a scene from life as the focus of his poem. Burns approaches his subject with an understanding of the genre and a vision of how it might be used to display, in humorous mode, some of the ideas and attitudes that he had more seriously and at greater length criticized in a number of his letters. But whereas the medieval examples of the 'brawl' were made up of farcical scenes contrived from the imagination of their authors, Burns uses a real event and introduces recognizable contemporary characters engaged in doing things that far exceed anything farcical that might have been created by the imagination.

'The Holy Fair' begins in similar fashion to Fergusson's 'Leith Races', with a lone observer on a beautiful morning espying people coming along the road.[67] On enquiring, Fergusson's observer discovers the lone figure to be 'Mirth'. Burns's observer tells of three 'hizzies', the third of which, when he says that he seems to know her, tells him that she is 'FUN' and that the other two are 'SUPERSTITION' and 'HYPOCRISY'. Burns very quickly tells us what the poem is about, as his narrator accepts FUN's invitation to accompany her to the Holy Fair at Mauchline, where she hopes to enjoy some merriment at the expense of the two somberly dressed in black, sour-faced figures of SUPERSTITION and HYPOCRISY. The subtlety of Burns's humour is immediately signalled by his noting that HYPOCRISY's black dress had 'lyart lining', that is it was grey in colour, implying that like all hypocrisy, the surface seldom shows the things that lie discretely hidden underneath. Most commentators settle for the interpretation of 'lyart', as meaning grey, but the usage in the eighteenth century, according to *The Concise Scots Dictionary*, would allow 'lyart' to mean 'variegated, multi-coloured, streaked with two colours, esp. red and white'.[68] Now although in the 'Cotter's Saturday Night' Burns uses the word 'lyart' to describe the greying hair of the Cotter, in 'The Holy Fair' he might be making use of the other usage of the word to hint that HYPOCRISY was even more of a 'scarlet woman' than the discreet grey, that the more common use of the word implied.

The poet then sets out to attack superstition and hypocrisy as they are to be found at a Holy Fair, a celebration that had gathered around the the most sacred of the ceremonies engaged in by the presbyterian Church of Scotland, the annual service at which the Sacrament of Holy Communion was administered. In using the genre of the medieval 'brawl' in this way Burns was doing something quite new, in that previously only secular subjects had been used, whereas now he was entering daringly into holy ground.

The women SUPERSTITION and HYPOCRISY, says the poet (using capital letters for added emphasis of their importance), are like 'sisters twin' and share the same unhappy look, implying that neither superstition nor hypocrisy can make people happy. By contrast, FUN is bright and cheerful, someone whom the narrator thinks is familiar to him. He remarks that he thinks that he has seen her face before and she reminds him that, for her sake, he has ignored all the Ten Commandments. So the first comments on religion in the poem are offered in a lightsome way. The next reference to religion comes at the entrance to the fair, where an Elder stands supervising the taking of a collection for the Church. Just as SUPERSTITION and HYPOCRISY are dressed in black, so the elder wears his covenanter style 'Black-bonnet'. He stands in sombre contrast to other people: farmers well turned out in their riding gear, the young men, 'swankies', in their best suits and the glittering 'silks an' scarlets' of the girls. The ominous black-bonneted guardian of the money on the offering plate is also described as having 'a greedy glow'r'. Thus far into the poem all the references to religion have been negative, associating it only with a sombreness, an unhappiness and an oppressive dourness.

'Then', says the poet, 'in we go to see the show'. In the crowd the poet spies the great mixture of types of people and the great variety of their different concerns:

> Here, some are thinkan on their sins,
> An' some upo' their claes;
> Ane curses feet that fy'ld his shins,
> Anither sighs an' prays.

Next, the poet spots 'a Chosen swatch', indicating the special nature of a group of people in the crowd, and in giving a capital letter to the word chosen signalling that they are those who consider themselves to be of the 'elect', that is those who have been destined by God for salvation and heaven. But even these great privileges do not seem to have had the effect of making them happy, for they sit, 'Wi' screw'd-up, grace-proud faces'. Here are those who have been assured of their salvation and of going to heaven but instead of it making them happier people it has given them an air of superiority. In that gathering at the fair, they give the impression that they are above the common herd, superior to their fellow men and women and deliberately sitting apart from those who were doing such ordinary playful human things as 'winkan on the lasses'. What had been forgotten by such people who believed in their being part of the chosen or the elect was that they were in that position not because of what they had done in terms of earning a place in that body, but that they were there by the arbitrary choice of God. Burns is inviting a judgment on this perversion of what he believed were the genuinely valuable aspects of the Christian religion. He had once written to Mrs Dunlop of the value of believing in Christianity, because of its capability of, 'making us better men, but also making us happier men'.[69] Quite clearly the religious people so far portrayed in 'The Holy Fair' are not happy people. The poet is suggesting that perhaps their version of Christianity is a misguided one and that another version, in which a belief in the benevolence of God is given its place, would result in better and happier lives.

The poet then cleverly uses words from the metrical version of Psalm 146 to signal that the assembled congregation have begun to worship. But instead of using the line 'O happy is that man an' blest!' as an expression of spiritual blessedness, he turns the phrase to use as a sign of a sensual pleasure: as a man in the crowd puts his arm across the back of the chair and gradually allows his hand to slip around his girl's neck, until it comes to rest upon her '*bosom*', Burns giving the word italics, as if to emphasize the physicality and sensuality of the act. For at least some within the crowd, the occasion is an opportunity for engaging with other human beings and, especially for the young, an opportunity for meeting with the opposite sex. So within the crowd there is this continuous interplay of spirituality and sensuality, of theological posing and physicality and of outward appearance and inward motivation. However, in using the words of Psalm 146, the poet reminds the reader of the far more generous God, in whom he believes, who is being mocked by those with their 'grace-proud faces', for the Psalm expands upon the nature of God:

> O Happy is the man and blest,
> whom Jacob's God doth aid;
> Whose hope upon the Lord doth rest,
> and on his God is stay'd
>
> Who made the earth and heavens high,
> who made the swelling deep,
> And all that is within the same;
> who truth doth ever keep:
>
> Who righteous judgment executes
> for those oppress'd that be,
> Who to the hungry giveth food;
> God sets the pris'ners free.[70]

The Psalm goes on to praise the God who helps the blind to see, who raises up those who are burdened, who loves those who morally strive, who cares for the stranger, the widow and the orphan. In using this Psalm, Burns is subtly inviting people to see the contrast between the God of the Psalm and the God who is being followed by the 'Chosen'. Their God is being shown in all his meanness of spirit, exemplified by their self-righteous conduct, their unhappy demeanour and by the way that they seem to think of themselves, and is seen to be vastly inferior to the God upheld by the Psalm and believed in by the poet.

Burns now turns from the religion of the people to the religion of the pulpit, as the first of five ministers begin to preach from the open air rostrum. The medieval 'brawl' is mirrored in what turns out to be almost a preaching contest, as each of the preachers, in turn, battle for the attention of the crowd. The Reverend Alexander Moodie of Riccarton is the first to do battle.[71] Burns had already written of Moodie as one of the protagonists in 'The Holy Tulzie'. In describing the content of the Auld Light preacher's sermon, the poet calls it 'tidings o' d–mn–t—n'. He emphasizes the negative and the threatening aspects of Moodie's delivery, as he says that the very sight of the preacher's face would have chased the Devil back to Hell. As Moodie goes over 'the points o' faith', that is the things that are necessary to believe, his body language takes over from the content, and he engages in histrionics:

> wi' rattlin an' thumpin!
> Now meekly calm, now wild in wrath,
> He's stampan, an' he's jumpan! (xiii)

These, combined with his facial contortions, weird unearthly squeals and strange gestures, are said by the poet to 'fire the heart devout, / Like cantharidian plasters.' This one-time medicine was otherwise known as Spanish Fly, which if applied externally brought the skin out in blisters and if taken internally was believed to be an aphrodisiac. So the hearers were being 'fired up' both outside and inside by the preacher. These reductionist tactics are being employed by Burns to invite his readers' judgement on such religious beliefs and practices as were held by Moodie and the other Auld Lights.

The next to mount the pulpit is the Reverend George Smith of Galston.[72] When he begins to preach, he is immediately identified by Burns as a New Light, because his preaching is characterised by 'cauld harangues / On practice and on morals' and in the opinion of the crowd with, 'ne'er a word o' faith in it'. Smith is seen by the Auld Lights as a typical New Light, more concerned with behaviour than theology, speaking more like some ancient Greek or Roman humanist pagan philosopher than a Christian. Burns indicates that the Auld Lights in the congregation are so angry at Smith's preaching that they leave in droves for refreshment at one of the nearby tents or hostelries. The poet rather neatly conveys the idea that if they cannot have their spirits lifted by the preacher's words, they can at least 'gie the jars an' the barrels / A lift'. But, he reminds us that these are 'the real judges', and skillfully reveals them as those who cannot bear to sit and listen to a preacher who is using the God given tool of his reasoning. Burns is negatively defining his own faith in this criticism of those who will not bring reason to bear upon what they believe, and even worse will not stay to hear the argument.

Next to the pulpit comes the Reverend William Peebles of Newton upon Ayr, who, the Auld Lights hope, will provide an antidote to counter the previous speaker's 'poosion'd nostrum' and set theological matters to rights again.[73] Burns dismisses him as curtly as he had done in 'The Holy Tulzie', in which he had labelled him shallow and says that as soon as Peebles began to speak, common sense left the place, 'Fast, fast that day'.

The preacher who follows Peebles is the Reverend Alexander Miller, who at that time was working as an Assistant Minister to the Reverend William Auld at Mauchline.[74] Burns implies that Miller disguises his real beliefs, which fit in with the New Lights, and pretends an Auld Light orthodoxy because he is looking for a charge. Sometimes, however, Miller nearly reveals what he truly believes, for he cannot always prevent his '*carnal* Wit an' Sense' from coming through in what he says. In using the word 'carnal', even italicising it, Burns is again revealing, to those who would read his work with an understanding of its theological nuances, his own thorough understanding of the preaching and theologically significant words of the Auld Lights. Allan H. MacLaine, in his notes on 'The Holy Fair' contained in *The Christis Kirk Tradition*, writes, '*carnal* was a cant term in Auld Licht preaching, used to discredit the idea that a man could earn salvation through his own *fleshly* good works and moral behaviour. Here [in the poem] it has the force of withering irony'.[75] Burns is engaging in the double irony of describing with an Auld Light term a minister who is in reality a New Light, and who is using the very faculty so condemned by the Auld Lights to pull the wool over their eyes, in order to further his own career. In this ironic comment on Alexander Miller, Burns shows that he is not a blind follower of the Moderates, but is acknowledging that in their ecclesiastical manoeuvering, some of them are as adept at connivance as any from the Auld Light party within the Church.

The next three stanzas enter into a digression worthy of Laurence Sterne, who in *The Life and Opinions of Tristram Shandy*, one of Burn's favourite books, not only digresses, but comments on the reason for it and what he wants to achieve by it. Sterne writes:

> That though my digressions are all fair, as you observe, and that I fly off from what I am about, as far as and as often too as any writer in Great Britain; yet I constantly care to order my affairs so, that my main business does not stand still in my absence.[76]

Burn's narrative suddenly breaks off from what is happening in the pulpit to what is happening in the pub. The scene is a noisy 'Change-house' filled with people clamouring for food and drink. These 'yill-caup Commentators', with a drink in their hand, are loudly discussing the sermon they have just heard, measuring it against 'Logic' and 'Scripture', yet with such vehemence that they are in danger of becoming further apart from each other and even more entrenched in their respective theologies to the extent that their differences might grow to provoke further angry division before the day's end. Burns hints at the respective positions of the protagonists' 'Logic', representing the New Lights and 'Scripture' the Auld Lights. This broad generalization being fairly accurate, as in the main the New Lights were characterized by their elevation of reason as a factor that must be brought to bear on Christian beliefs, whereas the Auld Lights always sought to abide by what the Bible said, even if it seemed to contradict the dictates of reason.

Burns then becomes expansive on the benefits of 'Drink'. Not lauding it in any bacchanalian way, but, dare I say it, attempting to soberly assess the effect a few drinks have on people. He pokes gentle fun at the way drink loosens the tongue and gives people the confidence to talk. Even more than 'School or Colledge' it seems to encourage wit, awakens learning and makes us tell of the things that we know. Yet within this playfulness there is again evidence of the poet's own deeper understanding of what is at work in people's minds as they expound their theories. Burns uses the word 'notion', a word that had particular philosophical nuance at the time of his writing. Burns had read Thomas Reid's *An Inquiry into the Human Mind, on the Principles of Common Sense* and knew of his theory of the reaction of the mind to what the senses suggest. Reid writes:

> sensation suggests the notion of present existence, and the belief that what we perceive or feel, does now exist; that memory suggests the notion of past existence, and the belief that what we remember did exist in time past; and that our sensations and thoughts do also suggest the notion of a mind and the belief of its existence and of its relation to our thoughts.[77]

Burns drops in the word 'notion' to remind us of the stimulus to our thinking brought about by sensation, perhaps even the sensation that arises from drink. In his digression, Burns, like Sterne, is not departing entirely from his subject, but has built into the apparent digression an element that adds to our understanding of the main argument. The poet concludes his little excursion with a stanza that draws attention again to the lads and lasses that are very much a part of the scene at the Holy Fair. They are held up to us perhaps as those who are getting the balance right in the living of their lives, in that they are concerned both for the soul and the body. There is also the hint at the presence of a loving interest in each other, an aspect that seems to be missing from any commentary on the more overtly religious people at the event. The little cameo of those 'cozie i' the neuk, / An' forming *assignations*', is in sharp contrast to the brawling of the preachers. Is Burns suggesting that the young lovers have more real understanding of the nature of 'love divine' than those who publicly declare it from the pulpit? He, I am sure, could better imagine such kind of young love being smiled upon by a benevolent God than the sometimes loveless pronouncements made by churchmen.

'But now the L—'s ain trumpet touts', and with this Burns returns to his main theme and brings the Reverend John Russel from Kilmarnock into the pulpit.[78] It is again significant that the poet describes Russel as 'Black', the colour that conjures up images of darkness, sombreness and death. But it is not just Russel's appearance that is being described as black, his theology also has a pervasive darkness about it that Burns relates with an almost visible shudder:

His piercin words, like highlan swords,
Divide the joints an' marrow;
His talk o' H–ll, whare devils dwell,
Our vera 'Sauls does harrow'
Wi' fright that day.

Burns was familiar with the religious controversy surrounding the book *The Marrow of Modern Divinity* by Edward Fisher, which was first published in 1646.[79] Its reprint in 1718 caused its theology to be adopted by some ministers, notably Thomas Boston, with whose work Burns was also familiar.[80] As the thrust of its theology was said to encourage an antinomian stance, whereby the elect could sin and still be assured of salvation, in 1720 the General Assembly pointed out its heresy and forbade ministers to use it. It seems likely, for Burns always chose his words carefully, that here he is hinting that the theology of John Russel, in its thunderous certainty, bordered on the antinomian heresy. Burns reduces the impact of Russel's words and the importance of the minister himself by telling of how after he has conjured up the 'raging flame' of Hell, the 'half-asleep', who think that they hear it 'roaran', come to realize that it was only 'some neebor snoran'. Russel and his theology are dismissed as if they were 'full of sound and fury, signifying nothing'. Here Burns is at his best in reductive satire. As for his own beliefs, at this point they remain hidden. The only thing of which we can be sure is that he does not share the beliefs of the Auld Light ministers featured in this poem. He so holds them up to ridicule as to invite an adverse judgement upon them. It is too much to make an argument for his positive beliefs from his silence here, but a case can be made for them when one attempts to reconstruct the stance from which the negative criticisms are made. Yet here and there are traces of those positive beliefs, as I have endeavoured to show in the very criticisms of the likes of Moodie, Peebles and Russel. In addition there are points made of a secular nature that give a hint as to his theology, for example in his affectionate reference to the lads and lasses that attend the fair who are mindful of both soul and body. In this there is an indication that here is a healthier form of religion than that which seems only to be concerned with the soul. There is also a warmth of respect being shown toward the genuine practice of religious duties in the reference to the old men, probably the fathers with their families, who are concerned not to start to eat before the grace is said:

> The auld *Guidmen*, about the *grace*,
> Frae side tae side they bother,
> Till some ane by his bonnet lays,
> An' gies them't, like a *tether*,
> Fu' lang that day.[81]

Amidst all the formality, a natural piety is glimpsed here. The people who are used to saying grace at home but who are too shy to take the lead among others are uncomfortable until one of them plucks up courage, lays down his bonnet and gives it out, like one giving a gentle signal by the reins, that tells that it is all right to go ahead. It is by such touches there comes a recognition that what the poet is writing is the product of his own observation, and in this case his genuine sympathy. So despite the ferocity of his satire and the sting of his ridicule directed towards hypocrisy, and what are deemed by the poet to be beliefs that cannot be held by anyone who applies his God given reason, Burns nevertheless has room in his religious understanding for those who display and hold honestly to what they believe.

One surprising omission from the poem is any detailed comment or criticism of superstition. 'The Holy Fair' had opened with SUPERSTITION and HYPOCRISY making their way to the fair, and FUN promising to have merriment at the pair's expense. While hypocrisy is dealt with at length, superstition does not get any mention whatsoever in the scenes that follow, neither is there any attempt by the poet to identify superstition with the beliefs or the practices of the people who participate in the religious service that is the focal point of the poem. Burns had begun by giving what appeared to be a key role to SUPERSTITION, but then seems to have forgotten that fact and ended up saying nothing at all about her. I have not as yet come across any commentator on the poem who has expounded on this seeming omission, and can only conclude that as the poem developed there was less cause to comment on superstition, as hypocrisy provided more than adequately as a source of fun. However, one word might be added about this odd omission. Perhaps as Burns explored the subject of religion he realized that however misguided some of its doctrines might at times seem, under the pressure of the increasingly rational ideas of his time it was beginning to depart from some of its more obvious attachments to superstition. Hence his omission of any further comment on superstition after his initial reference.

In adopting the genre of the medieval 'brawl' as the bearer of the tale of 'The Holy Fair', Burns daringly brings together the spiritual and the sensual in a rich brew. In this long romp of a poem Burns risks being provocative. He is not afraid to link a profession of religion with an enjoyment of life in a physical and sensual way. He is someone who dares to speak of '*faith* an' *hope* an' *love* an' *drink*' in the same breath, and not see any incongruity. He is someone who can acknowledge that men and women can be entirely serious about religion in the midst of a setting where, 'There's some are fou o' *love divine*; [and] / There's some are fou o' *brandy*'.[82] In 'The Holy Fair', Burns has taken an ancient form traditionally used in other ways, and introduced to it the controversial subject of religion as it is sometimes practised by men and women, in all their physicality and sensuality.

'The Cotter's Saturday Night'[83]

Between Burns's letter of 17 September 1785 to the Reverend John McMath, enclosing a copy of 'Holy Willie's Prayer', and his letter to Mr John Richmond on 17 February 1786, in which he tells of his having written 'The Cotter's Saturday Night', Burns wrote a strangely worded letter to Miss Margaret Kennedy, dated early October 1785. The stilted, artificial sounding words in which he describes in lofty tones the nature of a poet are similar to the wholly false-sounding first stanza of 'The Cotter's Saturday Night'. In writing of himself as a poet, Burns seems to be playing the role of the 'Man of Feeling':

> Poets, Madam, of all Mankind, feel most forcibly the powers of BEAUTY; as, if they are really Poets of Nature's making, their feelings must be finer, and their taste more delicate than the rest of the world. In The Chearful [*sic*] bloom of Spring, or the pensive mildness of Autumn; the Grandeur of Summer, or the hoary majesty of Winter; the Poet feels a charm unknown to the rest of [the world (deleted)] his Species; even the sight of a fine flower, or the company of a fine Woman, (by far the finest of God's works below) has sensations for the Poetic heart that the HERD of [our Species (deleted)] [his (deleted)] Man are strangers to.[84]

As the hesitations over the selection of words indicate, this letter is not written with the poet's usual fluency. Burns seems to be writing to impress the lady with his grasp of the ideas then in vogue, and reflected in the likes of Henry Mackenzie's novel *The Man of Feeling* (1771). But in attempting this style, the poet would appear to be ill at ease and it results in a very artificial sounding letter. In its peroration, the letter comes across as having been contrived for maximum effect; that of impressing the lady with an almost courtly, but certainly affected, style as he writes of 'ARROWS of Misfortune', and 'snares of Villainy', and expresses concern for her 'INNOCENCE' and 'HONOR' and makes a prayer for her 'PEACE'. It is difficult to avoid judging this letter as a blatantly insincere literary exercise. There may therefore be grounds for saying that 'The Cotter's Saturday Night' was begun around the same time as Burns was writing that letter to Margaret Kennedy. In his opening stanza of that poem, the same stilted artificiality is evident, as it also is in stanza ten, when Burns suddenly breaks from his description of young love to begin a vituperative diatribe against a hypothetical villain who might 'betray sweet Jenny's unsuspecting youth'.

Other commentators have criticized the opening stanza of the poem. David Daiches says that it, 'sounds as though it had been added to the poem as an afterthought, [and] is full of the posturing which Burns was led into when he wrote with the genteel tradition too much in mind'.[85] Maurice Lindsay agrees that it may have been a later edition and calls it, 'one of the most absurd stanzas he [Burns] ever wrote, and one in which his tactlessness is embarrassingly evident'.[86] However the first stanza is viewed, it might well be agreed that it is not one of Burns's best, and perhaps shows how ill at ease he could be with some of the conventions of the time.

The poem truly begins with its second stanza. Here we find the poet both at ease with his subject and the language in which he deals with it. The poem proceeds from stanzas two to eight with what seems to be an accurate and experienced description of a cotter's family life. A break comes at stanza nine, when the poet steps aside from the scene to reflect upon young love in a way that is reminiscent of his remarks in his *First Commonplace Book* in April 1783, 'If anything on earth deserves the name of rapture or transport, it is the feelings of green eighteen in the company of the mistress of his heart when she repays him with an equal return of affection.'[87] If only he had been able in stanza nine to convey those earlier sympathies more simply, then he might not have been led towards the totally out of keeping and context outburst of stanza ten:

> Is there a human-form that bears a heart –
> A wretch! a villain! lost to love and truth!
> That can, with studied, sly, ensnaring art,
> Betray sweet *Jenny*'s unsuspecting youth?
> Curse on his perjur'd arts! dissembling smoothe!
> Are *Honor*, *Virtue*, *Conscience*, all exil'd?
> Is there no Pity, no relenting Ruth,
> Points to the Parents fondling o'er their Child?
> Then paints the *ruin'd Maid*, and *their* distraction wild!

From a position of great understanding and sympathy for the poet, David Daiches comments:

> The ruined maid, who comes from *The Man of Feeling* and other sentimental works of the period, is an artificial and melodramatic figure in this humble cottage. This verse is, in fact, full of melodramatic gestures, such as 'Curse on his perjur'd arts' – we almost see the villain in a black cloak and curled black moustachios – and the redundant, conventional language ('Is there no Pity, no relenting Ruth?') shows how

> far away from good writing Burns could get when he moved into a tradition in which he was not at home.[88]

Mercifully, Burns break off from this use of artificial language, and his pose of the offended man of feeling, to return to the narrative of the domestic scene of the family gathering around the table for their simple supper. Then, as they arrange themselves around the fireside, Burns leads us into the scene that perhaps is the best remembered of all the scenes in 'The Cotter's Saturday Night', the little vignette of the family at worship.

Before entering upon any discussion of the detail of the poet's description of this, a word must be said as to the authenticity of the scene. Confirmation of the accuracy of Burns's account comes from at least three sources: his brother Gilbert, his former schoolteacher John Murdoch and the housekeeper of Mrs Dunlop, all of whom knew Burns personally. Gilbert Burns relates the poet's feelings for the opening words of the act of worship, 'Let us worship God': 'Robert had frequently remarked to me, that he thought that there was something peculiarly venerable in the phrase, "Let us worship God," used by a decent sober head of a family introducing family worship. To this sentiment ... the world is indebted for "The Cotter's Saturday Night."'[89] Gilbert goes on to say that he was 'electrified' by Robert's recitation of the poem: 'The fifth and sixth stanzas, and the eighteenth, thrilled with peculiar extasy through my soul.' When it is considered that Robert's recitation of the poem might even have taken place a few months before the death of their father, or shortly afterwards, Gilbert's words attest the authenticity of the verses relating to the atmosphere in the childhood home he had shared with Robert and the rest of the family.

On 22 February 1799, John Murdoch writes to the Irish author of *The Historical Memoirs of the Irish Bards*, Joseph Cooper Walker, of his experience in the cottage built by the poet's father: 'In this mean cottage, of which I myself was an inhabitant, I really believe there dwelt a larger portion of content, than any place in Europe. *The Cotter's Saturday Night* will give some idea of the temper and manners that prevailed there.'[90] Murdoch follows this up with a long laudatory passage on the character of William Burnes:

> ... I myself have always considered William Burnes as by far the best of the human race that ever I had the pleasure of being acquainted with – and many a worthy character I have known ... He was an excellent husband, if I may judge from his assiduous attention to the ease and comfort of his worthy partner; and from her affectionate behaviour to him ... He was a tender and affectionate father; he took pleasure in leading his children in the path of virtue; not in driving them, as some parents do to the performance of duties to which they themselves are averse. He took care to find fault but very seldom; and therefore when he did rebuke, he was listened to with a kind of reverential awe.

That William Burnes was a good man is attested by both these sources. That he was also a religious man is evidenced by the fact that he produced for the guidance of his children *A Manual of Religious Belief in a Dialogue Between Father & Son*. This little book, which took the form of a catechism, has as its first question, addressed by the son to the father, 'How shall I evidence to myself that there is a God?' to which the father replies, 'By the works of creation: for nothing can make itself; and this fabrick of nature demonstrates its Creator to be possessed of all possible perfection, and for that cause we owe all that we have to Him.'[91] The second question is very much a leading one, as the catechism continues: 'If God be possessed of all perfection, ought not we then to love Him, as well as fear and serve Him?' To which the father replies:

> Yes; we ought to serve him out of love, for his perfections give us delightful prospects of his favour and friendship, for if we serve him out of love, we will endeavour to be like him, and God will love his own image, and if God love us, he will rejoice over us to do good.

Here is further evidence for 'The Cotter's Saturday Night' being based on the actual experience of the poet, whose father was so concerned for the religious understanding of his children that he went to the length of writing a little book of religious instruction for them. It is also significant that this book differs considerably from the then standard *The Larger Catechism*, the second question of which is: 'How doth it appear that there is a God?' To which it gives the answer: 'The very light of nature in man, and the works of God, declare plainly that there is a God; but his word and Spirit only do sufficiently and effectually reveal him unto men for their salvation.'[92]

Apart from the language of Burnes's *Manual*, being more simple, the question is answered in a more direct way and in a manner that raises fewer questions than the answer to the similar question in *The Larger Catechism*. A real effort has been made by William Burnes to posit the existence of a Creator from all the signals that come from the surrounding natural world, and to attempt to evoke a response based on the goodness of a God that has so provided for humanity. He also introduces the concept of serving this God in love, and of this bond between God and human beings as the basis of their accountability towards him. From his earliest days, perhaps even before he was able to read for himself, Burns's father was teaching him of a benevolent God to whom he should respond in grateful love. That is the same kind of father that is found in 'The Cotter's Saturday Night'.

The third source that would confirm the authenticity of the scene of the family at worship in the poem are the words of Mrs Frances Anna Dunlop's housekeeper, who knew Burns from his calling at the house of her mistress. Kinsley tells of how Mrs Dunlop had given her a copy of 'The Cotter's Saturday Night' to raise her estimate of its author: 'She returned the volume with a strong shake of the head, saying, "Nae doubt gentlemen and ladies think mickle o' this, but for me its naething but what I saw i' my father's house every day, and I dinna see how he could hae tauld it ony other way" ' (Cunningham, ii.259).[93] Perhaps that is the most telling of all the testimonies as to the authenticity of the picture of the cotter's household as painted by Burns in 'The Cotter's Saturday Night'. But from this, and the other witnesses quoted, it would appear to have been painted from life and based upon the poet's childhood experience.

Turning now to the details of the act of worship engaged in by the family, the poet tells of how they gather around the fireside while the father opens up the big 'ha'-Bible' ('ha', meaning 'hame' or 'home'). This, usually large, family Bible was kept at home, and often was the place in which the family's births, marriages and deaths were recorded. One such bible owned by William Burnes records the following details in his own handwriting:

> William Burnes was born 11th November, 1721
> Agnes Broun, was born 17th March, 1732
> Married together, 15th December 1757.
> Had a son, Robert, 25th January, 1759
> Had a son, Gilbert, 28th Septr., 1760
> Had a daughter, Agnes, 30th Septr., 1762
> Had a daughter, Anabella, 14th Novr., 1764
> Had a son, William, 30th July, 1767
> Had a son, John, 10th July, 1769
> Had a daughter, Isobel, 27th June, 1771

The next entry is in the poet's handwriting: 'William Burness [*sic*] departed this life, 13th February, 1784 aged 63 years, 2 months, and 22 days.'[94]

The 'Call to Worship', 'Let us worship God', is given by the father and is followed by all of the family joining in the singing of one of the metrical psalms. Burns lists the psalm tunes that might have been used, and favourably compares them with the then fashionable 'Italian trills' which only tickle the ears, but 'no heart-felt raptures raise'. The poet is hinting that the foreign tunes only affect the surface whereas the sung in unison psalm tunes reach right down to the heart, which for one who confessed to his religion being the 'religion of the bosom' was the place that needed to be affected.

Then likening the father to the priest who mediates God to the people, Burns shows his knowledge of the Scriptures as he instances the Bible stories that the father might have chosen. The Scriptures are not merely listed, but by a simple sentence or phrase each story is singled out in a way that indicates the poet's familiarity with its content and significance.

Having read the Scriptures, 'The Saint, the Father, and the Husband prays'. The head of the family is at one and the same time a member of the Church, the father of his children and the husband of his wife. In describing the cotter in this way, Burns seems to be trying to say that this man gathered together all of his roles and brought them to God. Here was a whole man praying, concerned for the 'Communion of Saints' to which he belonged as a member of the Church, concerned for his children that they might know about God and concerned to acknowledge his wife as one who shared in all his aspirations. By using the words that he does to describe the cotter at prayer, the poet is paying tribute to a man who seemed to bring his whole life before God. In this act of prayer, various elements can be discerned: a hope of better days to come, a hope of a reunion in heaven, a hope of a time when tears will be things of the past and all will join in praise of their Creator. Elements of Burns's own religious thoughts are there: the belief in a good God who is the Creator of the world and who will preside over a time to come when all the causes of tears will be over.

The poet then compares this humble scene of family worship with the more formal acts of public worship engaged in by ministers and their congregations. He criticizes public worship for its artifice, and for its unnecessary and inappropriate pride, pompousness and show. Ministers again come in for criticism, or at least those ministers who 'display to congregations wide, / Devotion's every grace, except the heart!'[95]

The heartfeltness of religion was, for the poet, its most important aspect. The poet claims that his own religion is the religion of the heart. As it is with our personal relations with other people, so it is with God, 'The *heart* ay's the part ay, / That makes us right or wrang'.[96] In Burns's eyes, a preaching that was not heartfelt by its proclaimer and able to reach the heart of the one who heard it was a mere pretence. Further, Burns seems to imply that a religion that does not take account of the feelings of the heart is devoid of its essential content, and only consists of the superficialities of an outward show of piety, upheld merely by its formal structure and the skill of the artists who present it. There is nothing in such religion to meet the needs of the human heart. In this stanza, Burns suggests that God, whom he describes as 'The POWER', will become angry and impatient with organized religion as it is being practised, and will stop listening to, or being present at, these false displays of religion. Instead he will find his way to listen in to the worship offered up 'in some Cottage far apart', where he will hear 'the language of the *Soul*; / and in His *Book of Life* the Inmates poor enroll.'

In these few stanzas, the poet describes the scene of worship in the cottage in such a sympathetic manner that it is impossible to avoid sensing his identification with it. He may be looking back nostalgically, but if there is any sense of loss being experienced by him as he writes, it would appear that it is a loss regretted not because he no longer shares those feelings, but because he has left that period in his life behind. Burns still looks back with thankfulness for having known the benefits of such scenes as he describes in 'The Cotter's Saturday Night'.

The poem, as a work in praise of the rustic scene and the simplicity of the lives and religion of the cotter and his family, might well have been better to have ended with stanza 18, as the family gathering breaks up and 'homeward all take off their sev'ral way'. Although stanza 19 contains the much quoted lines:

From scenes like these, old SCOTIA's grandeur springs,
That makes her lov'd at home, rever'd abroad:
Princes and lords are but the breath of kings,
'An honest man's the noble work of GOD:'

from there on, it could be argued, the poem takes a downhill path ending with a patriotic outburst that nowadays might be thought of as bordering on jingoism. It is as if the poet has gone into another mode, the heroic one, and then gone so strongly with it that he has lost touch with what he had at first set out to do. The God of the last stanza, 'The Patriot's GOD, peculiarly thou art', cannot be reconciled with the God of the cotter, who seeks not his power for the fight, but his care of his family and his grace to live honestly.

The strengths of this poem are evident when the poet is describing the familiar scenes of the home and the family, in their being together in conversation, at supper and at worship. It is especially in the stanzas that deal with the religious practice of the family that the poet's sympathy and tacit approval emerge. It can be sensed that the poet is not just simply recording the quaint ways of an earlier age, but that he is genuinely dealing with things in which he himself participated, and of which he approves and believes in still. It is only when he adopts the pose and the language of the man of feeling, as in his condemnation of the hypothetical villain who would ruin a maid or when he begins to praise 'The Patriot's GOD' in the manner of a declamatory Augustan poet, that we sense an artificiality. Indeed an insincerity is introduced that ill befits the earlier ways in which he has spoken of a cotter's family that so closely resembles his own childhood experience in matters of custom and belief, as to make one think of there being almost an identity of the fictional family with the Burns family.

'The Ordination'[97]

Although 'The Ordination' is entirely concerned with a religious event, the ordination of a minister, Burns's own religious beliefs are not openly expressed in the poem. It is, however, possible to infer from his negative comments on ministers, on biblical texts, on doctrine and on the practices of the Church the things that he does not believe; and sometimes, from his not quite hidden approval, the things that he does. What he does value, in his own understanding of religion, is sometimes found by a process of extrapolation from the obverse of what it is that he is mocking, or even condemning. However, the very fact that Burns chooses to write about this local ecclesiastical event at all is an indication of his interest in religion. That he is prepared to mock the Auld Light ministers and to praise the New Lights who are named in the poem is also an indication of where his sympathies lie. But his own religious opinions and beliefs are often in this poem only negatively defined and are to be arrived at only by inference.

In December 1785, the Earl of Glencairn had presented the Reverend James Mackinlay, an Auld Light minister, for induction to the Laigh Kirk of Kilmarnock's second charge. The Moderates in the Presbytery of Irvine and Kilmarnock opposed the introduction of the minister, and caused his induction to be delayed until April 1786. The poem was written during the period prior to the induction and Burns deals with the issues that arose: the theological differences between Auld and New Lights, between those who opposed and those who supported Patronage, between congregation and presbytery, between different styles of preaching and between different methods of scriptural interpretation.[98]

In the poem, Burns relates the more recent history of church life in the Laigh Kirk, which had two charges within it. The minister of the first charge, and the senior minister, was the Reverend John Robertson, a Moderate who had been there since 1765. In the second charge there had served from 1764 to 1774 the Reverend William Lindsay, who was followed by the Reverend John Multrie from 1775 to 1785 when he died, thereby creating the vacancy. Both Lindsay and Multrie had been Moderates, so the proposed filling of the vacancy by an Auld Light minister such as the Reverend James Mackinlay was a break from the charge's most recent tradition.[99]

The first mention of the ministers who are involved in the story is made obliquely in verse two:

> Curst Common-sense, that imp o' h–ll,
> Cam in wi' Maggie Lauder;
> But O******* aft made her yell,
> And R***** sair misca'd her:

The first two lines refer to the Moderate's association with a common-sense view of the Bible, and more specifically to the view of the Reverend William Lindsay, whose wife's maiden name was Maggie Lauder. The following two lines refer to another two ministers, the Reverend James Oliphant of Kilmarnock High Kirk from 1764 to 1773 and his successor, the current minister, the Reverend John Russel. Both ministers were Auld Lights and opponents of the common-sense attitudes held by the Moderates. The verse concludes with the picture of Mackinlay taking up from where the other two ministers had left off, to beat common sense with a flail and to pin her down with a forked stick in the same way, apparently, as cruel children of the time sometimes did to the tail of a dog to enable them to abuse it. The imagery used by Burns implies the viciousness of the attack upon common sense that he expected the Auld Light minister to make, and is an indication of his own experience of the sometimes vitriolic exchanges between the opposing parties within the Church.

Then in Stanza III Burns gives further evidence of his personal experience of the Church, this time as he describes the psalm singing of the congregation. Burns's description of the singing is wickedly ironic. He creates an image of King David, traditionally the author of the Psalms, being so disturbed by the noise made by the congregation as they sing that he turns over in his grave. That this is likely to have been derived from Burns's own experience is corroborated by this description of an eighteenth century Scottish congregation at worship, quoted by Kinsley from W.D. Maxwell's *A History of Worship in the Church of Scotland*: 'No organs were permitted; the precentor led the praise .... Not content with the simple tune [congregations] fell to embellishing it with grace notes of their own devising, often invented on the spot .... Thus, together with lining [reading the line before singing it] and gracing, the cacophony created is mercifully unimaginable . . . '.[100]

All of this noise described by Burns is in celebration of the fact that an Auld Light minister, whose theology is deemed to be orthodox, will be able to deal with heresy as it is locally found and oust it from the place, and he will do this by the proper use of the Scriptures. Burns says, 'Come, let a proper text be read', implying that now, in Kilmarnock, there will be a return to the true message of orthodoxy. Burns then proceeds to give examples of what might be preached. His own contempt for the preaching of the Auld Lights becomes clear when the 'proper text[s]' are examined, for, arguably, Burns selects three of the seemingly most obscure and irrelevant texts as could be found anywhere in the whole of the Old Testament.

The first text, from Genesis 9:21–27 is from the story of Noah and his three sons, Ham, Shem and Japheth, and the incident in which Ham sees his father lying drunk and naked. He goes to tell his brothers who are so shocked that they contrive to walk backwards towards the old man, carrying a cloak across their shoulders to drop it down upon him to cover his nakedness without them looking upon it.

The second text, from Numbers 25:1–8, tells the story of Phinehas, who, after listening to a sermon warning against associating with foreign women, takes it upon himself to do something about it. So he picks up a javelin and goes into the tent of a young Israelite man who has been living with a

Midianitish woman and 'thrust both of them through, the man of Israel, and the woman through her belly'.

The third text quoted by Burns is from Exodus 4:24–26, and concerns the circumcision of Moses. The text is so ancient and so obscure that scholars today are unsure as to whether the story relates to Moses's circumcision or that of his son. An even earlier story seems to lie behind the one that is related in Exodus and the reason for its inclusion in the Old Testament book is difficult to understand, other than as giving supporting warranty to the already established practice of circumcision. The narrative immediately preceding this story tells of God calling Moses to be the leader of his people, to which Moses very reluctantly agrees. The story to which Burns refers then ensues. Moses has gone to an inn and, inexplicably we are told, 'the Lord met him and sought to kill him'. This tale of God setting out to kill the man whom he has just singled out to be the leader of his people probably relates to an older text in which it was said that a demon sought to kill Moses, and somewhere along the line 'demon' was transformed into 'the Lord'. When confronted in the inn by the threat of the demon, or the Lord, Moses's wife Zipporah, 'took a sharp stone, and cut off the foreskin of her son, and cast it at his feet, and said, Surely a bloody husband art thou to me. So he let him go: then she said, A bloody husband thou art, because of the circumcision.' This obviously muddled narrative with its doubly confusing meaning had somehow found its way into the book of Exodus, one of the books included in the list recorded in *The Westminster Confession of Faith* and referred to as 'Holy Scripture, or the Word of God'. After listing the 39 books of the Old Testament including Exodus and the 27 of the New Testament, the *Confession* continues: 'All of which are given by inspiration of God, to be the rule of faith and life.'[101] Here then, from this 'inspired' book, Burns selects these three odd stories, indicating the 'proper text[s]' and the kind of preaching that he thinks is likely to be engaged in by the Auld Light minister James Mackinlay.

When I first looked at these texts, I thought that Burns might just have been indulging himself in a bit of fun by looking for three examples of what he would later come to call 'religious nonsense'. But perhaps there was more method than madness in his selection of the texts, for all of them deal with taboos: the taboo of not looking at a parent's sexual organs, the taboo of mixed marriages and the taboo of the uncircumcised not being allowed into the elite house of Israel. All three taboos relate to the self-righteous and judgemental element of those religious people who think of themselves as the 'elect'. In the first story, the two brothers keep themselves right with God by not looking at their father's nakedness and the story ends with their being rewarded, while their brother is punished by having to become their servant in perpetuity. In the second story, the young man with the javelin exercises a self-righteous judgement in killing the couple. The third story tells of the self-righteousness of a people who think that a mere conforming to the physical act of circumcision saves them from destruction and brings them into relation with God. Even the later priestly writer of the book of Deuteronomy knew that there was more to the Hebrew faith than a mere conforming to the physical ritual of circumcision, when he wrote, 'And the Lord thy God will circumcise thine heart, and the heart of thy seed, to love the Lord thy God with all thine heart, and with all thy soul, that thou mayest live.'[102] Burns was in tune with the sentiment of the writer of Deuteronomy. For Burns, whose religion was the religion of the heart, if religion did not affect the heart, all else was but meaningless outward show. Perhaps, then, in his selection of these three texts Burns intended to say much more than is generally perceived by those who read his work.

In Stanza V of the poem Burns turns his attention to the preacher who will be tried and judged by his adherence to 'the creed'. He hints that there will be those around the minister, his watchful fellow ministers, his Elders and even ordinary members of his congregation who will, 'bind him down wi' caution', lest he stray from the accepted path that the orthodox have to walk if they are not to be condemned for straying from the faith. Burns then mentions 'Stipend', the minister's salary. Kinsley thinks that Burns unjustly criticizes Mackinlay, as in general stipends at that time were low when compared, for example, with what a master tradesman could earn. Perhaps in talking of stipend as 'a carnal weed', likening it to the luxury pleasure of smoking tobacco – something that is enjoyable but not the be all and end all of life – Burns was only saying that Mackinlay takes his stipend, 'for the fashion', that is, because it is customary to take it. The only sting in the remark is in the use of the word 'carnal', which was one of the cant words of the Auld Lights, and by applying this word to something as innocuous as a person's salary, Burns is again mocking their condemnation of such ordinary things as 'fleshly' as a way of showing how ridiculously out of touch they were with everyday life. Burns then turns to a subject that is truly carnal, and of which he has personal experience, when his narrator urges the minister to be particularly hard on the 'rams that cross the breed': the fornicators. As by that time Burns himself came officially into that category, he already knew what it was to be on the receiving end of the Church's condemnation.

Kilmarnock town is then likened to a cow that can look forward to good fodder, including 'gospel kail', the nourishing vegetable broth of the gospel, and the 'runts o' grace', the little titbits of gracious words. Burns's words are chosen carefully. 'Gospel kail' implies that the Kilmarnock people will be well fed with what is deemed to be the gospel, but that they will only be fed tiny morsels of grace. The runt was always the poorest of the litter and to link that word with grace is to create an impression of stinginess, of a grudgingly given message of the generous and gracious coming towards them of God. So although Burns sets out to tell the Kilmarnock people that they will be well fed with 'gospel kail', there is a hidden message in his use of the phrase 'runts of grace'. He is telling the people not to expect any generous spirited preaching from the likes of Mackinlay. Burns is clearly indicating to those who could see, that the Kilmarnock people are going to get little graciousness shown to them by their new minister.

The poet then goes on in Stanza VII to refer to Psalm 137, which was written to describe the miserable life of the people taken into captivity and exile in Babylon. It likens the lot of the Kilmarnock people, under the regime of the Moderates, to those who had endured a Babylonian captivity, and who have now been liberated by the Auld Lights. The poet returns to the theme of Patronage, and of how it has ruled over the Kirk 'wi' a rod o' airn' and shows his knowledge of the Fenwick case, where in 1780, the congregation had barricaded the church rather than accept the Moderate minister the Reverend William Boyd, who had been presented by the patron, the Earl of Glasgow. It took two years before the matter was resolved by the General Assembly, which ruled that he be ordained in 1782.[103]

Compared with this, the Kilmarnock patron, Lord Glencairn, had chosen well in bringing an Auld Light, 'a godly, elect bairn', to be the Laigh Kirk's minister. Here Burns is emphasizing the theology of the Auld Lights that pressed home a belief in election. Not only was the new minister wisely chosen by their patron but, even before that, God had already chosen him as one of the 'elect', one predestined for salvation.

The poem moves on to Stanza IX where John Robertson, Minister of the First Charge of the Laigh Kirk, and Mackinlay's senior, is told to 'harangue nae mair', to either shut up or put up, and depart for the 'wicked town of A**'. Burns is here referring to the fact that there were quite a number of Moderate ministers in Ayr. Dr William Dalrymple and Dr William McGill were ministers of the Auld Kirk of Ayr, and were well-known and outspoken Moderates. Burns goes on to say that the devil often sat like a cat watching both Robertson and his colleague Multrie, waiting for them to say something heretical that would result in them being punished in hell, but that now he could safely depart 'wi' a' his brimstone squadrons', for he will no longer be needed, so orthodox will the preaching be at the Laigh Kirk.

Orthodoxy is then portrayed as 'swingein thro' the city', wielding a 'nine-tailed cat'. Learning and Common Sense, meanwhile, have gone to complain to Dr James Beattie, Moral Philosopher and poet of the 'The Ministrel'. Morality is also suffering and is 'packed aff to h–ll' along with the other two. Mackinlay and Russel are then held up as 'the boys / That Heresy can torture', and the poem ends with a toast being raised, 'To ev'ry New-light mother's son, / From this time forth, Confusion.'

So Burns has described the scene of celebration at the prospect of the ordination of the Reverend James Mackinlay. All of Burns's own beliefs remain hidden within the criticisms that he makes of the Auld Lights, and the fears that he expresses at the likely outcome of such a regime in Kilmarnock.

His own views only emerge as the nature of the criticisms are examined. His religious beliefs and understandings and attitudes are discernible, but only emerge from a careful reading of the text.

'The First Psalm'[104]

Burns seems to have written this paraphrase of 'The First Psalm' in the winter of 1781–82, while at Irvine learning the craft of flax-dressing. Ill and depressed, he may well have turned to the Psalm for comfort. It was certainly conveniently placed for this to happen, being the first Psalm that would confront him when opening the book. Burns would have been familiar with the Psalms, both as they are found in the King James Bible and the metrical version that was the standard and usually the only praise book used for congregational singing in the Church of Scotland at the time. *The Scottish Psalter* had been in use in the reformed church in Scotland since 1564 and further editions had been published in 1615 and 1635. Both as a poet and as one with a lively interest in music Burns would have been familiar with the metres used and the tunes of the *Psalter*. *The Handbook to the Church Hymnary* says of the tunes:

> The tunes which were identified with particular Psalms came to be known as Proper tunes. But in course of time when the number of Psalms included in the Psalter exceeded the number of available tunes, the practice came in of regarding certain tunes as Common, i.e. not identifying them with any particular Psalms but using them for any Psalms in the corresponding metre.[105]

On reflection, this little piece of information on the history of the *Psalter* in the Scottish Church adds further weight and significance to Burns's use of the word 'proper' relating to the texts that he suggested might be used by the Auld Light preachers in 'The Ordination'. In selecting the word 'proper' he was applying a known ecclesiastical term.

Burns's version of the Psalm is modelled on the metrical version of the Psalm as it is found in the *Scottish Psalter*. For comparison the two versions are given here:

Scottish Psalter	**Burns**
That man hath perfect blessedness who walketh not astray In counsel of ungodly men, nor stands in sinners' way,	The man, in life where-ever plac'd, Hath happiness in store, Who walks not in the wicked's way, Nor learns their guilty lore!
Nor sitteth in the scorner's chair:	Nor from the seat of scornful Pride

But placeth his delight
Upon God's law, and meditates
on his law day and night.

He shall be like a tree that grows
near planted by a river,
Which in his season yields his fruit,
and his leaf fadeth never:

And all he doth shall prosper well.
The wicked are not so;
But like they are unto the chaff,
which wind drives to and fro.

In judgment therefore shall not stand
such as ungodly are;
Nor in th' assembly of the just
shall wicked men appear.

For why? the way of godly men
unto the Lord is known:
Whereas the way of wicked men
shall quite be overthrown.[106]

Casts forth his eyes abroad,
But with humility and awe
Still walks before his GOD.

That man shall flourish like the trees
Which by the streamlets grow;
The fruitful top is spread on high,
And firm the root below.

But he whose blossom buds in guilt
Shall to the ground be cast,
And like the rootless stubble tost,
Before the sweeping blast.

For why? that GOD the good adore
Hath giv'n them peace and rest,
But hath decreed that wicked men
Shall ne'er be truly blest.[107]

In his first verse Burns exactly follows the sentiments of the opening verse of the *Psalter*. However, in the second verse he changes the central character, around whom the Psalm is built, from a man who specifically delights to study and meditate upon God's law, to the more general one of a man who walks with humility and awe before God. By this device, Burns makes the happiness or blessedness of which the Psalm speaks much more accessible to the ordinary person. Blessedness is not just for the narrowly religious person who delights in acquiring a great understanding of God's law, but can be obtained by the person who lives with humility and a respect for God. In Burns's verse, there is a breaking away from the idea of the fixed source of information, revelation and inspiration that is the law of God that is to be found in the Scriptures, and a movement towards the idea that by the simple means of adopting an attitude of humility and reverence for God, blessedness can be found. In the third verse Burns uses the same simile of the flourishing tree as in the *Psalter*, but in the last line opts to extend it by describing the root taking a firm hold as against the psalmist's image of the never fading leaf. In verse four, Burns cleverly expands upon the simile of the growing tree, but turns the blossom to a guilt that like rotten fruit is thrown out and rejected, before rejoining the psalmist's theme of the fate of the wicked being like the chaff blowing away in the wind. He differs from the psalmist in that he does not use the word 'wicked' in this verse, reserving it for the last verse as if he was avoiding judging the 'rootless stubble'. The psalmist uses the word both in this and the fifth and sixth verses, as if to emphasize the difference between the godly and the wicked. Burns has no equivalent of verse five in the Psalm, one that is about the judgement of the 'ungodly' and the 'wicked'. One can only speculate as to why Burns writes no parallel to verse five. Is it because he does not like the idea of passing judgement on those who, 'gang a kennin wrang', and always remembers that 'to step aside is human'?[108] Is he turning away from the harshness of distinguishing between the godly and the ungodly, the just and the wicked? There might even be his memories of being part of a congregation, an 'assembly of the just', and knowing full well that it was far from being a gathering of the righteous, and indeed contained all sorts of people of varying degrees of honesty and dishonesty, goodness and badness; and so he shies away from this seperation of people into distinct categories to make a judgement upon them. I am sure that Burns's omission of a parallel verse to the psalmist's verse five is significant, because Burns finds himself at odds with the religious sentiments expressed within it. He clearly parts company with the theology expressed by the psalmist, and can find nothing to say that will not contest it. So he remains silent at this point, reserving his opinion for the last verse of his own version.

In the first two lines of verse six of the metrical Psalm there is kind of self-righteous, triumphalist air. Pride seems to be taken in the fact that God knows when people are godly. It has become as if they are saying, 'God knows that we are godly, and that is why we prosper.' This is followed by the last two lines in which there is a kind of attitude being encouraged that says, 'The wicked are going to get what they deserve, and we are glad, because they really do deserve it.' There is almost an air of gloating, a *Schadenfreude*, about these closing lines. It becomes very clear that Burns cannot share these sentiments expressed by the psalmist. Although he opens his last verse with the same question 'For why?', he offers a quite different answer. Why should these things be? There is nothing to gloat about, it is just the way that God has organized the world. The God that the good adore is adored because by believing in him, and walking in humility before him, men and women are able to experience 'peace and rest'. They are reconciled to themselves and to the world in which they live and are at home in it. That is the way it is, says Burns, therefore there is no reason to be exultant at the fate of those whom the world calls 'wicked' and no justification for thinking of yourselves as 'godly' or 'just'. You are blessed if you happen to attempt to live your life walking in humility and awe before God. Burns is sufficiently Calvinistic in his outlook to accept that God has 'decreed that wicked men / Shall ne'er be truly blest.' But as Thomas Crawford points out, Burns is a bit ambiguous as to what will be their final fate, he cannot consign them to perish utterly, only, however, allowing them a partial blessing.[109]

By these variations, Burns achieves a different theological tone in his version of the first Psalm. The theology that emerges from Burns's version is not the orthodox theology that can be extracted from the original version in the Old Testament, in which the theology is fairly accurately represented by the metrical version. The theology that does emerge from Burns's version is consistent with the views that Burns expresses in other parts of his writings, as he considers his own accountability, the mystery of life's ending and the desire to believe in a benevolent God.

'The First Six Verses of the Ninetieth Psalm'[110]

Psalm 90 in the King James Bible

1. Lord, thou hast been our dwelling place in all generations.
2. Before the mountains were brought forth, or ever thou hadst formed the earth and the world, even from everlasting to everlasting, thou art God.
3. Thou turnest man to destruction; and sayest, Return ye children of men.
4. For a thousand years in thy sight are but as yesterday when it is past, and as a watch in the night.
5. Thou carriest them away as with a flood; they are as a sleep: in the morning they are like grass which groweth up.
6. In the morning it flourisheth, and groweth up; in the evening it is cut down, and withereth.

'The First Six Verses of the Ninetieth Psalm', Robert Burns.

O THOU, the first, the greatest friend
Of all the human race!
Whose strong right hand has ever been
Their stay and dwelling place!

Before the mountains heav'd their heads
Beneath Thy forming hand,
Before this ponderous globe itself
Arose at thy command:

That Pow'r which rais'd and still upholds
This universal frame,
From countless, unbeginning time
Was ever still the same.

Those mighty periods of years
Which seem to us so vast,

Appear no more before Thy sight
Than yesterday that's past.

Thou giv'st the word; Thy creature, man,
Is to existence brought;
Again Thou say'st, 'Ye sons of men,
'Return ye into nought!'

Thou layest them with all their cares
In everlasting sleep;
As with a flood Thou tak'st them off
With overwhelming sweep.

They flourish like the morning flow'r
In beauty's pride array'd;
But long ere night cut down it lies
All wither'd and decay'd.

The God who emerges from Burns's version of the portion of Psalm 90 appears to be the same as the one portrayed in the equivalent verses of the Psalm in the King James Bible, in all but name, but a study of the manner in which Burns addresses or describes God allows us to see significant differences between the God of his poem and the God of the biblical Psalm. The biblical version hails God as 'Lord' and in the second verse declares, 'from everlasting to everlasting, thou art God'. The Burns version greets God, 'O THOU, the first, the greatest friend of all the human race!', and goes on to describe him impersonally as, 'That Pow'r which rais'd and still upholds / This universal frame'. Missing from the Burns version is the subservience implied by addressing God as 'Lord'. It is as if that word sticks in his throat. It might already have had a pejorative flavour to one who would go on to put it in the mouth of 'Holy Willie' no fewer than 12 times in the course of his prayer. Or it might even have been from Burns's early familiarity with the Gospel story that reminded the followers of Jesus that it was not just by the use of the word 'Lord' that discipleship was achieved that caused him to refrain from using it in his version of the Psalm. As someone who took a keen interest in matters of religion, 'Lord' could have become a devalued word for Burns because of its overuse by some of the more overtly religious people he had met. But there may have been another reason for not repeating or creating a similar phrase that used the word 'Lord'. Burns also avoids using the tense of the declaration of the stature of God that is in the Psalm, 'thou art Lord'. Perhaps it is because he cannot bring himself to articulate in such a specific way about the God that he believed in. It is just too much to incorporate in his version what amounts to a personal declaration of faith. However much he might have been drawn to a concept of the 'Eternal Now',[111] the omnipresence of a power that might be called God, he could not engage in such a personal commitment as to say, 'thou art God'.

In this Psalm, Burns addresses God as, 'O THOU, the first, the greatest friend / Of all the human race.' This seems to be almost as personal a way of addressing God as that adopted by the psalmist, but on examination it becomes less personal than it sounds. Burns placed a high value on friendship, as is evidenced by the many letters he writes to his friends. Friendship was one of the most supportive structures of his life. The warmth of his letters to those to whom he was close, like William Nicol, Alexander Cunningham or Robert Ainslie, or even the more formal ones, with the likes of Mrs Frances Dunlop or Peter Hill, show how he would go out of his way to maintain the friendship through compliments, the occasional gift or the expression of concern for other members of their families.[112] Burns likens the relationship with God to that of friendship; it is a sustaining relationship in times of illness, depression or weariness, but it is also a source of joy. He possibly thinks of God as akin to a corresponding friend, and writes to one of them that 'a correspondence fixed wi' heaven is sure a noble anchor'. Friendship is important to Burns, and God is addressed as one who is like a friend.

In his poem 'Epistle to Davie, a brother Poet', Burns makes a connection between love, friendship and God.[113] Stanza VIII declares the inestimable value of 'the *Pleasures o' the Heart*, / The *Lover* and the *Frien*'.' Stanza IX addresses the '*Pow'rs* who rule above' and singles out the one, God, 'whose very self art *love*' and commits Jean Armour, the object of Burns's love, into the care of God, who is described as 'Thou BEING, Allseeing'. Stanza X returns again to the theme of friendship being bestowed by some greater power, this time, given the title 'Fate'. These stanzas are like a wild romp of a 'Man of Feeling', passionate, demonstrative, an outburst barely controlled. It is difficult to separate the artistry from the sincerity in these stanzas. Sometimes the poet takes off in a panegyric declaration of love:

> O, all ye *Pow'rs* who rule above!
> O Thou, whose very self art *love*!
> Thou know'st my words sincere!

but Burns then reduces the impact of these words that are supposedly coming from the heart, by the ambiguity and possible sexual allusion of the next lines: 'The *life blood* streaming through my heart, / Or my more dear *Immortal* part.' As to whether he is referring to his soul or to his sexual organ is left in some doubt.

However, in these stanzas Burns is undoubtedly asserting that inner happiness comes only in love and friendship. Love is praised in such a way, Thomas Crawford says, as D.H. Lawrence would have approved. Crawford writes of these lines: 'It is a gospel of "Joy through Sex" that Burns is preaching here – not simply the sexual act itself . . . but all the emotions and sentiments which grow out of its soil.'[114] In a way that anticipates Lawrence, Burns brings God into this celebration of love, sex and friendship. In his Introduction to The Penguin Poets edition of *Selected Poems of D.H. Lawrence*, W.E. Williams writes: 'Beneath the varnish of civilization and social convention, he [Lawrence] believed, was to be found the true picture of human behaviour as God originally made it, and Lawrence's vocation (he concluded) was to clean and restore this true image – as art experts restore Old Masters.'[115] In his 'Epistle to Davie', Burns cannot speak of the emotional and physical aspects of love without bringing God into it as the one from whom these physical and emotional things come. His God he can only address as 'Thou, whose very self art *love*.' Lawrence writes in his poem, 'Pax':

> It is not easy to fall out of the hands of the living God
> They are so large, and they cradle so much of a man.
> It is a long time before a man can get himself away.
> Even through the greatest blasphemies, the hands of
> the living God still continue to cradle him.[116]

Despite all his efforts at asserting a more free-thinking theology, it is as if Burns still finds himself in 'the hands of the living God'. He cannot break away entirely from the sense of God having something to do with his life, especially when he is living that life amidst the relationships of friendship, sex and love. Therefore however clumsily he expresses these beliefs, or however cynically he uses conventional phrases to describe them, it is difficult to avoid feeling that it is because of this underlying belief in a loving God who is still holding on to him that he expresses himself in these ways.

In his version of the Psalms's first six verses Burns describe the activity and nature of this God. He is the God who has ever provided support and a place for man in his world; one who has ever been, and ever remains the same; one who brought not just the world, but the universe into being; one for whom time is almost insignificant, because he deals in eternity; one who brings humans into being and who sets limits upon their lives by death, returning them to the dust from which they have come; one, who at the end of lives that have been as brief and as beautiful as flowers yet also that have been full of worries and concerns, brings them suddenly 'all wither'd and decay'd' to an end, and gives them rest in sleep.

The question might be asked as to why Burns chose to write his own version of part of Psalm 90. The most likely answer is that while going through a rather depressing period in his life – probably brought about by a combination of a debilitating illness, his own lack of success in making his way in the world, bad weather resulting in poor harvests at Lochlie, financial worries and a father in his last illness – Burns is led to muse upon the transitoriness of human life, and found confirmation of it in Psalm 90. I suspect that the principal reason for choosing this Psalm is that Burns can identify with the portrait of God painted by the psalmist in his opening six verses. But, as I have outlined, although on the whole Burns went along with the description of what God had done and for what he was responsible, he made changes to this description that were significant: making God 'the first, the greatest friend / Of all the human race' and addressing him in the less personal way as 'That Pow'r which rais'd and still upholds / This universal frame'. In addressing God as 'That Pow'r', Burns is adopting the same attitude that he displays in 'Epistle to Davie', where he describes God as one of the 'Pow'rs who rule above'.[117] Burns then singles out from the 'Pow'rs' one particular God 'whose very self art *love*'. By addressing God as if he is one of a pantheon of Gods, Burns has moved away from any semblance of an orthodox Christian theology. But that is to press the analogy of what he means by 'Pow'rs' to the limit. Burns is probably using the term in a very general way to describe the forces that control the world. He does this in his 'To the Haggis', when he writes, 'Ye Pow'rs wha mak mankind your care'.[118] So, Burns is perhaps addressing God as one power in a world of many powers, such as nature and the State, but in his Psalm he singles out the creative and supportive power of God, whom he has elsewhere identified as love, as the power that is there for human beings to turn to.

By choosing this Psalm upon which to base his own version, and to a great extent not deviating from the main thrust of its theme, Burns is indicating what he believes, or at least is at ease with what others believe. Equally, by stopping his parallel version at verse six and not going any further, Burns is telling us what he does not believe. For in the King James Bible version the Psalm continues with a new theme in verses 7–12 and consequent upon that theme it delivers a homily in verses 13–17.

Psalm 90, verses 7–17.

7. For we are consumed by thine anger, and by thy wrath are we troubled.
8. Thou hast set our iniquities before thee, our secret sins in the light of thy countenance.
9. For all our days are passed away in thy wrath: we spend our years as a tale that is told.
10. The days of our years are threescore years and ten; and if by reason of strength they be fourscore years, yet is their strength labour and sorrow; for it is soon cut off, and we fly away.
11. Who knoweth the power of thine anger? even according to thy fear, so is thy wrath.
12. So teach us to number our days, that we may apply our hearts unto wisdom.
13. Return, O Lord, how long? and let it repent thee concerning thy servants.
14. O satisfy us early with thy mercy; that we may rejoice and be glad all our days.

15. Make us glad according to the days wherein thou hast afflicted us, and the years wherein we have seen evil.
16. Let thy work appear unto thy servants, and thy glory unto their children.
17. And let the beauty of the Lord our God be upon us: and establish thou the work of our hands upon us; yea, the work of our hands establish thou it.[119]

Verses 7–12 take up the theme of God's anger and man's iniquity. God, according to the Psalmist, is angry because of the sinfulness of man. He even knows of all the secret sins that have been hidden from others. Men are living under the threat of the wrath of God. Those who live in fear of God are the ones who are most aware of his wrath. As a consequence of this men should bring order into their lives. The Psalm then concludes with verses 13–17 being a plea for mercy and a plea that God will give recompense for the times of suffering with times of gladness.

Burns cannot come to terms with believing in the kind of God portrayed in verses 7–17 of the Psalm. He cannot believe in an angry God who had created man in the way that he had, then made the rules and alongside them a set of fearful punishments. His God had at least to be as kindly as he was, at least as willing to forgive as he was, at least as generous as he was. Therefore he could not go along with the sentiments expressed in the verses that followed the ones upon which his own version was based. Although Burns is still working under the influence of a Calvinistic understanding of an overarching and undergirding providence that governs the world, he bridles at what he deems to be the overprescriptive application of such a doctrine. He cannot accept the Doctrine of Predestination because he is unwilling to consign to hell those who have done nothing particularly wrong, far less evil, yet he seems to hold to there being a framework determined by God within which man has room to manoeuvre and work out his own salvation.

Burns therefore turns away from and avoids expounding such verses as are found in the second part of the Psalm. God is the friend of mankind not the seethingly angry judge that is portrayed in verse 11. An even more unacceptable aspect of the views of the psalmist is that it is the very people who are striving to be obedient to this God who are the ones most aware of God's wrath. The text might well have been explained at the time but a modern translation makes verse 11's meaning quite clear: 'Who feels the power of thy anger / Who feels thy wrath like those that fear thee.'[120] That is the kind of religion that Burns cannot believe in. A religion that causes even those who would be good, the 'God-fearing' people, to live in anxiety because they did not feel accepted by God.

In this Psalm Burns is identifying wholeheartedly with the psalmist when he is making a statement about the transitoriness of human life. But Burns parts company with the psalmist as to the nature of the God who presides over that transitoriness. Burns's God is in a relationship of friendship with mankind. If he is a power, his is not the omnipotent power of a tyrant who acts in an entirely arbitrary and unfeeling way towards those who are in his power, and before whom they have to plead for mercy. In his Psalm, Burns's God seems to be acknowledged as Creator and as a power that sustains the whole framework of life. But from other places we know that Burns regards the power of God, in terms of his nature, being love. God's power then is the power of love, and in this world love can be defeated. Therefore Burns's God is not an omnipotent power that dominates, but rather a sustaining and enlivening power that brings our humanity to its fullness of being.

As happens so often in Burns's writing on the subject of religion, as much can be learned about his beliefs from the things that he does not say as from the things that he does say. This Psalm confirms his belief in a benevolent God, as much by his only dealing with its first six verses as by his omitting to deal with the remaining verses. By his omission of any reference to the other verses, Burns is indicating his unwillingness to speculate on the final fate of mankind, preferring to leave that to the mercy of the God he believes in. Finally, the Psalm again reveals the attitude of a man who is aware of himself as a creature accountable for his very existence to his creator, and to this belief Burns subscribed to the end of his life.

Epilogue

'Think on these things, and think on.' That was the message that Robert Burns left for all who would consider religion. Yet he knew that much more important than religion was what lies behind religion – the humanity that contrives religion as a means of trying to meet the deepest urges of the inner life of thought and feeling. Throughout his life Burns was feeling his way towards a philosophy and a way of life that would satisfy and be in tune with what he called 'the senses of the mind'.

Burns knew the usefulness of 'a conversation fixed wi' heaven', but for him 'heaven' was always a metaphor for the highest and the best that humanity could know. He looked at his human nature and sighed, 'God knows, I'm no the thing I shou'd be, / Nor am I even the thing I cou'd be'. He looked at others, compassionately observing those who were judged by society to be sinners and musing on, 'the moving *Why* they do it'. He knew the motivation of love. He knew it as something that lit up his life, but he also knew that the same love that caused him 'to want to wipe away all tears from all eyes' nevertheless was the love that could lead him into the darkest corners of his life and bring him near to an abdication of all responsibility. And so he was left with the paradox that even 'the light that led astray / Was light from Heaven'.

Burns was fully aware of the dichotomy between religious aspiration and the acts of the religious, between a faith proclaimed and a failure of practice, but this did not put him off religion. He could write to James Candlish, with whom as a young man he had explored 'the daring path Spinoza trod', that he was not frightened by the strength of the arguments against it, but that it was, 'the experience of the weakness, not the strength of human powers, that made me grasp at revealed religion.' These words have sometimes been taken as Burns's rejection of the rigorous thought process of philosophy and as a retreating towards the easier option of religion. But I think that this is to misunderstand what Burns was seeking to defend: a philosophy that could embrace religion and take from it what (he thought) it could provide in its utility. Spinoza is referred to by Burns as if he were the epitome of philosophic logic and all the tough reasoning of those who go against the accepted norms, and in this Burns is adopting the then current labelling of Spinoza as atheistic and representative of the logical rejection of the orthodox religious position. But oddly enough, Spinoza, for all that he was branded as an atheist, was a man whose whole philosophy was built upon the premise of God – a God who was inseparable from the very substance of the world. Bertrand Russell says of Spinoza, 'He was born a Jew, but the Jews excommunicated him, Christians abhorred him equally; although his whole philosophy is dominated by the idea of God, the orthodox accused him of atheism.' Burns, though seeming to reject the rationality of the logic of philosophy in preference for the heart-sourced feeling of religion, is really saying that there is no conflict between philosophy and religion. He was seeking a philosophy that was well reasoned yet that could embody within it a feeling sensitivity to the non-rational elements of life as he knew it. Burns was perhaps nearer to Spinoza's 'daring path' than he knew, for Spinoza was one who saw God and nature, the world and man as of the same substance – indivisible – so much so that he could say 'No one can hate God'. Burns reached out to religion not because he sought an escape from thinking or a refuge from a harsh world; he used it not as a ghetto but as a gateway to further thought.

Burns's exploration of religion was to venture a long way from what he had called his infant 'idiot piety' to the last days of his life, when he still seemed to find himself addressed by the claims of the 'great unknown'. He seemed to be coming to the understanding that religion could not offer a *Weltanschauung* – a total explanation of reality – that there would always be insufficient data. Yet something within him (was it the continuance of that 'stubborn, sturdy something' in his disposition of which he wrote to Dr Moore?) that was unwilling to fully believe that his humanity was no better or different from the sod upon which he stood, or like a piece of broken down machinery that would be left to rust to dust when its usefulness was over. Yet equally he could not bring himself to an acceptance of the heavenly and hellish future presided over by a God who meted out rewards and punishments, as painted by those who claimed to be the orthodox Christians of their day. Their's was too small a vision, too neat and complete an explanation. Again he was faced with the paradox of the complexity of the questions raised by religion and what he felt was the simplicity of the answer. If there was to be a metaphysical explanation he felt sure that it had to be simpler than that proposed by the orthodox preachers of his day. He made his protest against their systems of right and wrong, rewards and punishments and the arbitrary nature of God's judgement. But if that protest against the inhumanity to man that was being propagated by the religious led him to the very edge of revolt against religion as it was then understood to be, it was a pleading along the lines of words that were once alleged to have been spoken by Oliver Cromwell to one with whom he was debating, 'I beseech you, by the bowels of Christ to consider whether or not ye might be mistaken.' Burns was pleading for common sense, humanity and love to be the factors that religion must hold on to if it was to keep in touch with the wonderful reality of life as something that was certainly 'given', and that might even be 'God-given'.

Even by the end of his life Burns's theology and philosophy, in broad terms his religion, was not fully defined or articulated, but still in the category of 'work in progress'; for example, while undoubtedly respecting the person of Jesus he could not commit himself to delineating the precise nature of Jesus's relationship to God. Yet religion remained a life-long interest, a source of comfort and enjoyment that contributed substantially to his thinking, and must be taken into account in any consideration of the life and work of this remarkably complex and yet ever loveable man, Robert Burns.

Appendix

Reverend William McGill

The Reverend William McGill (1732–1807), son of a Wigtonshire farmer, was educated at the University of Glasgow, licenced to preach in 1759 and appointed assistant minister at Kilwinning before being inducted to the second charge of the Auld Kirk of Ayr on 22 October 1760. He became the colleague of the Reverend William Dalrymple, minister of the first charge. The scholarly Dalrymple was awarded his doctorate by the University of St Andrews in 1779 and was soon to be joined in scholarship by McGill whose doctorate was awarded by the University of Glasgow in 1785.

In 1786, the same year that Robert Burns's *Poems Chiefly in the Scottish Dialect* was published, McGill published *A Practical Essay on the Death of Jesus Christ*. The title *Essay* is a bit misleading for it is a book of some five hundred and fifty pages. The book is in two parts: 'Containing the History of Jesus Christ from his Agony in the Garden to his Ascension into Heaven' and 'the Doctrine of Christ's Death'. That McGill expected controversy over what he had written is evidenced by his attempt at the beginning of the work to pre-empt criticism by appealing to would be critics to consider the difficulty of the subject and the need for judgement to be exercised with caution.

Within months the first of several criticisms appeared in print with John Russel's *The Reasons for our Lord's Agony in the Garden*. Russel was concerned at the lack of attention McGill had paid to what he considered were the real reasons for Jesus' agony: 'His father's countenance being withdrawn from him ... the inconceivably painful and dreadful sensations of divine wroth ... Satan and his infernal band now assailed him in most furious way'. Russel asserts that these were the real reasons for Christ's agony 'in opposition to the false or frivolous ones urged by men whose minds have never been thoroughly reconciled to the way of saving sinners by the substitution and sacrifice of the Son of God.'

McGill's speculations on the state of Jesus's mind are based on what might be the ordinary human reactions of anyone caught up in a situation in which they are facing imminent arrest, trial, torture and death. These reactions McGill asserts would be magnified when the person concerned knows his innocence and when he is of a particularly sensitive nature. He puts forward a basis for this approach that clearly brings him into conflict with those who work from a theologically imposed understanding rather than a human-centred one: 'Thus we have mentioned divers probable causes of our Saviour's agony in the garden; but have said nothing of God's withdrawing his countenance from him, or inflicting secret torments on his soul, because that seems injurious to the character of God, and not agreeable to the gospel history.' To write in such terms was to invite attack, and attack they did in various ways: by sermon (preached then printed), by books of protest, by innuendo and abuse and eventually by instigating an investigation through the courts of the Church with a view to a charge of heresy being proved that would result in McGill being deprived of his status as a Church of Scotland minister.

The plotting of the Reverend William Peebles, who was Clerk to the Presbytery of Ayr, was much in evidence, as was the polarization of the Auld and New Light factions. But throughout the years from 1786 to the final throwing out of any case against McGill in 1791, he continued to receive the respect of the people of the congregation and the townspeople of Ayr, who could not understand what all the fuss was about as they considered themselves well ministered to by Dr McGill.

The conflict over the book was only one battle in the verbal religious war in which many of the ministers and elders in Scotland were engaged at that time. That particular battle lasted for about five years until the General Assembly finally declared the matter settled in favour of McGill. The McGill case had no dramatic outcome and consequently did not acquire any national significance either at the time or later. But the issues it raised continued to be elaborated and its outcome, that favoured what today would be deemed the more liberal of the parties in contention, presaged the position of the present day Church of Scotland which in its 'Narrative' read at the Ordination and Induction of a Minister states:

> The Church of Scotland acknowledges the Word of God, which is contained in the Scriptures of the Old and New Testaments, to be the supreme rule of faith and life. The Church of Scotland holds as its subordinate standard the Westminster Confession of Faith, *recognizing liberty of opinion on such points of doctrine as do not enter into the substance of the Faith*, and claiming the right, in dependence of the promised guidance of the Holy Spirit, to formulate, interpret, or modify its subordinate standards: always in agreement with the Word of God and the fundamental doctrines of the Christian Faith contained in the said Confession, of which agreement the Church itself shall be sole judge.

The 'conscience clause' (italicized) that is contained in the 'Narrative' is one of the freedoms gained by the kind of battle engaged in by William McGill.

For further details see the Bibliography where some of the books by the protagonists in the McGill case are listed. The author's unpublished thesis, 'Literary, Philosophical and Theological Influences on Robert Burns' (University of Strathclyde, 1995), contains a detailed account of the controversy surrounding McGill's book.

References and Notes

Chapter 1: 'The Cultivation of the Finer Feelings of the Heart'

1. *The Letters of Robert Burns*, reprinted from Robert Burns: **The Letters, Volume I: 1780–1789** and **Volume II: 1790–1796** edited by J. De Lancey Ferguson, Second edition edited by G. Ross Roy (2nd edition, 1985) by permission of Oxford University Press. Hereafter referred to as *Letters*.
   Letters I, 5.
2. *Letters* I, 6.
3. *The Poems and Songs of Robert Burns*, © Oxford University Press 1968. Reprinted from **The Poems and Songs of Robert Burns, Volumes I–III** edited by James Kinsley (1968) by permission of Oxford University Press. Hereafter referred to as *Poems*.
   Poems I, 125.
4. *Letters* I, 138.
5. James Currie, *The Works of Robert Burns with an Account of his Life*, 4 vols, 8th edn (London, 1820), I, 64; hereafter referred to as Currie (1820).
6. James Currie, *Life and Works of Robert Burns* (1800) quoted in William Burnes, *A Manual of Religious Belief* (Kilmarnock, 1875), Preface, A.
7. *Letters* I, 135.
8. Currie (1820) I, 63–4.
9. *Letters* I, 135 (to Dr John Moore 2 August 1787).
10. Maurice Lindsay, *The Burns Encyclopedia* 3rd edn (London, 1980), p. 100.
11. *Letters* I, 135.
12. *Letters* I, 134.
13. *Letters* II, 39.
14. *Letters* I, 12.
15. Currie (1820) I, 64.
16. *Letters* I, 7. Note: Revelation 7:15–17.
    15. Therefore are they before the throne of God and serve him day and night in his temple: and he that sitteth on the throne shall dwell among them.
    16. They shall hunger no more, neither thirst any more; neither shall the sun light on them, nor any heat.

17. For the Lamb which is in the midst of the throne shall feed them, and shall lead them unto living fountains of waters: and God shall wipe away all tears from their eyes.

17. *Letters* I, 99.
18. *Letters* I, 183.
19. *Letters* I, 58–9.
20. *Letters* I, 17, quoting Pope: 'January and May', line 157.
21. *Letters* I, 22.
22. Currie (1820) I, 73, Gilbert's Letter to Mrs Dunlop.
23. J.H.S. Burleigh, *A Church History of Scotland* (London, 1960), p. 284.
24. *Letters* I, 22.
25. *Poems* I, 70–73.
26. *Letters* I, 144.
27. *Poems* III, 1043.
28. *Poems* I, 70–73. List of Ministers alluded to in 'The Holy Tulzie' other than the two principal characters: Robert Duncan, Dundonald; William Peebles, Newton upon Ayr; William Auld, Mauchline; William Dalrymple, Ayr; William McGill, Ayr; William McQuhae, St Quivox; David Shaw, Coylton; Andrew Shaw, Craigie; Patrick Wodrow, Tarbolton; John McMath, Tarbolton; George Smith, Galston. See also Chapter 9.
29. *Poems* I, 73; III, 1044.
30. *Poems* I, 133–4.
31. *Letters* II, 203 and *Poems* II, 617–18.
32. *Letters* I, 136.
33. *Letters* I, 36.
34. *Letters* II, 25, to Mrs Dunlop 10 April 1790.
35. *Letters* I, 45. G. Ross Roy notes: 'The date is conjectural from the reference to parting, but if we guess the enclosure to have been "The Court of Equity" [*Poems* I, 256], the month would be June after Jean's return from Paisley on the 7th.'
36. *Poems* I, 112, 235–40 and III, 1072.

Chapter 2: 'A Proven Fornicator'

1. See Chapter 9.
2. *Letters* I, 41, 42.
3. Deed of Assignment dated 22 July 1786 in *Letters* I, 43.
4. *Poems* I, 99.
5. *Poems* I, 101.

6. Tarbolton Parish Church records lodged with the Archives Dept. of Strathclyde Regional Council begin in 1795.
7. James Mackay draws attention to the note in the Mauchline kirk session minutes ('only 24 fornicators in the parish since last sacrament'), *A Biography of Robert Burns* (Edinburgh, 1992), pp. 140–41.
8. *Minute Book of Mauchline Kirk Session*, 20 May 1783 (p. 13) and 20 July 1784 (pp. 62–3).
9. *Presbytery of Ayr Minute Book* p. 362.
10. *Minute Book of Mauchline Kirk Session*, 17 July 1785, pp. 125–6.
11. *Poems* I, 74.
12. *Letters* I, 144.
13. *Poems* I, 124.
14. Mackay, *Biography*, pp. 179–91.
15. *Letters* I, 41–2.
16. *Letters* I, 42.
17. *Minute Book of Mauchline Kirk Session*, 6 August 1786, p. 171.
18. *Minute Book of Mauchline Kirk Session*, 5 August 1788, pp. 238–9.
19. *Letters* I, 419.
20. *Letters* II, 283.
21. *Poems* I, 286, lines 133 and 144–7.
22. P. Hately Waddell, *Life and Works of Robert Burns* (Glasgow, 1867), App., ix.
23. *Letters* I, 91, to the Earl of Buchan 7 February 1787.
24. *Letters* I, 303.
25. *The Westminster Confession of Faith*, Chapter X *Of Effectual Calling*, p. 18: 'All those whom God hath predestinated unto life and those only, he is pleased, in his appointed and accepted time, effectually to call, by his word and Spirit, out of that state of sin and death in which they are by nature, to grace and salvation by Jesus Christ....'
26. *Letters* I, 231.
27. *Letters* I, 433–4.
28. *Letters* II, 82.
29. *Letters* II, 118.
30. *Letters* II, 79.
31. *Letters* II, 146–7.
32. *Poems* I, 52.
33. *Letters* I, 195.
34. Ed. William Wallace, *Robert Burns and Mrs Dunlop*, (London, 1898), p. 41.
35. *Letters* I, 135.

36. *Letters* I, 230.
37. *Letters* II, 283.
38. Wallace, *Robert Burns and Mrs Dunlop*, p. 111.
39. *Letters* II, 56–7.
40. *Letters* I, 305–7.
41. *Letters* I, 135.
42. *Letters* I, 307.
43. *Letters* I, 210.
44. *Letters* I, 210, on which J. De Lancey Ferguson notes: 'One of several "Verses to Mr Hervey on his Meditations" found in the preparatory material of James Hervey's, *Meditations and Contemplations*, 2 vols (Glasgow, 1768). This poem dated 5 Aug. 1748 is by "A Physician". There were several earlier editions of the *Meditations*.' Author's note: See also on p. 98 of Chapter 7 and on p. 251 in note 19 where the physician is identified as Dr Nathaniel Cotton of St Albans, who treated William Cowper during his mental illness.
45. *Letters* I, 439; Job 38:23.
46. *Letters* II, 165–6.
47. *Letters* II, 283–4; Thomson, 'A Hymn on the Seasons', lines 1–3.
48. *Letters* II, 269–70.

Chapter 3: 'Still I am a Very Sincere Believer in the Bible'

1. *Letters* II, 73.
2. Ed. James A. Mackay, *The Complete Letters of Robert Burns* (Ayr, 1987), p. 16.
3. *The Westminster Confession*, p. 12.
   Note: (1) Romans 5:6, 8:7, 7:18; Colossians 1:21.
   (2) Genesis 6:5, 8:21; Romans 3:10–12.
   (3) James 1:14–15; Ephesians 2:2–3; Matthew 15:19.
4. *Poems* I, 134.
5. *Poems* I, 145–52, especially verses 14 and 15.
6. *Letters* I, 183.
7. *Letters* I, 349.
8. *Letters* I, 138.
9. John Taylor, *The Scripture Doctrine of Original Sin*, 2nd edn (London, 1741), p. 3.
10. John Goldie, *Essays on Various Important Subjects Moral and Divine* (Glasgow, 1779).

11. Goldie, *Essays*, p. 22.
12. Ibid, p. 70.
13. *Poems* I, 114–15.
14. *Poems* I, 71.
15. See Appendix.
16. *Letters* I, 136.
17. See Chapter 6.
18. *Confession*, p. 8.
19. King James Bible.
20. François Wendel, *Calvin* (London and Glasgow, 1972), pp. 112–18.
21. John Calvin, *Institutes of the Christian Religion*, a New translation by Henry Beveridge, Esq., 2 vols (Edinburgh, 1879), II, Book 3:5, p. 206.
22. *Institutes*, II, Book 3:4, 5, p. 206.
23. *Poems* I, 74.
24. Goldie, *Essays*, p. 324.
25. John Locke, *An Essay Concerning Human Understanding*, abridged and edited with an introduction by John W. Yolton (London and Melbourne, 1988), Book IV, XVIII, 5–11.
26. *Poems* I, 76 lines 43–54. Note: 'Leezie's lass' – a common way of describing a sister's daughter?
27. *Poems* I, 75.
28. Goldie, *Essays*, pp. 325–6.
29. *Poems* I, 75.
30. *Confession*, p. 12.
31. Goldie, *Essays*, p. 277.
32. Ibid, pp. 286–7.
33. Ibid, p. 291.
34. Ibid, pp. 189–90.
35. Ibid, p. 191.
36. *Letters* II, 146.
37. *Letters* II, 16. The works referred to are listed by De Lancey, Ferguson Letters I, ix:
    Thomas Boston, *Human Nature in its Four-fold state* (1720).
    Walter Marshall, *On Sanctification*.
    William Guthrie, *Trial of a Saving Interest*.
38. Burleigh, pp. 287–8.
39. *Letters* II, 16; II, 36.
40. *Letters* II, 66.
41. Burleigh, pp. 288–91.

42. *Letters* II, 20.
43. Thomas Watson, *A Body of Practical Divinity consisting of above 176 sermons on the Shorter Catechism*, 7th edn (Glasgow, 1782).
44. *The Shorter Catechism*, agreed upon by The Assembly of Divines at Westminster with the Assistance of Commissioners from the Church of Scotland (Edinburgh and London, 1959).
45. *Practical Divinity*, p. 9.
46. Ibid, p. 32.
47. Ibid, p. 35.
48. Ibid, p. 152.
49. Ibid, p. 143.
50. Ibid, p. 147.
51. *Letters* II, 21.
52. *Letters* II, 21.
53. John Locke, *An Essay Concerning Human Understanding*, First published 1689 (London, 1841), p. 44.
54. Locke, *Essay*, p. 31.
55. *Practical Divinity*, pp. 26–9.
56. Ibid, p. 137.
57. W.S. Gilbert, The Mikado, Act II, *Original Comic Operas*, Chappell (London, undated), p. 41.
58. *Practical Divinity*, p. 138.
59. *Confession*, X, p. 18.
60. *Practical Divinity*, pp. 222–3.
61. Ibid, p. 225.
62. *Letters* II, 75 and II, 146.
63. James Hervey, *Meditations and Contemplations* (London, 1855), p. 9. cf. *Letters* I, 447 'The Great Disposer of Events'.
64. *Hervey*, vi.
65. Ibid, pp. 61–2.
66. *Letters* II, 147.
67. *Letters* II, 73.
68. *Poems* I, 70.
69. *Poems* I, 71.
70. *Poems* I, 73.
71. *Letters* II, 66 and II, 20.
72. See Chapter 2.
73. *Poems* I, 99–102.
74. See Chapter 2.

75. McGinty, J. Walter, unpublished thesis and Chapter 9, William Peebles.
76. *Poems* I, 52.
77. *Poems* I, 124–5.
78. See Chapter 2.
79. *Letters* I, 120.
80. *Letters* I, 120.
81. See Chapter 9, William Peebles.
82. Ibid and *Letters* II, 18.
83. *Letters* I, 299.
84. See Chapter 9, William Peebles, William Auld and John Russel.
85. *Letters* II, 18 and *Poems* I, 498.
86. *Letters* II, 12–13.
87. See Chapter 9, William Dalrymple.
88. *Letters* II, 279.
89. *Poems* I, 126.
90. *Letters* I, 422.
91. *Letters* I, 258–9.
92. Lindsay, *Encyclopedia*, p. 298.
93. *Letters* II, 34.
94. *Letters* I, 385.
95. *Letters* I, 135.

Chapter 4: 'Though Sceptical on Some Points of our Current Belief'

1. *Letters* I, 58–9.
2. List of Titles and Descriptions of God in Burns's Letters in this chapter.
3. *Letters* II, 144.
4. *Letters* I, 336.
5. *Letters* I, 458.
6. *Letters* I, 419.
7. *Letters* I, 201.
8. *Poems* I, 245.
9. Richard H. Fowler, *Robert Burns* (London, 1988), pp. 77–8.
10. Ibid, p. 79.
11. *Letters* II, 183.
12. *Letters* I, 454.
13. *Letters* I, 349; II, 283.
14. Quoted by Fowler, p. 51.
15. Locke, *Essay*, p. 43.

16. See list of Burn's letters in this chapter.
17. *Letters* I, 233.
18. *Letters* I, 113.
19. *Letters* I, 320, 321 and I, 424.
20. *Letters* I, 232.
21. *Letters* I, 333.
22. *Letters* I, 347.
23. *Letters* I, 162 and I, 249.
24. *Letters* I, 347.
25. *Letters* I, 414.
26. *Letters* I, 418.
27. *Letters* I, 448 and I, 142–3.
28. *Letters* I, 447 and II, 129.
29. *Letters* I, 305, I, 450–51, II, 297 and II, 310.
30. *Letters* II, 282.
31. *Letters* I, 258–9 and II, 383.
32. *Letters* I, 349.
33. *Letters* I, 419.
34. *Letters* II, 311.
35. *Letters* II, 333.
36. William Shakespeare, *Macbeth*, V, iii (altered).
37. *Letters* II, 282–3.
38. Thomas Reid, *An Inquiry into the Human Mind on the Principles of Common Sense* pp. 10–11.
39. Francis Hutcheson, *An Inquiry into the Original of our Ideas of Beauty and Virtue* (London, 1725).
40. *Letters* II, 283–4.
41. *Letters* I, 204 and II, 73.
42. *Poems* I, 20–21.
43. *Poems* I, 22–3.
44. *Letters* I, 258.
45. *Letters* I, 58–9.
46. *Letters* II, 383.
47. Locke, *Essay*, pp. 87–8. Quote from John Baillie, *Our Knowledge of God* (London, 1959), p. 240.

Chapter 5: 'If There be Life Beyond the Grave'

1. *Letters* II, 16–17; quotation from Blair 'The Grave', lines 431–2 and 434.
2. *Letters* I, 456–7.
3. *Letters* I, 458.
4. *Letters* I, 458.
5. *Letters* II, 24–5.
6. *Letters* II, 34.
7. *Letters* I, 437–8.
8. *Poems* I, 322–3.
9. *The Lounger*, December 1786, text in *The Burns Encyclopedia*, p. 203.
10. Henry Mackenzie, *The Man of Feeling* (Oxford, 1987), see pp. 5, 8, 18, 19 and 34 as some examples of its tear-filled pages.
11. *Poems* I, 322–3.
12. Adam Smith, *The Theory of Moral Sentiments* (Indianapolis, 1982), III 2.34, p. 132; see also J. Walter McGinty, unpublished Ph.D. thesis 'Literary, Philosophical and Theological Influences on Robert Burns' (University of Strathclyde, 1995), pp. 30–137.
13. *Letters* II, 33–4.
14. *Letters* I, 135.
15. *Letters* I, 348.
16. Arthur Masson, *A Collection of Prose and Verse from the Best English Authors for the use of Schools* (Air, 1803), p. 257ff.
17. *Letters* II, 144.
18. *Letters* I, 242. Compare 'Verses written on a window of the Inn at Carron', *Poems* I, 348.
19. *Letters* I, 240.
20. *Letters* II, 164.
21. *Letters* II, 203.

Chapter 6: 'I am an Accountable Creature'

1. *Letters* I, 419.
2. Mackay, *Biography*, p. 424.
3. *Letters* I, 353.
4. Mackay, *Biography*, p. 424.
5. *Letters* II, 122.
6. Mackay, *Biography*, p. 425.
7. Ibid, pp. 317–19; *Letters* I, 124, I, 131 and I, 284.

8. *Letters* II, 21.
9. *Letters* I, 136–7; *Poems* I, 140, lines 93–100.
10. Currie (1820), p. 61.
11. *Letters* I, 135.
12. *Shorter Catechism*, p. 126.
13. *Confession*, p. 13.
14. Arthur Masson, *An English Spelling Book* (Air, 1819), p. 41.
15. *Letters* I, 255.
16. *Letters* I, 414.
17. *Letters* I, 414.
18. *Confession*, III, pp. 8–9 and X, pp. 18–19.
19. *Letters* II, 75–6.
20. *Letters* I, 418.
21. *Letters* II, 17, to Alexander Cunningham 13 February 1790, quoting Philippians 4:8 (slightly altered).

Chapter 7: William Cowper

1. *Letters* I, 296.
2. *Letters* I, 322.
3. *Letters* II, 269–70.
4. *Letters* II, 338–9.
5. *The Letters and Prose Writings of William Cowper Volume III: Letters, 1787–1791*, eds James King and Charles Ryskamp (Oxford, 1982), 15, 17–18, 139 and 145. Reprinted by permission of Oxford University Press.
6. David Cecil, *The Stricken Deer, The Life of Cowper* (London, 1929).
7. Ibid, p. 35.
8. Ibid, p. 108.
9. William Derham, *Physico-Theology or a Demonstration of the Being and Attributes of God* (Glasgow, 1758), p. 71.
10. Derham, *Physico-Theology*, p. 104.
11. Voltaire, *Candide* [first Published 1759] (Harmondsworth, 1985), p. 20. Note: Dr Pangloss taught 'metaphysico-theologo-cosmolo-nigology'.
12. Derham, *Physico-Theology*, p. 63.
13. Stephen Neill, *Anglicanism* (Harmondsworth, 1960), p. 149.
14. See Chapter 9, William Dalrymple.
15. See Chapter 3 on John Goldie and John Taylor.
16. Cecil, p. 18.
17. Ibid, pp. 71–4.

18. *Letters* I, 210, I, 226, II, 66 and II, 439.
19. Dr Nathaniel Cotton in *The Works of the English Poets from Chaucer to Cowper*, ed. Dr Samuel Johnson, with Additional Lives by Alexander Chalmers (1870), vol. XVIII, pp. 27–8.
20. Ibid, p. 5.
21. Cecil, p. 73.
22. Ibid, p. 74.
23. Ibid, p. 90.
24. Ibid, p. 99.
25. Ibid, p. 109ff.
26. Rev. Professor James Moffatt and Rev. Millar Patrick, eds *Handbook to the Church Hymnary, With Supplement* (London, 1951), p. 446.
27. *The Church Hymnary*, revised edition (London, 1929), Hymn 457 'O for a closer walk with God' and Hymn 692 'There is a fountain filled with blood'.
28. Ibid, Hymn 451 'Approach, my soul, the mercy-seat'.
29. Cecil, p. 159.
30. *Letters* I, 230 and I, 36.
31. *Poems* I, 208.
32. *Letters* I, 144.
33. *The Poetical Works of William Cowper Esq. With a Sketch of His Life*, by Rev. T. Greatheed (Glasgow, 1834), '*The Task*', Book I, p. 154.
34. 'The Task' II.
35. 'The Task' III, p. 171.
36. *Poems* I, 74.
37. 'The Task' III, p. 172.
38. 'The Task' II, p. 175.
39. *Poems* I, 126.
40. King James Bible, Ecclesiastes 1:2.
41. 'The Task' IV, p. 219.
42. Ibid, p. 226.
43. 'The Task' V, p. 236.
44. Ibid, pp. 238–9.
45. *Letters* I, 334–5 and J. De Lancey Ferguson, *Introduction to The Letters of Robert Burns*, p. 11; see also *Letters* II, 166, 171–2 and 174.
46. *Poems* II, 733, II, 815 and I, 436.
47. *Poems* I, 208, II, 663 and II, 707–8.
48. 'The Task' V, pp. 240, 242 and 243.

49. *The Scottish Psalter and Church Hymnary, Revised Edition,* authorized for use in the Church of Scotland (O.U.P., 1929), Hymn 692.
50. 'The Task' V, p. 243.
51. Richard Feingold, *Nature and Society, Later Eighteenth Century Uses of the Pastoral and Georgic* (New Jersey, 1978), p. 185.
52. 'The Task' V, p. 248.
53. *Letters* I, 348–9.
54. 'The Task' VI, p. 257.
55. Ibid, p. 258.
56. Ibid.
57. 'The Task' VI, pp. 759–804; compare with Isaiah Chapter 11 and 35.
58. 'The Task' VI, p. 274.
59. Michael Schmidt, *Lives of the Poets* (London, 1999), p. 364.
60. *Letters* II, 66, To Peter Hill, 17 January 1791, 'Well, Divines may say what they please, but I maintain that a hearty blast of execration is to the mind, what breathing a vein is to the body: the overloaded sluices of both are wonderfully relieved by their respective evacuations.'
61. Schmidt, pp. 367–8.

Chapter 8: Christopher Smart

1. *Poems* I, 112, lines 235–40.
2. John Milton, *Paradise Lost*, ed. Christopher Ricks (London, 1989), Book I, lines 25–6.
3. 'The Marriage of Heaven and Hell', in *William Blake, A Selection of Poems and Letters*, edited with an introduction by J. Bronowski (Harmondsworth, 1958), pp. 93–109.
4. See Chapter 7.
5. Quoted by Schmidt, p. 351.
6. *The Works of the English Poets from Chaucer to Cowper*, ed. Dr Samuel Johnson, vol. XVI, pp. 1–13; see also Michael Schmidt, p. 352.
7. Moira Dearnley, *The Poetry of Christopher Smart* (Routledge & Kegan Paul Ltd: London, 1968), p. 5.
8. Ibid, p. 2.
9. *English Poets*, XVI, p. 8.
10. Christopher Smart, Prologue to 'A Trip to Cambridge', in Dearnley, p. 50.
11. *English Poets*, XVI, p. 4.
12. James Boswell, *The Life of Samuel Johnson*, Collins (London and Glasgow, undated), p. 154.

13. Dearnley, p. 37.
14. *Poems*, I, 125.
15. Dearnley, pp. 114–15.
16. King James Bible, Isaiah 38.
17. *English Poets* XVI, p. 27.
18. See Chapter 9.
19. Dearnley, p. 226 ff.
20. Seatonian Prize Poems:
    1750 'On the Eternity of the Supreme Being'.
    1751 'On the Immensity of the Supreme Being'.
    1752 'On the Omniscience of the Supreme Being'.
    1753 'On the Power of the Supreme Being'.
    1755 'On the Goodness of the Supreme Being'.
    In 1754 George Bally won the prize with his poem, 'On the Justice of the Supreme Being'.
21. Isaac Newton, *Principia* and *Opticks*; William Derham, *Physico-Theology* and *Astro-Theology*. *Philosophiae naturalis principia mathematica* by Isaac Newton was published in 1687. Commonly known as *The Principia* it was revised in 1713 and again in 1726. His second treatise *Opticks* was published in 1704. For details of William Derham's works see Bibliography pp. 266–7.
22. *English Poets* XVI, p. 28.
23. The Holy Bible, containing the Old and New Testaments (Glasgow, 1949), p. 7 has a central column of references and opposite verse 1 of Genesis's account of the creation signals the date as 4004 BC.
24. *English Poets,* XVI, p. 29.
25. Ibid, p. 33.
26. Dearnley, p. 152.
27. *English Poets* XVI, p. 34.
28. Ibid, p. 32.
29. Ibid, pp. 26–7.
30. I Samuel: 16–31, II Samuel: 1–24 and I Kings: 1–8.
31. Schmidt, p. 350.
32. Dearnley, pp. 170–76.
33. 'Essay on Criticism', *The Poetical Works of Alexander Pope* (London 1882), p. 53, lines 150–55.
34. Dearnley, p. 60.

35. *The Religious Poetry of Christopher Smart*, ed. Marcus Walsh (Carcanet Press Limited, Manchester, 1972). All references to 'A Song to David' are from pp. 54–72.
36. Verse LXXXVI of 'A Song to David' in Walsh, p. 72.
37. *Rejoice in the Lamb*, ed. W.F. Stead (1939).
38. Schmidt, p. 350.
39. *English Poets*, XVI, p. 12 refers to a visit from Dr Lowth to Smart in 1764.
40. Christopher Smart, *Jubilate Agno*, re-edited from the original manuscript with an introduction and notes by W.H. Bond, Curator of Manuscripts at the Houghton Library, Harvard (London, 1954), Introduction p.20.
41. Bond, Introduction p. 24.
42. Walsh, p. 32.
43. Ibid, p. 33.
44. Ibid.
45. Ibid, p. 34.
46. Ibid.
47. Ibid, p. 35.
48. *The Apocrypha, The New English Bible* (O.U.P., 1970), First Book of Esdras pp. 1–19.
49. Text from Bond, pp. 40–41.
50. Bond, p. 43.
51. Ibid, p. 45.
52. Ibid, p. 51.
53. Ibid, pp. 66–7.
54. Ibid, 'Introduction'. p. 23.
55. Ibid, p. 65.
56. William Blake, *Poems*, p. 94.
57. Quoted by Peter Ackroyd, in *Blake* (London, 1995), p. 335.
58. Ackroyd, p. 147.
59. Ibid, p. 311.
60. William Blake, *Poems*, p. 94.
61. Jacob Boehme, quoted in Ackroyd, p. 149.
62. See Chapter 3.
63. *Letters* II, 146–7 and *Poems* I, 74–8.
64. See Chapter 3.
65. Ibid and *Letters* I, 349.
66. *Letters* I, 123.
67. *Letters* I, 17.
68. *Poems* I, 131–2.

69. Dearnley, p. 119.
70. *Jubilate Agno*, Fragment B2. lines 504–6.
71. *Letters* II, 383.
72. *Jubilate Agno*, B1. line 132.

Chapter 9: The Ministers of 'The Kirk of Scotland's Garland – a New Song'

1. *Poems* I, 472, 'The Kirk of Scotland's Garland – a new Song', also known as 'The Kirk's Alarm'.
2. 'Ode to Liberty' appended to *A Sermon by Rev. William Peebles preached to the Magistrates and Council of the Burgh of Newton upon Ayr, 5th November 1788* (Kilmarnock, 1788).
3. *Sermon* II, 5 November 1788, p. 49.
4. William Peebles, *Burnomania: The Celebrity of Robert Burns considered in a Discourse Addressed to all real Christians of every denomination to which are added Epistles in Verse respecting Peter Pindar, Burns &c.* (Edinburgh, 1811). Originally published anonymously.
5. *Poems* I, 72.
6. William Peebles, *Sermons on Various Subjects to which are subjoined Hymns suited to several discourses* (Edinburgh, 1794), Sermon I, p. 1.
7. Peebles, *Sermons*, V, p. 117.
8. Ibid, V, p. 119.
9. Ibid, II, p. 34.
10. *Poems* I, 70–73.
11. *Larousse Encyclopedia of Mythology*, with an introduction by Robert Graves (London, 1959), pp. 118, 128, 154, 203.
12. *Minute Book of Newton upon Ayr Kirk Session 1780–1830*. The Act and Proceedings of the Kirk Session of Newton upon Ayr commencing from the month of May 1780, pp. 1–4.
13. Ibid, p. 5.
14. Ibid, pp. 6–7.
15. Ibid, p. 7.
16. Ibid, p. 30.
17. Ibid.
18. Ibid, p. 33.
19. *The Statistical Account of Scotland*, ed. Sir John Sinclair, Bart. The Parish of Newton upon Ayr (1791) by the Reverend Mr. Peebles, vol. VI, p. 485.
20. *Statistical Account*, vol. VI, Appendix by Sir John Sinclair, p. 501.
21. 'The Holy Fair', *Poems* I, 133–4.

22. Note: Dr Dalrymple contributed the report on the Parish of Ayr in 1791, and Dr McGill contributed a supplementary report that just missed the printer's deadline and was not published until 1799 in the *General Appendix of The Statistical Account of Scotland*, vol. XXI, p. 44. Robert Burns's account of the Monkland Friendly Society appears in the account of the Parish of Dunscore, vol. III, pp. 598–600. See also *Letters* II, 106–8.
23. *Statistical Account*, vol. XXI, p. 44.
24. 'Some Eminent Men', John McCartney, M.A., in *The Royal Burgh of Ayr Seven Hundred and Fifty Years of History*, ed. Annie I. Dunlop (Edinburgh, 1953), pp. 285–7.
25. Peebles, *Burnomania*, frontispiece.
26. Peebles, *Burnomania*, pp. 5–7.
27. Ibid, p. 8.
28. Ibid, pp. 29–30.
29. Ibid, pp. 76–7.
30. James Wright, A.M., *A Treatise on the Causes of Sedition – On the best Remedy against this great evil and on what ought to be the Disposition of the British People at the present great crisis of the alarm of an invasion by the French* (Air, 1798), p. 52.
31. Wright, James, p. 53.
32. Ibid, p. 60.
33. Peebles, *Burnomania*, p. 64.
34. Ibid, pp. 63–4.
35. Ibid, p. 65.
36. Ibid, p. 10.
37. Ibid, p. 102.
38. *Poems* I, 471.
39. William Burnes, *A Manual of Religious Belief in a Dialogue between Father and Son* (Kilmarnock, 1875).
40. *Fasti Ecclesiae Scoticanae*, vol. III, p. 10. Publications of William Dalrymple:
    - 1766 *Christian Unity – Illustrated and recommended from the example of the primitive church.*
    - 1787 *A History of Christ for the use of the unlearned.*
    - 1787 *Family Worship explained and recommended in four sermons.*
    - 1790 *Faith in Jesus Christ.*
    - 1791 *A Sequel to the Life of Christ.*
    - 1792 *The Acts of the Apostles, made easy to the young and unlearned.*
    - 1794 *The Mosaic Account of Creation.*

1795 *Meditations and Prayers.*
1796 *Legacy of Dying Thoughts.*
1799 *Solomon's Ethics or the Book of Proverbs made easy.*
1803 *The Scripture Jewish History, chiefly for the benefit of the unlearned.*

41. William Dalrymple, *A History of Christ for the use of the Unlearned* (Edinburgh, 1787), Preface.
42. James Ramsay, *A clear Scriptural Detection of Satan transformed into an Angel of Light, or The Socinian Creed as held by Drs McGill and Dalrymple, Ministers of Ayr.*
43. Dr William McGill, Supplementary Report on the Parish of Ayr (1791), *The Statistical Account of Scotland*, vol. XXI, p. 43.
44. Dalrymple, *A History of Christ.*
45. William Dalrymple, *A Sequel to the Life of Christ* (Ayr, 1791), p. 126.
46. Dalrymple, *Sequel*, p. 128.
47. Ibid.
48. *Poems* I, 125.
49. Dalrymple, *Sequel*, p. 223.
50. Ibid, p. 242.
51. Ibid, *Preface* p. viii, referring to Thomas Reid, *An Inquiry into the Human Mind on the Principles of Common Sense* (1764).
52. *Poems* I, 73.
53. Dalrymple, *Sequel*, pp. 259 and 262.
54. Ibid, p. 265.
55. Ibid, pp. 265–6.
56. Ibid, p. 275.
57. Ibid, p. 276.
58. *Robert Burns and Mrs Dunlop, Correspondence now published in full for the first time with Elucidations by William Wallace* (London, 1898), p. 195.
59. *Poems* I, 470.
60. *Burns and Dunlop*, p. 195.
61. *Poems* I, 73.
62. Dalrymple, *Sequel*, p. 84.
63. *Poems* I, 87 'Epistle to J. L*****k, An Old Scotch Bard'.
64. *Poems* I, 471.
65. *Fasti*, vol. III, p. 108.
66. A. Burns Jamieson, M.A., *Burns and Religion* (Cambridge, 1931), p. 20.
67. *Letters* I, 27.
68. *Poems* I, 217, also III, 1164, notes on 'The Ordination'.

69. *Fasti*, vol. III, p. 108.
70. *Letters* I, 69–70.
71. *Letters* I, 94.
72. John Russel, A.M., *The Nature of the Gospel Delineated. A Sermon Preached in the Parish Church of Kilmarnock on Thursday, August 18th 1796* (Air, 1796), frontispiece.
73. Russel, *Sermon* (1796), frontispiece.
74. *Statistical Account*, VI, p. 286 ff.
75. *Fasti*, III, pp. 107–8.
76. *Poems* I, 472.
77. *Poems* III, 1310 and *The Burns Encyclopedia*, p. 237.
78. *Fasti*, vol. III, p. 57.
79. *Statistical Account*, vol. III, Parish of Monkton and Prestwick, pp. 458–67.
80. *Poems* I, 472.
81. *Fasti*, vol. III, p. 18.
82. *Statistical Account*, vol. VI (1982), Parish of Barr, pp. 56–64.
83. *Statistical Account*, vol. VI, (1982), general editor's Introduction, Preface, p. iii.
84. *Statistical Account*, vol. VI, (1982), pp. 56, 57 and 60–64.
85. *Poems* I, 472.
86. *Statistical Account*, vol. VI (1982), Parish of New Cumnock, pp. 107–8.
87. *Presbytery of Ayr Minutes*, pp. 454–60.
88. *Poems* I, 472. Note by Kinsley that James Young 'had lately been foiled in an ecclesiastic prosecution against a Lieut. Mitchel'.
89. *Poems* I, 473.
90. Reverend George Smith, born 2 March 1748, was presented to Galston by John Wallace of Cessnock on 26 July 1777, and ordained 3 February 1778. *Fasti*, vol. II, p. 4.
91. *Poems* I, 73.
92. *Poems* I, 133.
93. *Statistical Account*, vol. VI (1982), Parish of Galston, p. 227.
94. *Poems* I, 473.
95. *Poems* III, 1311, Kinsley quoting Chambers-Wallace III, p. 94.
96. *Statistical Account*, vol. VI (1982), Parish of Muirkirk, pp. 470, 471, 478 and 479.
97. *Poems* I, 473–4.
98. *Fasti*, III, p. 50.
99. See Chapter 2.

100. *Fasti*, III, p. 50.
101. *Presbytery of Ayr Minutes*, p. 419 and 423.
102. *Fasti*, III, p. 50.
103. *Poems* I, 473.
104. *Fasti*, vol. III, Parish of Ochiltree, p. 62; *Poems* III, notes p. 1311.
105. *Letters* I, 465.
106. *Poems* I, notes p. 473.
107. *Presbytery of Ayr Minutes*, 15 July 1789, pp. 453–4.
108. See Chapter 9, Peebles.
109. *Popish Bill, Introduction giving a short history of the Rise, Progress and Effects of the Alarm in Scotland respecting the Popish Bill and a Collection of Declarations, Resolutions &c. and Appendix: A Short View of the Statutes at present in Force in Scotland against Popery*, by John Dickson, Advocate. First published December 1778 (Edinburgh, 1780). Introduction p. vi. Note: in the 1780 edition, Dickson dedicates his pamphlet 'To the Friends of the Protestant Interest and Particularly their Committee of Correspondence in Edinburgh.'
110. *Poems* III, 1311.
111. Richard B. Sher, *Church and University in the Scottish Enlightenment* (Edinburgh, 1985), pp. 294–5.
112. *Poems* I, 472.
113. *Poems* I, 72.
114. *Poems* I, 132.
115. *Statistical Account*, vol. VI (1982), Parish of Riccartoun, p. 513.
116. *Statistical Account*, vol. VI (1982), Parish of Mauchline, pp. 448–9.
117. *Poems* I, 471.
118. Russel's sermon *The Reasons for our Lord's Agony in the Garden*, published in 1787, contained an attack on William McGill's *A Practical Essay on the Death of Christ* (1786).
119. *Acts and Proceedings of the Kirk Session of Newton upon Ayr commencing from the month of May 1780*, pp. 4–6.
120. *Letters* I, 204.
121. *Poems* I, 71, I, 213, I, 135–6 and I, 471.
122. *Letters* I, 94.
123. Russel, *Sermon* (1796), p. 5.
124. Ibid.
125. Ibid, p. 9.
126. Ibid, pp. 7, 17 and 19.

127. William McGill, *A Practical Essay on the Death of Jesus Christ* (Edinburgh, 1786).
128. King James Bible, Psalm 40; Russel, *Sermon* (1796), p. 7.
129. Luke 23:21–7 and Hebrews 13:12.
130. Russel, *Sermon* (1796), p. 49.
131. Ibid, p. 32.
132. Ibid.
133. Ibid, p. 63.
134. Ibid, p. 64.
135. *Letters* I, 422.
136. *Poems* I, 70–71.
137. *Poems* I, 135.
138. Quoted by Lindsay, *Encyclopedia*, p. 321.
139. Burleigh, pp. 288–91.
140. *Poems* I, 213.
141. *Letters* I, 453–4.
142. *Poems* I, 470.
143. *Letters* I, 175.

Chapter 10: Poems Reflecting the Recurrent Themes of a Benevolent God, Life After Death and Accountability

1. *Poems* I, 20–21.
2. *The Poetical Works of Alexander Pope*, p. 227.
3. *Poems* I, 76 (particularly vv. 7–10).
4. Heinrich Heine (1797–1856): 'Dieu me pardonnera, c'est son métier' ('God will pardon me, it is his trade.'); words on his deathbed from Alfred Meisner, *Heinrich Heine*, Chapter 5.
5. *Poems* III, 1012–13 and Letters 1, 6–7.
6. *Poems* I, 22.
7. *Poems* I, 22.
8. *Pope*, note on p. 227.
9. *Poems* I, 23.
10. *Poems* I, 37.
11. Smith, p. 85.
12. *Poems* I, 52–4.
13. *Robert Burns Commonplace Book*, Printed from the original manuscript in the possession of John Adam, Esq., Greenock (Edinburgh, 1872), p. 9.
14. *Poems* I, 52, lines 10–12.

15. Smith, p. 105.
16. Alexander Pope, 'Essay on Man', Epistle II, lines 231–8.
17. *Poems* I, 70–73.
18. *Poems* III, note on verse 15, pp. 1045–6. For a fuller discussion see Burleigh, pp. 277–9.
19. John R. McIntosh, *Church and Theology in Enlightenment Scotland: The Popular Party, 1740–1800* (East Lothian, 1998), p. 23.
20. See Chapter 9, John Russel.
21. Goldie, *Essays*.
22. Burleigh, pp. 281–2; see diagram appended on the history of the secessions.
23. Burleigh, p. 279.
24. Ibid, p. 282.
25. G.D. Henderson, *The Church of Scotland, A Short History* (Edinburgh, c. 1960) p. 107.
26. Ibid, p. 108.
27. *Poems* I, 70 note; III, 1043–4.
28. *Poems* I, 71, lines 21–4.
29. Owen Chadwick, *The Reformation*, The Pelican History of the Church vol. 3, (Harmondsworth, 1972), p. 220.
30. Gerald R. Cragg, *The Church and the Age of Reason 1648–1789*, The Pelican History of the Church vol. 4, (Harmondsworth, 1960), pp. 144–5.
31. *Poems* I, 74–8.
32. *The Confession of Faith* (Edinburgh and London, 1959) References: Chapters III, V, VI, X, XIV, XXXII and XXXIII.
33. *Letters* II, 146.
34. See Chapter 3.
35. Masson, *English Spelling Book*. Note: During research in preparation of his Ph.D., the author explored the editions of the spelling and the reading books used by John Murdoch while Burns was under his tutulage at Alloway. See J. Walter McGinty's unpublished thesis, pp. 1–29 and *Letters* I, 135.
36. Masson, *Prose and Verse*.
37. *Poems* I, 114–15.
38. See Chapter 9, John Russel.
39. *Poems* I, 115, lines 25–30.
40. Goldie, *Essays*, p. 191.
41. Ibid.

42. Thomas Reid, *An Inquiry into the Human Mind on the Principles of Common Sense* (first published 1764); *Poems* I, 90, line 10; and *Poems* III, note on 8–16.
43. *Letters* II, 19–20 and II, 66.
44. *Letters* I, 418–19.
45. *Poems* I, 116.
46. Maurice Lindsay, *Robert Burns, The man, his work, the legend* (London, 1954) p. 117.
47. *Poems* II, 1087.
48. See Chapter 5.
49. *Confession of Faith*, XXXII, pp. 46–7.
50. *Poems* I, 124–6.
51. *Poems* III, 1091 and III, 1047; *The Concise Dictionary of National Biography* (O.U.P., 1992) ref. to Robert Wodrow, p. 3270.
52. See Chapter 3; *Poems* III, 1047–8.
53. *Poems* II, 1047–53.
54. Mackay, p. 171; John D. Ross, *Who's Who in Burns* (Stirling, 1927), pp. 197–8.
55. *Poems* I, 128–37.
56. *Poems* I, 124, line 14.
57. *Poems* III, 1094–6; also Allan H. MacLaine, *The Christis Kirk Tradition* (Glasgow, 1996), Introduction and pp. 1–17.
58. Mackay, p. 124.
59. MacLaine, 'Peblis to the Play', anon, Stanza 2.
60. MacLaine, 'Christ's Kirk on the Green', Allan Ramsay, p. 10.
61. MacLaine, 'Christ's Kirk on the Green', Stanza 13, p. 14.
62. *Robert Fergusson Selected Poems*, ed. James Robertson (Edinburgh, 2000) pp. 87–91.
63. *Fergusson*, pp. 152–9.
64. *Letters* I, 17.
65. *Poems* III, 1094.
66. *Letter from a Blacksmith to the Ministers and Elders of the Church of Scotland*, printed by George Faulkner, Essex Street, Dublin, MDCCLIX. (Ed. notes that the letter is signed at the end by A.T. Blacksmith, Inverary, 1758.) The 'Letter' is sometimes attributed to the Reverend John Witherspoon, then a minister in Paisley, who became one of the leaders of the Popular Party in the Church of Scotland and was the author of *Ecclesiastical Characteristics* (1753), a satirical pamphlet highly

critical of the Moderate Party. He moved to America in 1768 to become Principal of New Jersey College, now Princeton University.

67. *Poems* I, 128–37.
68. *The Concise Scots Dictionary* (Aberdeen, 1985), p. 390.
69. *Letters* II, 144.
70. The Psalms of David in Metre, *The Scottish Psalter* (O.U.P., 1929), p. 185.
71. See Chapter 9, Alexander Moodie, and *Poems* III, 1100 note 116.
72. See Chapter 9, George Smith.
73. See Chapter 9, William Peebles.
74. See Chapter 9, William Auld, and MacLaine, note on line 145, p. 198.
75. MacLaine, note on lines 151, pp. 198–9.
76. *The Life and Opinions of Tristram Shandy, Gentleman*, Laurence Sterne [first published 1759–67] (Harmondsworth, 1986), p. 44.
77. Reid, Chapter II, section 7, p. 64.
78. See Chapter 9, John Russel.
79. For an account of the controversy see Burleigh, pp. 288–90.
80. *Poems* I, 225 'Letter to J[ame]s T[ennan]t, Gl[enconne]r', lines 21–2 and letter to Alexander Cunningham 14 February 1790,'; *Letters* II, 16, II, 36 and II, 66.
81. *Poems* I, 136, lines 212–16.
82. *Poems* I, 137, lines 239–40.
83. *Poems* I, 145–52.
84. *Letters* I, 26–7.
85. David Daiches *Robert Burns The Poet* (Edinburgh, 1994), p. 143.
86. Lindsay, p. 110.
87. *Commonplace Book*, p. 3.
88. Daiches, *Robert Burns*, p. 146.
89. *Poems* III, 1111–12.
90. Quoted by James Currie in *Life of Robert Burns*, pp. 86–92.
91. Burnes, p. xxxix–xl.
92. *The Larger Catechism*, Question 2 and Answer in *The Confession of Faith* (Edinburgh, 1959), p. 51.
93. Quoted by James Kinsley, *Poems* III, 1112.
94. Biographical Preface to Burnes, p. xxxiii.
95. *Poems* I, 150, Stanza xvii, lines 147–8.
96. *Poems* I, 67, Stanza v, lines 69–70, 'Epistle to Davie, A Brother Poet'.
97. *Poems* I, 213–17.
98. See Chapter 9, James Mackinlay.

99. *Poems* III, 1164–5.
100. *Poems* III, 1165, note on verses 19–20.
101. *The Confession of Faith*, Chapter I, p. 4.
102. King James Bible, Deuteronomy 30:6.
103. *Poems* III, lines 64–7, p. 1166.
104. *Poems* I, 24–5.
105. Moffatt and Patrick, eds, p. xxii.
106. *The Scottish Psalter 1929* (Oxford 1929), p. 1.
107. *Poems* I, 24–5.
108. *Poems* I, 53 'Address to the Unco Guid', lines 51–2.
109. Thomas Crawford, *Burns: A Study of the Poems and Songs* (Edinburgh, 1994), p. 14.
110. *Poems* I, 25–6.
111. Paul Tillich, *Systematic Theology*, vol. I (London, 1955), p. 232, and vol. 3 (London, 1964), p. 422.
112. *Letters* I, 120, II, 14–17, II, 211–12, II, 61–2 and II, 314.
113. *Poems* I, 65–9.
114. Crawford, p. 88.
115. W.E. Williams, *Selected Poems of D.H. Lawrence*, (Harmondsworth, 1960), *Introduction*, p. 8.
116. D.H. Lawrence, p. 124.
117. *Poems* I, 68, line 113.
118. *Poems* I, 312.
119. King James Bible, Psalm 90: 7–17.
120. The New English Bible, Psalm 90:11 (O.U.P., 1970), p. 691.

Bibliography

Primary Sources

Anon., *Dr McGill Vindicated from the Charge of Heresy and the Erroneous Assertions of his Adversaries Briefly Refuted,* by a Friend of Truth, printed and sold by Charles Elliot (Edinburgh, 20 May 1789).

——*Proceedings of the Very Reverend The Synod Ayr held at Ayr on the 13th & 14th April 1790. Relating to some late Publications of the Rev Dr William McGill with the Final Decisions in that cause*, published by Authority of The Synod, entered in Stationer's Hall.

——*A Warning Against Socinianism: Drawn up and published by a Committee of the Associate Synod* (Falkirk, 1788).

——*Letter from a Blacksmith to the Ministers and Elders of the Church of Scotland* (Dublin, 1759).

——*The Procedure of our Church Courts in the case of Dr William McGill of Ayr with a Complaint lately exhibited against him and a Narrative of the Rise, Progress and Termination of a Prosecution carried on against him before our Church Judicatories, by the Laity of Scotland. To which is added a conclusion, containing Reflections on the Defection of our Church Courts &c*, by the Friends of Truth ([Text defaced], 1792).

Boston, Thomas, *Human Nature in its Four-fold State*, 2nd edn 1729, Reprinted J.P. Wilson (Air, 1797).

Boyle, A.M., *The Ayrshire Book of Burns Lore* (Ayr, 1986).

Bronowski, J., ed., *William Blake, A Selection of Poems and Letters* (Harmondsworth, 1958).

Burnes, William, *A Manual of Religious Belief in A Dialogue Between Father and Son* (Kilmarnock, 1875).

Burns, Robert, *The Poems and Songs of Robert Burns Volumes I–III*, ed. James Kinsley (Oxford, 1968).

——*Robert Burns: The Letters, volume I: 1780–1789* and *volume II: 1790–1796*, ed. J. De Lancey Ferguson, 2nd edn ed. G. Ross Roy (Oxford, 1985).

——*The Complete Works of Robert Burns*, edited and introduced by James A. Mackay (Ayr, 1986).

——*The Complete Letters of Robert Burns*, edited and introduced by James A. Mackay (Ayr, 1987).

——*The Poems and Songs of Robert Burns*, edited and introduced by James Barke (London and Glasgow, 1976).

——*The Life and Works of Robert Burns*, ed. Robert Chambers, revised by William Wallace, 4 vols (Edinburgh and London, 1896).

——*Robert Burns Commonplace Book*, [1783–85], printed from the original manuscript in the possession of John Adam, Esq., Greenock (Edinburgh, 1872).

——*Robert Burns The Kilmarnock Poems* (Poems, Chiefly in the Scottish Dialect, 1786), edited with an introduction and notes by Donald A. Low (London and Melbourne, 1985).

——*Commonplace Book – April 9th 1787*, published in MacMillan's Magazines, nos 233–37 (March–July 1879).

——*Robert Burns and Mrs Dunlop, Correspondence now published in full for the first time with Elucidations* by William Wallace, editor of Robert Chambers *Life and Work of Robert Burns* (London, 1898).

Calvin, John, *Institutes of The Christian Religion*, a new translation by Henry Beveridge, Esq., 2 vols (Edinburgh, 1879).

Cowper, William, *The Poetical Works of William Cowper, with a Sketch of his Life* by Reverend T. Greatheed (Glasgow, 1834).

——*The Poems of William Cowper*, eds J.D. Baird and C. Ryskamp, vol. I 1748–82 (Oxford, 1980).

——*William Cowper, Selected Poems*, ed. Nick Rhodes (Manchester, 1988).

——*The Letters and Prose Writings of William Cowper, Volume III: Letters, 1787–1791*, eds James King and Charles Ryskamp (Oxford, 1982).

——*The Works of the English Poets from Chaucer to Cowper* including the series edited, with prefaces, biographical and critical by Dr Samuel Johnson; and the most approved translations. The Additional Lives by Alexander Chalmers, F.S.A., vol. XVIII (London,1810).

Dalrymple, William, *Family Worship explained and recommended in four sermons* (Kilmarnock, 1787).

——*A History of Christ for the use of the Unlearned* (Edinburgh, 1787).

——*A Sequel to The Life of Christ* (Ayr, 1791).

Derham, William, *Physico-Theology: or a Demonstration of the Being and Attributes of God from his Creation, Being the Substance of Sixteen Sermons preached in St Mary le Bow Church, London; at the Honourable Mr. Boyle's*

Lectures in the Years 1711 and 1712. With large Notes and many curious observations, the 3rd Scots edition (Glasgow, 1758) [first published 1713].

——*Astro-Theology: or a Demonstration of the Being and Attributes of God from a Survey of the Heavens* [From the same source as the previous volume] the 7th Edition (Glasgow, 1757) [first published 1715].

Dickson, John, *Popish Bill*, Introduction giving a short history of the Rise, Progress and Effects of the Alarm in Scotland respecting the Popish Bill and a Collection of Declarations, Resolutions &c. and *Appendix: A Short View of the Statutes at present in Force in Scotland against Popery*, first published December 1778 (Edinburgh, 1780).

Fasti Ecclesiae Scoticanae The Succession of Ministers in the Church of Scotland from the Reformation, by Hew Scott, D.D., new edition vol. III (Edinburgh, 1921); vol. IV (Edinburgh, 1923).

Goldie, John, *Essays on various important subjects Moral and Divine being an attempt to distinguish True from False Religion* (Glasgow, 1779).

——*Essays on various subjects Moral and Divine* in one volume, 2nd edn (1785), to which is added *The Gospel Recovered from its Captive State in five volumes by a Gentile Christian*, printed for the author and sold by C. Dilly in the Strand, W. Creech and C. Elliot (Edinburgh, 1784).

Grose, Francis, *The Antiquities of Scotland*, 2 vols (High Holborn, 1791).

Hervey, James, *Meditations and Contemplations* (London, 1855).

Hume, David, *A Treatise of Human Nature*, edited with an introduction by Ernest C. Mossner (London, 1984).

——*Dialogues concerning Natural Religion*, edited with an introduction and notes by Martin Bell (London, 1990).

Hutcheson, Francis, *An Inquiry into the Original of our Ideas of Beauty and Virtue (1725) and Alterations and Additions made in the second addition of the Inquiry into Beauty and Virtue* (1726), published by George Olms Verlag (Hildesheim, Zurich, New York, 1990).

Jamieson, John, *A Friend to Truth. Socinianism Unmasked in Four Letters to the Lay Members of the Church of Scotland and especially to those of the Collegiate Church of Ayr: occasioned by Dr McGill's Practical Essay on the Death of Jesus Christ*, 2nd edn (Edinburgh, 1790).

Johnson, Samuel, ed., *The Works of the English Poets from Chaucer to Cowper*, including the series edited, with prefaces, biographical and critical by Dr Samuel Johnson; and the most approved translations. The Additional Lives by Alexander Chalmers F.S.A., vol. XVI (London 1810).

Lawrence, D.H., *Selected Poems*, with an Introduction by W.E. Williams (Harmondsworth, 1960).

Locke, John, *An Essay Concerning Human Understanding*, an abridgement selected and edited by John W. Yolton (London and Melbourne, 1988).

——*An Essay concerning Human Understanding* (London, 1841).

——*Two Treatises of Civil Government*, Introduction by W.F. Carpenter (London, 1949).

Mackenzie, Henry, *The Man of Feeling*, edited with an introduction by Brian Vickers (Oxford, 1987).

McGill, William, D.D., *A Practical Essay on the Death of Jesus Christ* (Edinburgh, 1786).

——*The Benefits of the Revolution, A Sermon preached at Ayr on 5th of November 1788 by William McGill, D.D., to which are added Remarks on a Sermon preached on the same day at Newton upon Ayr* (Kilmarnock, 1789).

——*The Friends, a sermon preached 27th December 1778 at the Annual Meeting of the Society of Freemasons at Ayr* (Edinburgh, 1779).

McLehose, W.C., *Ed. The Correspondence between Burns and Clarinda with a memoir of Mrs McLehose (Clarinda)*, arranged and edited by her grandson Mr W.C. McLehose (Edinburgh, 1843).

Masson, Arthur, *A Collection of Prose and Verse from the Best English Authors for the use of schools* (Air, 1803).

——*An English Spelling Book in three parts for use in Schools*, 35th edn, corrected, improved and enlarged (Air, 1819).

Milton, John, *Paradise Lost*, ed. Christopher Ricks (London, 1989).

Mitchell, Thomas, *A Letter to The Rev. William McGill, D.D., one of the Ministers of Ayr from a Brother Clergyman of the Church of Scotland by Law Established* (Edinburgh, 1791).

Moir, James, *The Scripture Doctrine of Redemption by the Death of our Lord Jesus Christ Stated and Defended. Being an Answer to A Practical Essay on the Death of Jesus Christ by William McGill, D.D., one of the ministers of Air* (Edinburgh, 1787).

——*A Distinct and Impartial Account of the Process for Socinian Heresy against William McGill, D.D., one of the ministers of Ayr with observations on his Explanations and Apology and on the Proceedings and Final Decision of the Reverend Synod of Glasgow and Ayr in that cause* (Edinburgh, June 1790).

Ordinal and Service Book for Use in the Church of Scotland, prepared by the General Assembly's Committee of Public Worship and Aids to Devotion, 3rd edn (London, 1962).

Peebles, William, *A Sermon by Rev. William Peebles preached to the Magistrates and Council of the Burgh of Newton upon Ayr, 5th November 1788* (Kilmarnock, 1788).

——*Sermons on Various Subjects to which are subjoined Hymns suited to the several discourses* (Edinburgh, 1794).

——*Burnomania: The Celebrity of Robert Burns considered in a Discourse addressed to all real Christians of every denomination to which are added Epistles in Verse reflecting Peter Pindar, Burns &c.* (Edinburgh, 1811) [note: originally published anonymously].

Pope, Alexander, *The Poetical Works of Alexander Pope*, edited with notes and introductory memoir by Adolphus William Ward, M.A. (London, 1882).

Ramsay, James, *Minister of the Gospel in Glasgow, A clear Scriptural Detection of Satan transformed into an Angel of Light, or The Socinian Creed as held by Drs McGill and Dalrymple, Ministers of Ayr, exhibited in distinct Articles, illustrated from their own works and contrasted with the Holy Scriptures* (Glasgow, 1790).

Reid, Thomas, *An Inquiry into the Human Mind on the Principles of Common Sense*, with a new introduction by Paul B. Wood, Kingston, Canada. Reprint of the 1785 edn Thoemmes Antiquarian Books Ltd (Bristol, 1990).

Russel, John, *The Reason of our Lord's Agony in the Garden, and the influence of Just Views of them on Universal Holiness in a Sermon by John Russel one of the ministers of Kilmarnock* (Kilmarnock, 1787).

——*The Nature of the Gospel Delineated, A Sermon preached in the Parish Church of Kilmarnock on Thursday, 18th August, 1796* (Air, 1796).

——*Sermons by the Late Rev Mr Russel, Stirling along with the Sermons of his son Rev John Russel of Muthill* (Glasgow, 1826).

Shakespeare, William, *The Complete Works of William Shakespeare*, with introduction by St John Ervine, Collins (Glasgow, undated).

Sillar, David, *Poems* (Kilmarnock, 1789).

Smart, Christopher, *Jubilate Agno*, re-edited from the original manuscript with an introduction and notes by W.H. Bond, Curator of Manuscripts at the Houghton Library, Harvard (London, 1954).

——*Rejoice in the Lamb*, ed. W.F. Stead (1939).

——*The Religious Poetry of Christopher Smart*, ed. Marcus Walsh, Carcanet Press Limited (Manchester, 1972).

Smith, Adam, *The Theory of Moral Sentiments*, eds D.D. Raphael and A.L. Macfie (Indianapolis, 1982).

——*The Wealth of Nations Books I–III*, with an introduction by Andrew Skinner (London, 1986).

Sterne, Laurence, *The Life and Opinions of Tristram Shandy, Gentleman*, ed. Graham Petrie with an introduction by Christopher Ricks (Harmondsworth, 1986).

Taylor, John, *The Scripture Doctrine of Original Sin*, 2nd edn (London, 1741).

The Confession of Faith, agreed upon by The Assembly of Divines at Westminster with the Assistance of Commissioners from the Church of Scotland, as a part of the covenanted uniformity in religion betwixt the churches of Christ in the kingdoms of Scotland, England, and Ireland. Approved by the General Assembly 1647, and ratified and established by Acts of Parliament 1649 and 1690, as the publick and avowed Confession of the Church of Scotland, with references to the Proofs from the Scripture (Edinburgh and London, 1959). Included in this volume are *The Larger Catechism, The Shorter Catechism, The Directory For Publick Worship* and *The Form of Presbyterian Church Government*.

The Larger Catechism, agreed upon by The Assembly of Divines at Westminister with the Assistance of Commissioners from the Church of Scotland, as a part of the covenanted uniformity in religion betwixt the churches of Christ in the kingdoms of Scotland, England, and Ireland. And approved Anno 1648, by the General Assembly of the Church of Scotland, to be a Directory *for catechising such as have made some proficiency in the Knowledge of the Grounds of Religion.* With references to the Proofs from the Scripture (Edinburgh and London, 1959).

The Shorter Catechism, description as above except: *for catechising such as are of weaker Capacity* (Edinburgh and London, 1959).

The Scottish Psalter and Church Hymnary, Revised Edition, authorized for use in the Church of Scotland (O.U.P., 1929).

The Holy Bible, King James Version 1611 (Glasgow, 1949).

The New English Bible with the Apocrypha (Oxford, 1970).

The Statistical Account of Scotland (1791–99), ed. Sir John Sinclair, Bart. vol. VI Ayrshire, with a new introduction by John Strawhorn (Wakefield, 1982).

The Statistical Account of Scotland, ed. Sir John Sinclair, Bart. vol. III (Edinburgh, 1791); vol. XII (Edinburgh, 1793); vol. XXI (Edinburgh, 1799).

Waddell, P. Hately, *Life and Works of Robert Burns* (Glasgow, 1867).

Watson, Thomas, *A Body of Practical Divinity consisting of above 176 sermons on the Shorter Catechism*, 7th edn (Glasgow, 1782) [first published 1692].

Wright, James, A.M. (Minister of the Gospel at Maybole), *A Treatise on the Causes of Sedition – On the best remedy against this great evil and on what ought to be the Disposition of the British People at the present great crisis of the alarm of an invasion by the French* (Air, 1798).

Kirk Session, Presbytery and Synod Records

The Session Book for the Associate Congregation of Tarbolton, 1778 (presently held as part of the records of Tarbolton Parish Church).
Presbytery of Ayr Minute Books (South Ayrshire Council Archives, Ayr).
Synod of Glasgow and Ayr Minute Books (Scottish Register House).
Minute Book of Newton upon Ayr Kirk Session 1780–1830. The Acts and Proceedings of the Kirk Session of Newton upon Ayr commencing from the month of May 1780 (South Ayrshire Council Archives, Ayr).
Minute Books of Mauchline Kirk Session (South Ayrshire Council Archives, Ayr).

Secondary Sources

Ackroyd, Peter, *Blake* (London, 1995).
Anon, *The Contemporaries of Robert Burns* (Edinburgh, 1840).
Bawcutt, Priscilla and Riddy, Felicity, eds, *Longer Scottish Poems vol. I, 1375–1650* (Edinburgh, 1987).
Bell, M. Charles, *Calvin and Scottish Theology, The Doctrine of Assurance* (Edinburgh, 1985).
Boswell, James, *The Life of Samuel Johnson*, Collins (London and Glasgow, undated).
Broadie, Alexander, *The Tradition of Scottish Philosophy: A New Perspective on the Enlightment* (Edinburgh, 1990).
Burleigh, J.H.S., *A Church History of Scotland* (London, 1960).
Cecil, David, *The Stricken Deer, The Life of Cowper* (London, 1929).
Chadwick, Owen, *The Reformation*, The Pelican History of the Church vol. 3 (Harmondsworth, 1972).
Cox, James T., D.D., *Practice and Procedure in The Church of Scotland*, 6th edn, ed. Rev D.F.M. Macdonald, M.A., LL.B., Principal Clerk of the General Assembly (Edinburgh, 1976).
Cragg, Gerald R., *The Church and the Age of Reason 1648–1789*, The Pelican History of the Church vol. 4 (Harmondsworth, 1960).
Crawford, Thomas; Hewitt, David; and Law, Alexander, eds *Longer Scottish Poems*, vol. II, 1650–1830 (Edinburgh, 1987).
Crawford, Thomas, *Burns: A Study of the Poems and Songs* (Edinburgh, 1994).
Currie, James, *The Works of Robert Burns with an Account of his Life*, 4 vols, 8th edn (London, 1820).
Daiches, David, *Robert Ferguson* (Edinburgh, 1982).

——*Robert Burns The Poet* (Edinburgh, 1994).

Dakin, A., *Calvinism* (London, 1949).

Dearnley, Moira, *The Poetry of Christopher Smart* (Routledge & Kegan Paul Ltd: London, 1968).

Douglas, W. Scott, *The Works of Robert Burns*, 5 vols. (Edinburgh, 1879).

Dwyer, John and Sher, Richard B., eds, *Sociability and Society in Eighteenth-Century Scotland* (Edinburgh, 1991).

Feingold, Richard, *Nature and Society, Later Eighteenth Century Uses of the Pastoral and the Georgic* (New Jersey, 1978).

Fielding, Henry, *The History of Tom Jones, a Foundling*, with an introduction by Alan Pryce-Jones (London and Glasgow, 1955).

Fowler, Richard H., *Robert Burns* (London, 1988).

Gilbert, W.S., *Original Comic Operas*, Chappell (London, undated).

Hecht, Hans, *Robert Burns the man and his work*, translated by Jane Lymburn (Ayr, 1981).

Henderson, G.D., *The Church of Scotland, A Short History*, published in Edinburgh by the Church of Scotland Youth Committee c.1960.

Heron, Alasdair I.C., *The Westminster Confession in the Church Today: Papers prepared for the Church of Scotland Panel on Doctrine* (Edinburgh, 1982).

Jamieson, A. Burns, *Burns and Religion* (Cambridge, 1931).

Lindsay, Maurice, *Robert Burns, The man, his work, the legend* (London, 1954).

——*The Burns Encyclopedia*, 3rd edn (London, 1980).

Low, Donald, ed., *Critical Essays on Robert Burns* (London, 1975).

Mackay, James, *A Biography of Robert Burns* (Edinburgh, 1992).

MacLaine, Allan H. ed., *The Christis Kirk Tradition, Scots Poems of Folk Festivity* (Glasgow, 1996).

MacQueen, John and Winifred, eds, *A Choice of Scottish Verse 1470–1570*, selected with an introduction (London, 1972).

McGuirk, Carol, *Robert Burns and the Sentimental Era* (Athens, Georgia, 1985).

McIntosh, John R., *Church and Theology in Enlightenment Scotland: The Popular Party, 1740–1800* (East Linton, 1998).

McKay, Archibald, *Burns and his Kilmarnock Friends* (Kilmarnock, 1864).

——*History of Kilmarnock*, 4th edn (Kilmarnock, 1880).

McVie, John, *Robert Burns and Edinburgh* (Kilmarnock, 1969), ed. by J.M. Cohen (Edinburgh, 1984).

Moffatt, the Rev. Professor James, and Patrick, the Rev. Millar, eds *Handbook to the Church Hymnary, With Supplement* (London, 1951).

Neill, Stephen, *Anglicanism* (Harmondsworth, 1960).

Robertson, James, ed., *Robert Fergusson Selected Poems* (Edinburgh, 2000).
Ross, John D., *Who's Who in Burns* (Stirling, 1927).
Russell, Bertrand, *History of Western Philosophy and its connections with political and social circumstances from the earliest times to the present day* (London, 1979).
Schmidt, Michael, *Lives of the Poets* (London, 1999).
Sher, Richard B., *Church and University in the Scottish Enlightenment* (Edinburgh, 1985).
Simpson, Kenneth, *The Protean Scot: The Crisis of Identity in Eighteenth Century Scottish Literature* (Aberdeen, 1988).
Smout, T.C., *A History of the Scottish People 1560–1830* (Bungay, 1973).
The Concise Dictionary of National Biography, 3 vols. (Oxford, 1995).
The Concise Scots Dictionary, editor in chief Mairi Robinson (Aberdeen, 1985).
The History of Scottish Literature, vol. 2, 1660–1800, ed. Andrew Hook, general ed. Cairns Craig (Aberdeen, 1989).
Thornton, R.D., *James Currie, The Entire Stranger and Robert Burns* (Edinburgh and London, 1963).
Tillich, Paul, *Systematic Theology*, 3 vols (London, 1955–64).
Voltaire, *Candide*, translated with an introduction by John Butt (London, 1985).
Wendel, Francois, *Calvin, The Origins and Development of his Religious Thought*, translated by Philip Mairet (London and Glasgow, 1972).
Wright, David F., ed., *The Bible in Scottish Life and Literature* (Edinburgh, 1988).

Articles

Crawford, Thomas, 'Enlightenment, Metaphysics and Religion in the Boswell-Temple Correspondence', *Studies in Scottish Literature* XXV (1990).
Horne, John, 'Black Jock Russell', *Burns Chronicle* no. 34 (1925).
Kinsley, James, 'Burns and the Peasantry, 1785', *Proceedings of the British Academy* (1974).
——'The Rustic Inhabitants of the Hamlet', *Review of English Literature* (1 January 1960).
Landsburgh, Reverend David, 'John Russel', *The Kilmarnock Standard* (11 January 1879).
Landsman, Ned C., 'Presbyterians and Provincial Society: The Evangelical Enlightenment in the West of Scotland 1740–1775', *Sociability and Society in*

Eighteenth-Century Scotland, ed. John Dwyer and Richard B. Sher (Edinburgh, 1991).

Law, Alexander, 'Scottish School Books of the 18th and 19th Centuries', *Studies in Scottish Literature* XVIII (1984).

Low, Donald, 'Introduction' in *Critical Essays on Robert Burns*, ed. Donald Low (London, 1975).

McCartney, John, 'Some Eminent Men', *The Royal Burgh of Ayr Seven Hundred and Fifty Years of History*, ed. Annie I. Dunlop, for the Ayrshire Archaeological and Natural History Society (Edinburgh, 1953).

Orr, Norma F., 'Robert Burns and the Ayrshire Ministers', *Burns Chronicle* no. 28 (1919).

Simpson, Kenneth, 'Burns and Scottish Society', *Sociability and Society in Eighteenth-Century Scotland*, ed. John Dwyer and Richard B. Sher (Edinburgh, 1993).

Watkins, Morgan George, 'Notes on John Goldie', *Dictionary of National Biography* vol. III (1890).

Index